INVESTING IN
THOROUGHBREDS
Strategies for Success

INVESTING IN THOROUGHBREDS

Strategies for Success

ARNOLD KIRKPATRICK

ECLIPSE
PRESS

Lexington, Kentucky

The Library of Congress Number: 00-108855

ISBN: 1-58150-041-6

Printed in the United States
First Edition: April 2001

a division of The Blood-Horse, Inc.

PUBLISHERS SINCE 1916

CONTENTS

PREFACE

"Don't check your brains at the door."

— *A.K., Successful Thoroughbred Investment, 1984*

When I was training as a PADI scuba diving instructor, I learned that you always tell students what they are going to be taught, teach it to them, and then tell them what they just learned. That's why this book begins, repeats, and ends with the phrase above. If this book accomplishes nothing other than to emblazon that one concept ("Don't check your brains at the door") in your mind, I will have done a good job.

The reason: The Thoroughbred business is one of the easiest places in the world to fall in love and let your heart overrule your head.

It's easy to understand why the horse has inspired art, poetry, and music, and why it has been regarded over millennia as a symbol of strength, courage, and virility. The Thoroughbred embodies all those qualities, refined over generations into the finest athlete God put on this earth. Born to run, the Thoroughbred competes with every fiber and sinew of his being.

It's easy to fall in love with this game as you watch a field of two-year-olds dance wide-eyed with excitement to the post on an

October afternoon at Keeneland.

It's easy to fall in love with the glamour and the pageantry of a day at the racetrack, particularly as you stand in the paddock watching your own silks hoisted aboard your own horse. Then and there, with no particular skill and talent, you can experience the same pounding heart, dry mouth, and sweaty palms that a leader of the U.S. Open feels as he strides up the fairway toward the eighteenth green.

It's easy to fall in love with a group of foals as they romp across a grassy pasture chasing each other, already testing their speed and honing their competitive nature.

And while it's easy to get wrapped up in a top-class horse that is winning for you in stakes company, it's also possible to fall in love with the courage and perseverance of a less-than-talented claimer that tries time and again to compete with horses of superior ability.

In short, the horse business is one of the most exciting activities you can pursue professionally outside of bed. And, with luck and the proper attitude, it can be financially, as well as aesthetically, rewarding.

However, you often do silly and crazy things during that giddy period of first being in love. So you must fight hard to keep from falling in love with your horses. As in life, it's okay to fall in love once or twice, but it's very expensive both financially and emotionally if you fall in love too often.

That brings to mind another precept with which I'll beat you over the head. You need to assess your horses at least once a year — more often if possible — to determine which ones are carrying their weight, which ones have potential, and which ones fall under the category "none of the above." Then you must do the hardest thing of all for most people: get rid of those that fall in the latter group — even if it means taking a loss. I can assure you that you'll be better off in the long run underestimating the abilities of a horse on occasion than overestimating the abilities of a number of horses over the long term.

During more than forty years in the Thoroughbred business, I have seen literally hundreds of smart business people take a beating, sometimes a thrashing, because when they entered the horse business they did not apply the same business principles that earned them enough money to become involved in the horse business.

If you owned a successful manufacturing business and decided to branch out into, say, venture capital, you wouldn't abandon the principles that made you a success in the first place. So, when you decide to get involved in the horse business:

Don't check your brains at the door.

Having repeated that most important admonition one more time, on to a few more considerations.

If you're a product of the education systems of Kentucky, Ohio, or West Virginia, you may not understand evolution — in fact, you may have never heard the term — but this book is the result of an evolutionary process. It is the culmination of the wisdom, as well as the mistakes, that were contained in two previous works, *How to Make Money Investing in Thoroughbred*s, which Jack Lohman wrote in 1978, and *Successful Thoroughbred Investment in a Changing Market*, which Jack and I co-authored in 1984.

This book is going to include a lot of things from *Successful Thoroughbred Investment*, because all of the principles are just as valid; and so are most, if not all, of the stories. Finally, I figure, what the hell, if Dick Francis and John Irving can keep writing the same book over and over, why can't I?

There will be a lot of changes, too, because the Thoroughbred business has changed enormously since 1984.

This book and its predecessors are the product of a crusade that Jack Lohman and I carried on through our long years of friendship. We were of the opinion — and I still strongly believe — the horse business can be profitable and exciting for investors at all levels and from all backgrounds. However, this business is not all roses in the winner's circle on the first Saturday in May. People who want to come into the horse business should know what they are getting into. They should recognize the risks, as well as the emotional and fiscal benefits, before they get into the hard, often harsh realities of the game.

That brings me to the first of a number of anecdotes I'll share, some apocryphal but most true.

A millionaire came down to Kentucky with the idea of getting his feet wet in the horse business. "I've got a lot of money," he told a number of people whom he encountered, "what I need is someone with experience in the horse business to help me out." To the surprise of absolutely no one, he quickly found someone with years of experience to help him out.

Pretty soon after that, the millionaire was heard telling a friend about his new agent, "It wasn't long before *he* had the money, and *I* had the experience."

This book is about avoiding these types of situations.

Since you're reading this book, it is logical to assume that you are either thinking about becoming involved in the horse business or someone thinks you're interested enough to give you this book. The whole purpose of writing it is to provide you with some basic knowledge that will help you to avoid — or, at the very least, warn you about — some of the problems you may experience as you navigate the complex world of Thoroughbred racing and breeding.

If you've got any spirit, any gamble in you at all, I'm convinced you'll love the horse business — in fact, I'll guarantee it. But I'll also guarantee that your enjoyment will be inverse to the number of unpleasant surprises you encounter.

Having you start out with a sound foundation will help you

avoid a number of potential pitfalls and pratfalls.

The rewards in the Thoroughbred business are commensurate with the amount of risk you take. Some ways of investing in Thoroughbreds are relatively safe — and I emphasize the "relatively" in that phrase — and some are more exciting.

I'll discuss those later, but first I need to insert one additional caveat: the economics of the horse business as a whole do not make any sense...never have, never will.

If you're looking for a risk-free investment; if you don't feel a rush when a closely bunched pack of horses strains with every last ounce of their being for the finish line; if you don't get a thrill out of watching a foal romp, jump, and buck its way across a spring pasture; then put your money in municipal bonds, and forget about the horse business.

If, on the other hand, your heart beats faster at the feel of a soft muzzle searching you in a quest for something good to eat; if you care at all about the wonders of nature; if you would be thrilled by standing in the winner's circle of a racetrack; then this is for you.

This book is basically organized in the order in which you would encounter the Thoroughbred business. I strongly urge you to read the first two chapters before skipping to any chapters of particular interest, although I believe that you'll enjoy and learn from each chapter. To make this more lively than a strict "how to" book, I've sprinkled each chapter with stories of how and why people have achieved success and/or met with failure.

As you read these stories, you'll notice the role that luck — good and bad — plays. Luck is part of the Thoroughbred business. And though guarantees in this business are few, I can assure you that along the way you're going to have some bad luck: a prize foal with contracted tendons, a top yearling prospect that gets hurt right before the sales, a stakes horse that chips a sesamoid right before the Derby, etc., etc., etc.

Good luck is far more elusive and rare. But like any other endeavor, sound decisions enhance good luck.

"It's a big help to be lucky in the Thoroughbred business" is another phrase I'll repeat, along with "it's better to own a piece of a good horse than all of a bad one," "you get what you pay for," and "be patient."

These redundancies are intentional, for they are among the points that will make this business a better experience for you. If you remember them.

In fact, this is probably as good a place as any to trot out my five rules for getting into the horse business:

(1) Learn all you can about the business. I probably wouldn't even have to say this if we were talking about going into any other business. People seem to think they can go into the horse business, which is one of the most complex I can think of, without first studying it. Study, or at least read, horse magazines and other sources of information (see the list of suggested reading at the end of the book).

(2) Obtain sound, honest advice. The person whom you choose as your advisor can save (or cost) you millions. He will make the difference between a pleasant and an unpleasant experience, between profit and loss, and between loss and ruin. You have my word that someone not involved in the horse business full time cannot compete with the professionals who spend all their time concentrating on the business.

(3) Work out a plan for your involvement. Establish your goals and level of commitment to the business early on. Unlike some of my friends, I do not think that time-management guru Stephen Covey is the Second Coming of Christ, but sitting down with your advisor and summarizing what you want out of the horse business will be useful. Review your plans every so often to see whether you're really getting what you want and how much it's costing.

(4) Emphasize quality. As you'll see throughout the book, but mostly in chapters 5 and 6, the closer you are to the top of the business, the better off you'll be financially. And the better off you are financially, the better time you'll have. You don't have to make money to have fun here, but if you're spending a lot of money and not having any fun, it can and will get old very fast.

(5) Be patient. Only one person, the late Fred Hooper, has ever won the Kentucky Derby with the first horse he bought. Hooper won in 1945 with Hoop, Jr., who came from a crop of 6,427 foals. The odds are that this is not likely to happen again for a long, long time. As you'll see in Chapter 2, the projected foal crop for 2000 was 36,700, which is about six times the size of Hoop, Jr.'s foal crop, and in 2000, there were 12,642 yearlings offered at auction as compared with 873 when Hoop, Jr. was a yearling.

Another point to remember throughout this book is that the masculine pronoun "he," used with respect to humans, means "he or she," because in the Thoroughbred business, brains count, so women can and do compete equally and successfully with men. For example, Jenine Sahadi is one of the best trainers in the country. She won the Breeders' Cup Sprint back to back in 1996 and 1997 with Lit de Justice and Elmhurst. Alice Chandler is one of the smartest and most successful farm operators in the world (besides which, women have actually run many of the other farms for years, while the men who owned them were out strutting around). Jockeys such as Julie Krone and Abby Fuller have made their male counterparts stand up and take notice. And many of the most successful owners in the business are women. So, when somebody tells you the horse business is basically an "old boys' club," you can just tell them for me that it might be true now, but the old boys had better be looking over their shoulders because brains will overcome tradition and brawn most of the time.[1]

The jargon of the business is also important. I spent a lot of time and effort compiling the glossary that appears at the end of the book. I urge you to study it, because it will help make your trip through the business smoother and easier.

Finally, unless you are experienced, knowledgeable, and a full-time participant in the business, invest only your disposable income, not your survival funds.

There is a very appropriate saying about your venture into the horse business prominently displayed in many track kitchens:

"It's okay to eat with your bettin' money, but don't bet with your eatin' money."

Have fun…and good luck.

---

[1] Since most of the people who know me well think that I can be somewhat opinionated on occasion (the understatement of the millennium — the old one and the new one), the paragraph above contains the first of what will undoubtedly be many expressions of opinion in this book. I will try to differentiate them from fact whenever it's necessary, but it's my guess you won't have much trouble telling the difference.

CHAPTER ONE

SOME SUCCESS STORIES

"It's true, I have been lucky in the horse business, but I find the harder I work, the luckier I get."

— Hall of Fame trainer Hirsch Jacobs

O ne of the most enjoyable parts of writing a book about investing in the Thoroughbred business is recounting many of the success stories.

Some of the horses in the following stories were overlooked as yearlings and two-year-olds, while others started out at the top of the heap. Yet all of them generated substantial financial rewards and provided enormous enjoyment for the people associated with them.

Each of these stories also contains at least one lesson, the first and foremost of which is: it certainly doesn't hurt to be lucky.

Success Story #1:

Back in the 1960s, Bold Ruler, who stood at Claiborne Farm, was arguably the most successful stallion of modern times — leading sire eight times, sire of eighty-two stakes winners, great sire of sires, and the reason you see "Bold" or "Ruler" in the names and/or pedigrees of so many outstanding horses, even today.

Bold Ruler was owned by the Wheatley Stable of Mrs. Henry Carnegie Phipps, one of the great names in racing and a lady who, to put it delicately, didn't really need any more money.

Mrs. Phipps lived in the era when improvement of the breed was not an anachronism. She was an astute breeder, as well as owner, of many fine racehorses; and she didn't reach her exalted status in racing by standing still. Since her principal goal was to improve her bloodstock, A. B. Hancock, her principal breeding advisor, devised a plan whereby a breeder with a really good mare could breed her to Bold Ruler not for money, but to improve his and the Phipps' bloodstock holdings.

The breeder would agree to send his mare to Bold Ruler for two breeding seasons. When the first foal arrived, the breeder and a Phipps family representative would flip a coin to see who got first choice of which foal.

Well, in 1968, Christopher T. Chenery's Meadow Stable sent a nice mare, Somethingroyal, to Bold Ruler. The resulting foal was a filly, which the Phippses generally preferred because (a) they already had Bold Ruler, and (b) with access to the exceptional Claiborne stallion roster, they really didn't need much in the way of stallion prospects.

In the fall of 1969, Ogden Phipps chose "tails" in a coin toss at Belmont Park and won the right to the filly, who was ultimately named The Bride, but probably would have been better named "The Bridesmaid," because she didn't turn out to be much of a runner or producer.

Having lost the toss, Meadow Stable was entitled in 1970 to the "other" foal...the one they named Secretariat.

Success Story #2:

The next account is the most impressive financial success I can recall in this business. Although the story of a big, nearly black colt named Seattle Slew was written about extensively in *Successful Thoroughbred Investment*, it deserves repeating and in particular, an update.

The story began July 19, 1975, when Mickey and Karen Taylor accompanied their friend, partner, and advisor, Dr. Jim Hill, to the Fasig-Tipton Kentucky Summer yearling sale in Lexington. There, for $17,500, the young couple purchased a muscular dark bay colt by Bold Reasoning out of My Charmer, by Poker. They bought the colt from the two-horse consignment of a small breeder, the late Ben Castleman, whose farm was just about two miles from the then-temporary sales arena on Newtown Pike.

The colt was later named Seattle Slew — Seattle because the Taylors lived near Seattle, and Slew, the story goes, for the swampy areas around Hill's hometown of Fort Myers, Florida (although most people in-the-know contend that the latter half of the name comes from the fact that the colt's a bit slew-footed in the right fore).

On the track, he was a wonder to behold. Slew went undefeated at age two, winning the Champagne Stakes by nearly ten lengths and earning the Eclipse Award as champion two-year-old colt of 1976. He opened his three-year-old campaign by setting a track record of 1:20⅗ in a seven-furlong allowance prep for the Flamingo Stakes, which he also won with ease. He followed with a three and a quarter-length victory in the Wood Memorial Stakes, his last prep race before the Kentucky Derby.

Slew swept through the Triple Crown the way you'd expect Genghis Khan to sweep through a group of conscientious objectors, winning the Kentucky Derby, Preakness Stakes, and Belmont Stakes, each with increasing ease. He became the first undefeated horse in history to win the Triple Crown.

But, there are only two kinds of horses — those that have been beaten and those that are going to get beaten. Shipped to California for the Swaps Stakes, Slew finished out of the money for the first defeat of his career and his only finish worse than second.

He wound up the year with Eclipse Awards, both as Horse of the Year and champion three-year-old male, not to mention earnings of $641,370.

At four, Slew set a track record when he won the Woodward Stakes. He also won the Marlboro Cup Invitational and Stuyvesant Handicaps. His greatest race of the year, though, and perhaps the greatest race of his career, was a second to Exceller in the mile-and-a-half Jockey Club Gold Cup. In that race, Slew went to the front at the start, pressed by the likes of that year's Triple Crown winner Affirmed and Life's Hope. On a track listed as sloppy, the three of them blistered through murderous early fractions of :22⅗ for the first quarter, :45⅕ for the half, and 1:09⅖ for six furlongs (as a point of comparison, Secretariat's fractions when he set the world record for the same distance in the Belmont Stakes, on a fast track, were :23⅗, :46⅕, and 1:09⅘).

At that point, beginning a spectacular move on the inside was Exceller, who blew past the other horses as though they were standing still, collared and passed Seattle Slew at the head of the

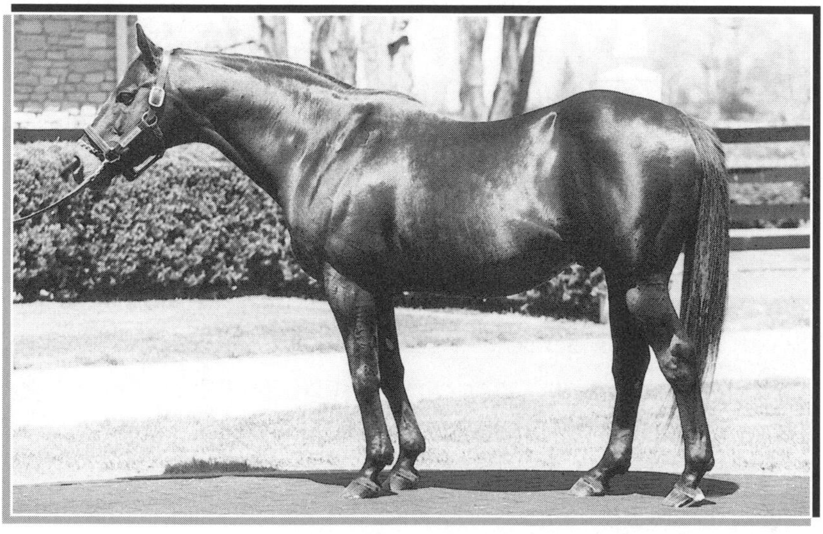

Seattle Slew, a champion on the track and at stud.

stretch and looked as though he would draw out to win by daylight, a lot of daylight. Exceller opened up a lead of about three-quarters of a length, but Slew reached down into that big heart of his and began to fight back. Stride by stride, inch by inch, he cut into Exceller's lead, but it was a dead-tired horse working against a relatively fresh one and a very good one. At the end, Slew failed by a short nose to catch Exceller, and many spectators thought he would have caught the winner in another couple of jumps. But that's what makes horse racing.

Win, lose, or draw, the performance was one of the most courageous ever seen on a racetrack. The loss probably cost Seattle Slew a second title as Horse of the Year, but he gained the admiration of the racing world. Affirmed, incidentally, went on to be named Horse of the Year off his victories in the Triple Crown.

Seattle Slew was retired with earnings of $1,208,726, a profit of $1,191,226, and a return on investment of 6,807 percent.[1]

He was then syndicated by Brownell Combs to stand at Spendthrift Farm for $300,000 a share, which in a forty-share syndicate increased his worth to the Taylors and the Hills by another $12 million and raised their return on investment to 75,378 percent.

That was just the beginning of the story. Tightly held — the Taylors and Hills only sold half the available shares — Slew became an example of good stallion management and a lifelong meal ticket for his connections. As a stallion he was as fast out of the gate as he had been on the track. His first two crops included champions Landaluce, Slew o' Gold, and the 1984 Kentucky Derby and Belmont Stakes winner Swale, in addition to the grade I stakes winners Slewpy, Adored, and Seattle Song — possibly one of the most fantastic early success stories for a stallion in history.

---

[1] Return on investment figures only take into account the initial purchase price because it is difficult to project how much money went into upkeep, vet bills, training, insurance, etc., for each horse.

By the time Slew's third crop was running, his stud fee was well in excess of what his original cost per share had been. In fact, I remember when a no-guarantee season was sold for $750,000 (that would be the equivalent of a price well in excess of $1 million for a live-foal season). In his heyday, two shares in the horse changed hands for sums in excess of $2 million each; the second one for $2.9 million.

While you can't extrapolate that directly into a total value for the horse because the price for a single share is exaggerated due to scarcity, the value of Seattle Slew in the mid-1980s could be estimated in the range of $80 million to $90 million, a return on investment of 457,143 percent at the bottom figure, 514,286 percent at the top.

The Taylors and Hills parlayed their good luck into majority ownership of a bank and several horse farms, partial ownership of a number of other good and very good racehorses, and numerous other investments. While Slew's contribution to their coffers is inestimable, I would estimate conservatively that he contributed between $125 million and $150 million to the coffers of Wooden Horse Investments, Tayhill Stable, and Pearson's Barn; just a few of the companies the horse's revenues generated. Not a bad return on an initial investment of $17,500.

No story, however charmed, is without its down side. By 1992, the magic friendship and golden partnership between the Taylors and the Hills had disintegrated into a morass of vituperation, recriminations, and nasty lawsuits. In November of 1992, Wooden Horse dispersed twenty-three horses for $3,976,500 at the Keeneland November breeding stock sale while Hill was suing the Taylors for misappropriating and wasting its corporate funds. Following an extended trial, a federal jury awarded Hill $4.4 million in damages.

At the time this book was written, Slew's offspring had earned in excess of $64 million on the racetrack; yearlings sired by him had brought more than $145 million at the sales (including one for $6.5 million in 1984); and his reputation had been established as both a sire of sires and a leading broodmare sire.

Unfortunately, at twenty-six the vagaries of age were taking a toll. Two vertebrae in his neck had become arthritic and were causing him pain, making it difficult to service mares as the 2000 season got under way. Slew underwent successful surgery in April of 2000, followed by extensive rehabilitation by the Taylors, stud groom Tom Wade, and the Three Chimneys staff. As this book was going to press, he was pronounced healthy and was expected to return to the breeding shed in 2001 and service shareholder mares.

Success Story #3:

Another story of lightning in a bottle surrounds a small, ill-bred colt that was back at the knee (considered by most conformation experts to be one of the most serious flaws a horse can have). He was bred by the highly successful Golden Chance Farm near Paris, Kentucky. The farm raced most of the horses it bred, but this one was considered to be so small and badly conformed that it sold him as a yearling in the 1976 Keeneland January horses of all ages sale. The few yearlings that are included in this sale are there because their breeders don't think it's worth carrying them until July, August, or September when most yearlings normally are sold.

The little colt brought a final bid of $1,100 from J. E. Colloway, who kept him for precisely a year and sold him at the same sale in 1977 for double that price. The buyer was Hal Snowden Jr., who broke the colt, had him gelded, and sold him to a Japanese client, who "promptly returned him because of the knees."

Not too long afterward, Snowden found two other buyers who apparently didn't know or care about horses being back at the knee. They took the young gelding down to Louisiana where he won a few races, including the Lafayette Futurity. He earned a little more than $50,000 before Snowden bought him back in March of 1978. A month later, after the little gelding finished fourth in an allowance race at Keeneland, Snowden sold him for $25,000, sight unseen, to Sam Rubin, a bicycle importer and horse player from New York.

The ill-bred, badly conformed, smallish gelding, named John Henry, earned a total of $6,591,860 — which at the time he retired was twice as much as the second-leading money-winning horse of all time. In 1981 when he was Horse of the Year for the first time, he won Thoroughbred racing's first million-dollar race, the Arlington Million Stakes (a feat he repeated in 1984) and set an all-time annual earnings record of $1,798,030. In 1984, he earned $2,336,650 and was again Horse of the Year.

To put it into perspective, John Henry was the first horse to reach earnings levels of $3 million, then $4 million, then $5 million, and then $6 million.

Return on investment for Rubin was 26,167 percent, and

John Henry sold for $1,100 and earned more than $6 million.

despite all the aforementioned faults, John Henry sure as hell looked good crossing the finish line. And that, as Paul Harvey says, is the rest of the story.

Unfortunately, being a gelding, John Henry's life after the racetrack was not as illustrious as that of Seattle Slew. John Henry was retired to wile away his days at the Kentucky Horse Park, where he grazes contentedly between showings at the Hall of Champions. He remains an icon to dreamers throughout the Thoroughbred business and a star to thousands of visitors a year.

Success Story #4:

In 1996, the overall North American yearling average was $34,545 when trainer Bob Baffert paid less than half that, $17,000, on behalf of his good friend Mike Pegram for a moderately bred bay colt by Quiet American—Really Blue, by Believe It, at the Keeneland September yearling sale.

The stable crew nicknamed him "The Fish" because he was so slab-sided (a racetrack expression for not having much body definition) and narrow in front. But the colt reaffirmed the axiom

Trainer Bob Baffert (left) and owner Mike Pegram (right)
celebrating Real Quiet's Kentucky Derby victory.

that looks aren't everything on the racetrack. He missed winning the Triple Crown by a dirty nose in the 1998 Belmont after impressive wins in the Kentucky Derby and Preakness Stakes. A grade I winner at two and four as well, Real Quiet finished his racing career with $3,271,802 in earnings, a 19,246 percent return on investment. He has now gone to stud at Vinery in Kentucky, where he was bred to 102 mares in 2000 at $25,000 a pop, which, assuming average fertility, has added another $2 million to his earnings.

Success Story #5:

This rags-to-riches story shows that even the most experienced horse people need a little luck along the way.

If one were to draw up a list of the best and brightest horsemen in Central Kentucky, I think Arthur Hancock would have to be ranked at or near the top. One of the scions of Claiborne Farm, he went off on his own to breed countless good horses, including the subject of this story.

In 1987, Arthur took a colt by Halo, out of a moderate mare, Wishing Well, to the Keeneland July yearling sale for a client of his. The kindest description for this colt at the time might well have been "unobtrusive," and for the first part of his life anyway, he was what we in Kentucky call "snakebit," i.e., everything that could possibly go wrong with him did...and then some.

As a weanling, he nearly died from a case of the scours (diarrhea). Then as a yearling he was entered in the Keeneland July sale, but Arthur bought him back, mistakenly thinking that the breeder didn't want to sell him for so little. The $17,000 price tag was less than half the overall yearling average for the year and only about five percent of the average for that sale. Typically, Arthur blamed himself and took ownership of the horse. Sent to California for a sale of two-year-olds in training, the colt again failed to meet the reserve and was bought back by his owner, this time for $32,000.

On the way back from California after the sale, the van carrying the colt overturned, but the skinny little snakebit fellow only suffered minor injuries.

About that time Arthur's friend Paul Sullivan, who owned half of the colt, wanted out, so Arthur arranged for Hall of Fame trainer Charlie Whittingham to buy a half interest in the colt for $25,000. As part of the deal, Whittingham took the colt into his barn.

The unwanted colt, Sunday Silence, blossomed into a "freak." This may not have the best connotation in the vernacular, but it is a term of high approbation at the racetrack.

In fourteen starts he never finished worse than second. He was Horse of the Year at age three when he earned more than $4.5 million in a brilliant series of duels with another spectacularly talented horse named Easy Goer, who denied Sunday Silence the Triple Crown when he beat him in the Belmont Stakes. In the Breeders' Cup Classic, Sunday Silence again turned the tables on Easy Goer, although he emerged from the race with chips in his knees. Following arthroscopic surgery, Sunday Silence returned to the track as a four-year-old with a winning effort in the Californian Stakes. Whittingham, however, discovered some heat in the ankle on the colt's left fore following a second to Criminal Type in the Hollywood Gold Cup, and it was decided to retire him.

Sunday Silence leads the 1989 Derby field to the wire.

In all, Sunday Silence earned $4,968,554, which is not bad for a colt who undoubtedly could have been bought for $20,000 as a yearling. Return on investment: 24,843 percent, thus far.

Sunday Silence was retired to stud at Hancock's Stone Farm near Paris, Kentucky, where he received limited attention at a reported stud fee of $50,000 live foal. Then, Zenya Yoshida, who had purchased a quarter interest in Sunday Silence for $2.25 million when he was still in training, suggested they ship the horse to stand at Shadai Stud in Japan, and once again the rest is history. As 2000 neared a close, Sunday Silence was poised to conclude his sixth consecutive season as Japan's top stallion with anticipated progeny earnings in excess of of $50 million for the year.

Success Story #6:

Of course, not all the success stories in the Thoroughbred business involve horses that were overlooked.

For instance, the top-priced yearling of 1990 was a rangy son of Seattle Slew—Weekend Surprise, by Secretariat, who was purchased by the British Bloodstock Agency for $2.9 million on behalf of a Japanese client, Tomonori Tsurumaki. This well-balanced half-brother to classic winner Summer Squall was named A.P. Indy (the "A.P." for Auto Polis, a Formula-One race car track that Tsurumaki owns in Japan and the "Indy" presumably for the Indy cars that race there), and he became the first multimillion-dollar yearling to earn back his purchase price on the racetrack before even going to stud.

At age two, A.P. Indy won the Hollywood Futurity. During his three-year-old campaign, he became Horse of the Year after winning the Belmont Stakes, the Breeders' Cup Classic, two other races, and $2.6 million. In all, at the end of the 1992 racing season, A.P. Indy retired with earnings of $2,979,815, a return on investment of 103 percent, which again is only the beginning of the story.

In July of 1992, William S. Farish and W. S. Kilroy, who had bred A.P. Indy, got together with a third partner, Harold Goodman, and purchased a half interest in the colt.

Then, when A.P. Indy retired he was syndicated to stand at Farish's Lane's End Farm, where he has already shown a great deal of promise as a stallion. He has sired twenty-six stakes winners in his first five crops, and, perhaps more importantly, has a lifetime yearling average of $387,648, including a 2000 yearling average of $850,000.

Largely because of that yearling average and also because of the success of his offspring on the track, in 2000 he was bred to 130 mares at $150,000 a pop, which, assuming average fertility and not too many discounted seasons, would equate to an annual income of about $16 million. As a comparison, in 1999 he stood for $100,000 and bred 125 mares generating about $12 million.

Success Story #7:

The next story contains another important lesson. At the 1994 Fasig-Tipton Saratoga yearling sale, Ernie Paragallo's Paraneck Stable went to $200,000 to acquire a good-looking roan colt by Unbridled—Trolley Song, by Caro. As it is today, paying $200,000 to pinhook a colt is a dangerous proposition. But this investment paid off in spades, at least temporarily. When the colt went through the Barretts select sale of two-year-olds in training in 1995, he became the most successful pinhook in history, bringing a final bid of $1,400,000 from another Japanese buyer, Hiroshi Fujita.

The sale quickly soured, however. Veterinarians for the new owner rejected the colt, claiming that post-sale X-rays revealed bone chips in the left fore ankle that would compromise the colt's racing ability.

The consignor took the colt back and put him in training. Named Unbridled's Song, he broke his maiden in August at

Saratoga then won the $1-million Breeders' Cup Juvenile before heading to Florida to prepare for the classics. He won the Florida Derby and Wood Memorial, in addition to finishing second in two more stakes. He ran unplaced in the Kentucky Derby before it was discovered he had injured himself, as happens to so many good horses during the rigors of a Triple Crown campaign.

Unbridled's Song returned to the races at four and won the Olympic Handicap at Gulfstream Park. A fractured cannon bone ended his career, and he was retired to stud with total earnings of $1,311,800.

Today, Unbridled's Song is kept busy shuttling between stud duties at Taylor Made Farm in Kentucky and Arrowfield Farm in Australia. Once again, if he is of average fertility and not too many of his seasons have been discounted, I would estimate he has generated stud fees in the neighborhood of $15 million during his first three seasons in the Northern Hemisphere alone. Further, his first crop of yearlings in North America averaged $254,400, nearly eight and a half times his stud fee, which bodes well for his future as a stallion.

Success Story #8:

Finally, as this book is being completed, one of the most noteworthy of all financial success stories involving Thoroughbred ownership has unfolded. And, it's a story with a couple of different lessons.

In 1996, a Japanese entrepreneur named Fusao Sekiguchi came to the Keeneland July yearling sale where he endeared himself to many, including the Keeneland management, by purchasing seven yearlings for a total of $5.75 million.

The romance almost soured when Sekiguchi returned to Japan to discover he had been displaced as CEO of a personnel company he had founded, and he could not pay for the horses. He quickly showed the class that we would like to see in all participants in the

Thoroughbred business when he immediately contacted the Keeneland management, arranged for the yearlings he had purchased to be sold privately, and made up the difference in a timely manner.

As a result, Sekiguchi was welcomed again when he returned to Keeneland in July of 1998. Through his advisor, John Ward, he paid $4 million for the sale topper, a strapping bay son of Mr. Prospector—Angel Fever, by Danzig, who had been consigned by breeders Arthur Hancock and Robert McNair.

After the sale, Sekiguchi told the press that he had wanted the colt so badly that he would have bid as much as "$5 million, or whatever it would cost to buy him."

As you've no doubt guessed, the colt was Fusaichi Pegasus, who turned in one of the most impressive performances in recent memory to win the 2000 Kentucky Derby, his fifth victory in six starts to that point.

While a whole lot of people, myself included, thought Fusaichi Pegasus might be the second coming of Secretariat, he stumbled slightly in the Preakness, losing to Red Bullet. As so often happens with horses that are beginning to show a little tarnish, his connections announced he had suffered a minor injury, would miss the Belmont Stakes, and would be taken out of training for a while.

However, Sekiguchi apparently must also subscribe to the philosophy that "it's better to sell and repent than to keep and repent." Sekiguchi soon announced he would sell the colt.

Fusaichi Pegasus.

In mid-June, following a ferocious bidding war among most of the top stud farms in Kentucky, Fusaichi Pegasus was sold to Coolmore Stud for a record price, reported to be between $60 million and $70 million. Just for the sake of argument, let's say $65 million is the syndication price. That would be a return on investment of "only" about 165 percent for Sekiguchi. However, when you think of it as a profit of $60 million, it sounds a whole lot better.

Fusaichi Pegasus finished a disappointing sixth in the 2000 Breeders' Cup Classic, then immediately was retired to Coolmore's Kentucky operation, Ashford Stud, just outside Versailles. During his brief racing career, he tallied six victories from nine lifetime starts and earned nearly $2 million. He is standing for a fee of $150,000. In consideration of Coolmore's propensity to breed well over 100 mares each to their stallions, that will probably equate to an annual return of $20 million or more. This might justify the syndication price, particularly with the prospect of dual-hemisphere breeding.

However, at the risk of being repetitive, I must point out that the laws of supply and demand do apply to the Thoroughbred business. I think it will be exceedingly difficult to sell eighty to 100 seasons at $150,000 a pop without seriously discounting them, particularly when breeders realize that as many as seventy or eighty yearlings by that stallion could show up at the yearling sales two years down the road.

While the last four stories may not have the astronomical percentage return on investment of Seattle Slew or John Henry, the horses most certainly proved to be great investments, and I don't think anyone is going to kick at an income of $5 million to $10 million a year in stud fees.

And even if they had not been the phenomenal financial successes that they turned out to be, their connections would have had a helluva time watching them run.

YESTERDAY, TODAY & TOMORROW

"I know no way of judging the future but by the past."

— *Patrick Henry*

As I mentioned in the preface, this book is part of an evolutionary process. It is the culmination of the wisdom and mistakes in two previous versions, *How to Make Money Investing in Thoroughbreds*, published in 1978, and *Successful Thoroughbred Investment in a Changing Market*, published in 1984.

Since then, the Thoroughbred business has undergone prodigious change.

For example: The foal crop of 1978 was 31,510, the first time in history that registrations exceeded 30,000. The average racehorse in North America earned $5,840. Nineteen percent of the total yearling crop (5,777 yearlings) was sold at auction for an average of $19,846. And the top-priced yearling was a handsome son of Northern Dancer—Special, by Forli, who turned out to be a huge bargain at $1.3 million. Named Nureyev, he became the champion miler in France before being syndicated for $14 million to stand at Walmac International near Lexington, Kentucky. One of the world's leading stallions, he has sired winners of more than $62 million, including 120 stakes winners, sixty-seven of which won graded stakes.

Nureyev selling as a yearling.

In 1984, when *Successful Thoroughbred Investment* was written, the annual foal crop was 49,247. Average earnings per racehorse had grown to $7,774. The yearling sales included 9,268 lots (19.6 percent of the crop) that averaged $41,396; seven of the top-ten yearling prices of all time were achieved that year (without those seven yearlings the average was $36,428). The highest-priced yearling, at $8,250,000, was a son of Northern Dancer—Ballade, by Herbager.

In contrast to Nureyev, this colt turned out to be pretty much of a bust, although he did play an important part in the history of the Thoroughbred world market. In March of 1985, Sheikh Mohammed bought a half interest in him as a two-year-old from Robert Sangster, signaling the end of the epic monetary battles the Sangster group had waged with the Arabs in the sales ring. The horse was named Imperial Falcon, and he won two cheap races in Ireland as a three-year-old before becoming an obscure stallion. He now stands for $1,000, live foal, at Cloverleaf Farm in

Florida. (Did you ever notice how really good horses usually have good names? Well, Imperial Falcon is the exception to the rule. Here's a truly wonderful name wasted on a truly ordinary horse.)

The other six didn't exactly set the world on fire, either. Jareer ($7,100,000), by Northern Dancer—Fabuleux Jane, won a race at age two in England and now stands in Italy. Amjaad ($6,500,000), by Seattle Slew—Desiree, was unplaced and now stands in Venezuela. Obligato ($5,400,000), by Northern Dancer—Truly Bound, was unplaced and now stands in New York. Wassl Touch ($5,100,000), by Northern Dancer—Queen Sucree, won a minor stakes in England and was later reported standing in Japan. Parlando ($4,600,000), by Northern Dancer—Bubbling, was unraced and now stands in Mexico. Professor Blue ($4,000,000), by Northern Dancer—Mississippi Mud, was placed in France and now stands in the Philippines.

There is an important lesson here. If the Sangster team and several groups of Arabs can go to the select sales with all their vast financial and intellectual resources, spend an average of $5 million per yearling, and still strike out, you really shouldn't feel bad if the first yearling you buy doesn't turn out to be a champion.

When *Successful Thoroughbred Investment* was published, we made a conscious decision to add the ponderous phrase "in a Changing Market" to the title as a subtle warning that the Thoroughbred market was oversaturated and a correction was imminent. Actually, I had forecasted that the Thoroughbred business would undergo a substantial correction as early as 1982 in an article I wrote for a European magazine called *Pacemaker*, but I didn't realize just how sharp or enduring the decline would be.

Neither Jack Lohman nor I being particularly afflicted by a surfeit of subtlety, we noted in the text:

> As this book is being written, the Thoroughbred
> business is in an extremely volatile period of

> change. We feel it is probably in the second year of
> a four- to six-year shakeout. A study by the excel-
> lent publication *Racing Update* in March of 1984
> concluded, "...the commercial yearling market is
> in poor health as things stand now...In our opin-
> ion, certainly no more than two of every seven
> 1983 Kentucky auction yearlings showed a profit,
> and the figure is probably closer to one in four."

At the 1984 September yearling sales, only about ten percent of
the stallions represented by yearlings at the sales achieved a median of three times their retail stud fees, which is the traditional rule
of thumb for determining whether a breeder makes money on a
yearling. While this doesn't mean that a full ninety percent of the
yearlings at that sale were losing propositions, it did mean that a
high percentage of the yearlings that were sent through the ring
were not profitable for their breeders. This should have served as a
conspicuous warning for breeders that the business was in for a
serious shakeout.

> As we write this book, we feel that many stud fees
> will drop in 1985 and subsequent years to a rate of
> about half to one-third of what they had been in
> the late '70s and early '80s. This, of course, will be
> reflected in the syndication value of good horses
> at the racetrack, and, unfortunately, we feel that a
> number of people will be disappointed with the
> stud value of horses they had been expecting to
> make them rich.
> Further, since the price of broodmares is also a
> function of yearling prices, we expect an adjust-
> ment in the overall broodmare market during this
> shakeout period.

As can be seen from the following chart of the 1984-2000 yearling sales, and as predicted in *Successful Thoroughbred Investment,*

the yearling market took a sharp dive beginning in 1985-86. The decline steadily continued until it hit bottom in 1992. Since then, it has been on a long, steady upward drive.

A certain level of arrogance prevails in the horse business that leads otherwise sensible people to accept the fallacy we are somehow exempt from the laws of economics.

This abdication of accountability (or, more likely, refusal to acknowledge reality) led many of those in the Thoroughbred industry to blame the problems our industry faced in the late '80s and early '90s on the Tax Reform Act of 1986.

However, other than giving people who didn't want to face reality something to blame for the problems that resulted from overproduction and excesses in the sales ring, the Tax Reform Act of 1986 had little to do with the decline.

In fact, I believe that the single most important factor in the "depression" was a meeting in Sheikh Mohammed's palace in Dubai in March of 1985.

The meeting is best described in *Horsetrader*, the biography of Robert Sangster by Nick Robinson and Patrick Robinson, which is

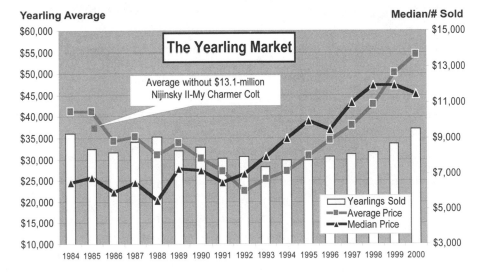

excellent, if I do say so myself even though I collaborated with them on it:

The summit was held behind closed doors. The only upshot of it was an announcement that Sheikh Mohammed had taken a share in two hors-

es which Robert had bought at the last sale. One of them was the $8.25 million Northern Dancer—Ballade colt, now being prepared by Vincent [O'Brien]. But no word was ever uttered about the essence of the meeting...

Whatever had been decided at the summit, the market was about to crash. The Arabs and the Brethren from Coolmore

Sheikh Mohammed. would not drive each other up again. The years of craziness were ended, as suddenly and abruptly as they had begun. Kentucky breeders would not need their

Brinks trucks to pick up the cash any longer. They needed crash helmets. Nothing, repeat noth- ing...would be the same again... ...The 1985 Keeneland Summer Sales...still had its show-busi- ness glamour...but the mighty bidding duels between the Tipperary traders and Sheikh Mohammed were over. The Sheikh was now an owner of Vincent O'Brien's and, when his

Robert Sangster. men went in to buy, they did so unopposed by the agents repre-

senting the Coolmore team. When Joss Collins stepped forward for the Irishmen, they were not challenged by the men from the Gulf.

The Sangster team[1] would be forced to go to the mat one more time in 1985 when it had to bid $13.1 million to obtain a son of Nijinsky II—My Charmer. The opposing group comprised Bob French, Mel Hatley, and Eugene Klein, who were represented by Wayne Lukas. It was ludicrous. Rich men fighting each other with money; money that essentially was being thrown away based on the breeding potential of horses that seldom, if ever, seemed to pan out.[2]

Just how insane was it? As a comparison, $13.1 million was a little more than three times the entire purse money available in Ireland that year. When you include the Nijinsky II colt, the average for the 1985 Keeneland July sale was $537,129, and without him it was $488,502, so he alone raised the sales average $48,627.

As you can see from the previous chart, when you include the Nijinsky II—My Charmer colt, the overall yearling average for the year was $41,311, while without him it was $38,945, six percent less. As pointed out in *Horsetrader*, the debacle had begun.

The Thoroughbred business is subject to the laws of supply and demand, just like any other business, and as much as people would like to find an excuse for the difficulties faced by the industry, the problems are usually the result of its inner workings not exterior forces.

For example, as predicted in that 1982 *Pacemaker* article, one primary engine behind the crash of the mid-'80s was that the number of stallions being syndicated was so high that there

---

[1] In this instance, the team comprised sixty-five percent Coolmore, twenty-five percent Stavros Niarchos (formerly another fierce competitor), and ten percent Danny Schwartz, a frequent partner.

[2] For the record, while he didn't exactly set the world on fire, the $13.1-million colt was not as big of a bust as some of his predecessors. Named Seattle Dancer, he won two group II races in Ireland, the Derby Trial and Gallinule Stakes, and finished second in the group I Grand Prix de Paris. He knocked around a bit as a journeyman stallion in Ireland and Australia, before being sold to Japan in 1996.

weren't enough mares to go around, even if syndicate managers gave away seasons.[3] The picture is further muddled by consistent allegations that more than just a few of the million-dollar yearling sales in those days just might have been predicated on false pretenses. While it is judicious not to point fingers, many people suspect that several of the top-priced yearlings that went through the auction ring in those days had actually been purchased from consignors for substantially less money and were sent through the ring at outrageously inflated prices, following which they were syndicated as racing prospects at the inflated sums.

A good advisor will keep you from buying into these schemes. Making money in this business is difficult enough without paying five times what a horse is worth before you even start.

In 2000 the foal crop was estimated at 36,700; the average starter earned $16,560; a total of 9530 yearlings (twenty-six percent of the total foal crop) were sold for an average of $54,506 and a median of $11,500; and the top-priced yearling of 2000 brought $6.8 million. Of course, it's too early to tell what will happen with any of the top-priced yearlings, but keep an eye out, because seeing how they pan out is always fun.

When an industry experiences a shakeout, no matter the cause, it often emerges stronger. The horse industry is no different, and during the last half of the '90s, the Thoroughbred business was more robust than ever before. For instance, both the North American yearling average and median[4] were at record levels in

---

[3] More than 100 new stallions were retired to Kentucky alone in 1982, which, even accounting for average attrition and a normal book (about forty-five mares in those days), would require the addition of about 3,600 new broodmares to the breeding pool in order to balance out the added seasons that were available.

[4] In the mid-'70s when Bill Robertson and I were editors of *The Thoroughbred Record*, we were met with general derision when we began to publish sales medians in addition to averages as a measure of central tendency, because sales results were already reaching the point where one or two yearlings could skew the average so badly that it would become insignificant.

1999, and as will be discussed later, many of the major yearling sales in 2000 made their 1999 counterparts look like they were held in a recession.

Today's market also has more overall substance. I can't remember it ever being as broad in strength and participation. Thanks to a number of factors, most notably new ways to get into the business, coupled with unprecedented national economic prosperity, a wider range of people can now afford to get involved in the Thoroughbred business than ever before (see Chapter 8).

Most of the prime economic indicators for the horse business are at all-time highs. As mentioned, almost all the indicators of strength in the yearling market have soared to their highest levels in history during the past several years, and the yearling market is the true indicator of the economic health of the business.

While some people might think that the racing segment is the primary indicator of the health of the business, I believe it is only a secondary indicator. The health of racing may, but does not necessarily, influence the yearling market. If potential earnings had real bearing on the yearling market, I think average earnings per runner and the yearling average would correlate, but as you can see in the following chart, they usually don't.

Further, if what went on at the racetrack had any real bearing on the economic strength of the Thoroughbred business, we would probably be in pathetic shape, even now when the market is at a pinnacle.

Purses in North America crossed the billion-dollar mark in 1999 and reached an all-time high of $1.165 billion in 2000 thanks largely to simulcasting and other ways of stretching the betting dollar. According to the International Federation of Horse Racing Authorities, horse owners were able to recoup about forty-two percent of their expenses in the form of purses in 1999. The percentage of return had been around forty-five percent since the

Yearling Average   **Average Earnings/Rnr**

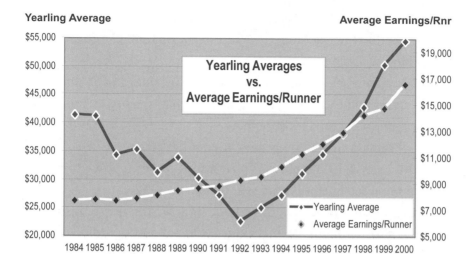

Federation began publishing these figures. Based on a forty-five percent return of expenses, that means that North American horse owners spent more than $2.2 billion in 2000 in order to earn slightly more than $1 billion in purses.

Breaking it down a little further, the average earnings per runner in 2000 was $16,560, and fewer than twenty percent of the runners earned more than $25,000, which for the past twenty years has been the traditional benchmark for a horse earning its own way. Even if a horse did only have to earn $25,000 a year to pay its way, when you consider it is the custom (actually, today it's a require-ment) to give ten percent of the winning purse to the trainer, one or two percent to the groom, and another ten percent to the rider, not to mention tipping everybody at the racetrack to celebrate, I think that the average horse has to earn between $32,500 and $35,000 a year, conservatively, to break even at the track. That, then, reduces the percentage of horses that are actually earning their way to somewhere around twelve percent. Worse still, it is projected that about half of the horses running in North America in 2000 earned $6,000 or less. Perhaps more discouraging, about seventy percent of all runners earned less than $15,000, while about ten percent failed to earn anything at all.

It doesn't make much economic sense, does it? What most owners are hoping is their racing operation will make their horses more valuable as breeding prospects so they can produce yearlings and get into the money-making part of the business. And, most of them are having a pretty good time while hoping to luck onto a good horse so they can have an even better time.

Further proof the yearling market is the primary engine driving the horse business is in the below chart, which shows how the broodmare and weanling markets follow the yearling market. As you can see, the trend line for broodmares follows the yearling line almost exactly, and while the weanling line bounces around a little more, the overall trend also follows the yearling market. The market for seasons and shares follows the yearling market, as well.

If nothing else, the chart below should tell you that by the time the major yearling sales are winding down in mid-September, a savvy advisor ought to have a good line on how strong the breed-

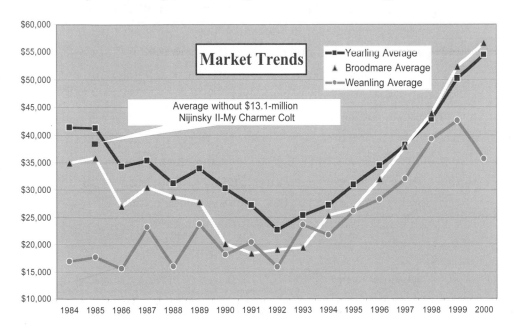

ing stock sales are going to be later in the fall.

Another reason why the market is stronger than ever before is that today's Thoroughbred business is more honest than ever before. This is an information-intensive business, and a lot more information is readily available to owners and breeders. This should enable investors not only to check up on the business, but to check out what their people are telling them.

One more important point needs to be made. Like any other enterprise, the Thoroughbred business is cyclical, and the hair on the back of my neck rises whenever I hear people talking about the boom going on forever.

As mentioned earlier, the strength of the overall economy and creative marketing have combined to produce more ways to participate in the Thoroughbred business than I can ever remember. This has both good and bad points. For instance, in the '80s the health of the Thoroughbred business basically depended on the whim of five or six people who could wreak havoc by deciding, as they should have done years earlier, that it was idiotic for them to keep battling each other at the select sales.[5] Now with broader participation, the economic health of the Thoroughbred business is less dependent on a few individuals and more dependent on the vagaries of the overall world economy.

If, indeed, the health of the Thoroughbred business is a direct result of the health of the world economy, then we need to be keeping an eye on the activities of Alan Greenspan and the governors of the Federal Reserve who, as this is being written, have begun to raise interest rates and take other steps to cool the economy.

For that reason alone, I would not be at all surprised to see a

---

[5] To an impartial observer, it would also seem that the British Bloodstock Agency, which represented most of the major players in those epic battles in the sales ring during the early '80s, might have felt some sort of fiduciary responsibility to their clients to stem the bleeding, rather than leaving it to Sheikh Mohammed to initiate the truce/compromise.

touch of softness or a correction in the bloodstock market some time during the next couple of years, and from many consignors' reactions to the major sales in 2000, I think it has already begun. I don't know how long it will last or how deep it will run, but I'm convinced that (a) a correction is already underway, and, more importantly, (b) it will not be nearly as destructive as the last one.

Today's auction market remains very strong at the top — and somewhat surprisingly shows some strength at the lower levels — with the primary weakness showing up in the middle. However, the strength at the top of the market appears to be more broadly based than it was in the '80s when a very few horses were propping up the averages. While averages have continued to rise, medians have declined only moderately, with the exception of weanlings, which took a major hit because weanling to yearling pinhookers took a bath in the select sales.

The worrisome problem to emerge in 2000 was an increase in sales results where horses that are not at the top of the market generate little or no interest at all…or at least they do not generate enough interest to tempt their consignors to sell them.

Consequently, the rate of RNAs (reserve not attained) is creeping up at sales across the country, particularly sales of two-year-olds in training. RNAs are horses that did not bring the reserve prices consignors place on them at an auction, which, incidentally, is perfectly legal. A rise in the number or percentage of RNAs usually is a sign that fewer sales animals are generating bids sufficient to make a profit (see Chapter 6). At the major sales of two-year-olds in training in 2000, RNAs reached a record high. More than thirty-seven percent of the horses cataloged failed to meet their reserves.

This makes me a little nervous because during the past five years or so pinhookers have become more of a significant influence on the yearling market. Pinhookers are people or groups who buy a horse at one sale in order to sell it again at a later sale, i.e., they purchase a weanling to sell back at the yearling sales or a yearling to sell at a sale of two-year-olds in training. When they don't make a profit on the two-year-olds that they sell, they can't pay as much for yearlings, or when they don't make a profit on their yearlings, they can't pay as much for weanlings, etc.

Pinhookers have been active in the yearling market at major sales during the past several years. In addition to the horses that they actually buy, pinhookers account for a substantial portion of the underbidding on a large segment of the overall market, as well.

However, another strong reason I have for believing that any shakeout we are facing or experiencing will be neither as devastating nor as long term as the last one is that whatever softness we are currently feeling has absolutely nothing to do with decreased demand. In fact, I am fully convinced that demand is higher in the Thoroughbred business than it has ever been.

In my opinion, our current problems are the result of overproduction and overpricing, not a lack of demand for our product.

Remember my earlier diatribe about supply and demand, and, in particular, the egocentric attitude prevalent in the horse business that we are exempt from the laws of supply and demand? Well, at the risk of being redundant, let me state once again that the horse business is not exempt from any economic laws, particularly supply and demand.

If you catalogue 4,700 horses in a yearling sale, or 5,100 horses in a breeding stock sale as Keeneland did in 2000, inevitably the sale is going to have weak spots. It is no reflection on Keeneland — they are simply providing a service — but anyone who thinks a sale that big can be strong throughout is crazy.

Further, on the subject of supply and demand, stud fees are increasing once again to the point where it is becoming more difficult for the average mare owner to produce a profitable yearling.

Stallion numbers and the number of mares to which they are

being bred are beginning to creep up to worrisome levels. This is an inevitable result of rising stud fees, because as the stallion business gets more profitable, more people want to get in it.

Back when I was working on the *Pacemaker* article, I think I was the first person to publicly examine the ratio of seasons to available mares. When too many nominations or seasons are available, many go to waste no matter how reasonably a stallion is priced. There just aren't enough mares to go around, even if the stallion managers give away the seasons.

In 2000, a total of eighty-two stallions (sixty-three of which stood in Kentucky) were bred to 100 mares or more, and an additional sixty-five stallions (thirty-nine of them in Kentucky) were bred to between eighty-one and 100 mares. Keep in mind that a "normal" book of mares used to be about forty-five and now is closer to between sixty-five and seventy. This means an increasing number of stallions won't get enough mares to be economically feasible.

As noted in the *Thoroughbred Times* November 6, 1999 article:

> ...the gap between the haves and have-nots has never been wider. The top 100 stallions — those with books of 90 or more — were bred to a total of 10,651 mares in 1999. On the opposite end of the spectrum, 1,744 stallions covered five or fewer mares. In other words, 2.6 percent of the stallions serviced 18.5 percent of available mares, while the bottom 46.5 percent got just 7.8 percent of the total mare population. Fully sixty percent of North American stallions covered eight or fewer mares in 1999.

This doesn't take into account that approximately thirty-five to forty new stallions retired to stand in Kentucky in 2000. With normal attrition through death, movements, retirements, etc., this means another 1,000 to 1,500 nominations are probably available.

As a breeder, this is sort of a good news/bad news story. If there is an overabundance of seasons on the market, stallion managers will (or should) be forced to reduce fees to some stallions in order to attract mares. On the other hand, remember how I keep insisting supply and demand does apply to the horse market? If you go to the yearling sales with, say, a daughter or son of Tale of the Cat (who was bred to 175 mares this year and with normal fertility should produce between 135 and 150 foals), you damned well better have one that's nearly perfect, because forty to forty-five others may be in the sale as well. In fact, seven stallions had forty or more yearlings catalogued in the 2000 Keeneland September yearling sale. Consequently, if yours isn't perfect, he will generate little, if any, interest. You may see this as a weak spot in the sale, but I view it as an oversupply of yearlings by a particular sire.

In summary, I am saying that no one should get into the Thoroughbred business based on the assumption that it's going to be capable of sustaining the strength and growth it has experienced during the past five or six years.

Having said that, I would like to close this chapter with a final thought I included in *Successful Thoroughbred Investment*, a conviction that I believe in as strongly today as I did in 1984:

> ...Throughout history, in times of market fluctuation, in times of recession or depression, there have been people who continued to make money, good money. They were the people who were smart, who studied, who worked hard, and who were able to anticipate trends and capitalize on that anticipation. There are a lot of people like that in the horse business today, and, if you hook up with one or more of them, your chances of success will improve dramatically.

CHAPTER
THREE

CHOOSING YOUR ADVISOR OR AGENT

"You may be Albert Einstein in the building business or the rag trade, but you're going to need help in the Thoroughbred business."

— *A.K.*

Take my word for it, choosing your advisor or agent probably will be the most important step you'll take in the horse business, short of buying this book.

The choice will, quite literally, make the difference between a pleasant and an unpleasant experience, between profit and loss, or between loss and ruin. This is no exaggeration. I know numerous examples of the first two of those categories and several of the final one! People have been ruined in this business because it's extremely easy to get in over your head — it can happen very quickly, and it usually happens after some early success.

So, here we go again:

Don't check your brains at the door.

Many highly successful business people have taken a terrible beating in the horse business because they either were too careless in the selection of their advisors or, worse, decided that they were smart enough to go it alone.

Most of these people would no more think of hiring someone to drive a $75,000 tractor-trailer rig without a thorough background check than they would think of trying to swim the Pacific Ocean. Yet, they'll give a half-million dollars to some guy to buy and train the most expensive and fragile animals in the world, and all they know about him is they met him in a bar someplace and he said he was a horse trainer. Anyone you hire or take on as an advisor should be happy to give you a number of references, and you should check those references carefully.

Why do you even need an advisor? For one thing, the horse industry, especially the Thoroughbred business, is very complicated. I can assure you that you cannot hope to learn about it quickly enough to keep up with the constant changes without working on it full time.

This business is full of absolute fanatics — people who think about nothing but horses; they don't read books or magazines unless they're about horses; they don't see movies unless it's something like *National Velvet* or *Simpatico*; and they don't listen to music unless it's Dan Fogelberg's inane "Run for the Roses"...or maybe the Light Cavalry Overture.

You'll be competing in the same arena with those people. After meeting many of them, you may decide, quite correctly, that someone with average intelligence is way out in front in this game, but you'll have no chance unless you have someone who is equally fanatical on your side.

As a matter of fact, most of the successful people who operate in the horse business full time use experts to help them. For instance, the Coolmore group, which arguably has enjoyed greater financial success the past three decades than anyone else in the Thoroughbred business, employs a team concept. When Michael Tabor and John Magnier go to the sales, they are accompanied by a number of people, all the way from trainers and bloodstock agents to business managers and several veterinarians, all of whom serve a purpose on the team when it selects a horse at a sale.

Carrying the process one step further, Fusao Sekiguchi engaged a head-hunting firm to find an agent to advise him in the purchase of yearlings in America. The firm came up with John Ward, who bought Fusaichi Pegasus for Sekiguchi.

Bob and Beverly Lewis can attribute much of their success to bloodstock agent John Moynihan, who in conjunction with trainers such as Wayne Lukas and Bob Baffert, helped them purchase Charismatic and other good horses.

In short, this is a very complex business, and even the experts have advisors who help them in the selection of their bloodstock, so why shouldn't you?

Before going any further, it should be noted that your advisor can be any one of a number of people: a "general advisor," a bloodstock agent, a horse trainer, a farm operator, or a combination thereof. Most likely, it will be a team, because the business today is so complex that it is virtually impossible for a single person to embody all the skills necessary to achieve success. One person will probably be your primary or principal advisor, but if he says he can do it all himself, be wary from the start. It also is highly advisable to have a lawyer and/or an accountant as part of your team.

Bob and Beverly Lewis have gotten good advice.

As you'll discover in Chapter 7, even the Internal Revenue Service places considerable emphasis on your choice of advisors and experts in determining whether your horse operation qualifies as a business. In the unlikely event that you can find a lending institution that is willing to grant a loan to you for your equine endeavors, it also will be highly interested in the quality and reputation of the people who are assisting you.

So your advisor is going to be one of the best investments you'll make in the horse business.

Just to emphasize this most important point, I'd like to digress for a moment to recount a couple of horror stories about people going into the horse business. Both of these were in *Successful Thoroughbred Investment,* but each is such an egregious example of what can happen if you're not careful that they both bear repeating here. Some of the names have been eliminated to protect the stupid, but as you're shaking your head at the lunacy of the characters, remember that both of these stories are absolutely true and the second one is not all that uncommon. The first is the story of how a bad, a very bad, advisor cost his client a great deal of money, while the second is a story of how two people got smart too fast, and it wound up costing them money.

On February 27, 1982, a gentleman in Louisiana paid $750,000 for a three-year-old that was the leading contender for the HITS Parade Invitational Derby, a minor stakes, now defunct, that was restricted to horses sold in the HITS Parade Invitational two-year-olds in training sale, a minor sale, also now defunct. The horse, whose name was Real Dare, could run a little bit — he had won the HITS Parade Futurity (same restrictions) the previous year and had earned nearly $140,000 — so he was obviously the class of the field for the "Derby" the next day. The odd thing was that Real Dare was a gelding, and not too many geldings, with the possible exceptions of Kelso, Forego, and John Henry, are worth that sort of price tag, let alone one who is obviously several levels below a top horse.

Sure enough, the next day Real Dare returned $60,000, a substantial portion of his purchase price, as he easily won the HITS Parade Derby. Then the story came out as to why the new owner paid such a sum for a gelding:

After the race, an incredulous reporter from *The Thoroughbred Record* asked Real Dare's proud new owner how he could justify paying such an exorbitant sum for a gelding. The reply was (and I promise you this is a true quote from *The Record*): "We are researching the possibility of having microsurgery performed on Real Dare after this year. There's a urologist in California who, I understand, has performed this surgery about 200 times without a failure...on sheep, hogs, and horses. What the surgery does is make a gelded animal fertile again. They would take the testicles from another horse. The testicles only produce the sperm; the genetics are all in the prostate."

Well, anyone who got a grade above a D- in biology knows that the genetics are contained in the sperm, which is produced by the testicles, but the gentleman in question took the word of his bloodstock agent and didn't take the time to ask a veterinarian if what the agent told him was possible.

Needless to say, Real Dare is still a gelding. He continued to race for several more years, and now is probably pulling a buggy in the French Quarter. At the time this book was written, he was only about $600,000 short of returning his purchase price to his owner. The agent, who is out of jail now, still laughs about the big lick he hit down in New Orleans...and still works occasionally as a blood-stock agent. Once again, an agent with a sharp line had struck, and someone who failed to check out a story was left holding the bag, a rather considerable one in this case.

The second horror story involves a good advisor and two clients who got too smart way too fast.

Bill Lockridge is a knowledgeable horseman who has as keen an eye for a horse as anyone I can think of. In addition to many of the good horses that he has purchased for his clients, he was the original syndicator of Storm Bird, and he sold Terlingua to W. T. Young at the conclusion of her racing career. Bred to Storm Bird, Terlingua produced the phenomenally successful stallion Storm Cat.

In 1970, two fellows came to Kentucky for the Keeneland July yearling sale and asked Bill to find a nice filly for them. When they told him how much they had to spend, he was candid enough to let them know that they didn't stand much chance of buying anything decent at the July sale for that kind of money, and he took them out to a farm and showed them a daughter of Crimson Satan—Bolero Rose, by Bolero. After some dickering, he sold them the filly privately for $11,000.

The next year they came back for the Keeneland July sale and asked him to pick out another filly for them. This time they were able to go a little higher, so he went to the sale and paid $25,000 (you could do that in those days) for a daughter of Jacinto—Turkish Belle, by My Babu.

By the time the two guys came back for the 1972 sale, the first filly, now named Crimson Saint, had won two stakes and equaled a world record. The other, named Bold Liz, had won the $50,000-added Hollywood Lassie Stakes. She brought her earnings up to $168,235 by defeating colts in the $100,000-added Hollywood Juvenile Championship Stakes two days before the sale.

I was present when Bill asked if they'd like him to pick out another filly for them and was utterly dumfounded when they replied "no thanks; we can do it ourselves."

Just for the record, the two guys did not succeed nearly as well on their own and the two good fillies ultimately changed hands.

Crimson Saint ended her career with two track records, four stakes wins, and earnings of $91,770. Her eight yearlings to sell at auction (her last was in 1993) grossed $16,975,000 and included a Nijinsky II colt that brought $3,500,000 at the 1988 Keeneland July sale and a Secretariat colt that brought $1,800,000 at the 1983 Keeneland July sale. The Nijinsky II colt was named Royal

Academy, and he went on to become an Irish champion and winner of the 1990 Breeders' Cup Mile. The Secretariat colt, named Pancho Villa, became a multiple graded-stakes winner. Crimson Saint also is the dam of the aforementioned Terlingua, who was a multiple graded-stakes winner in her own right.

Bold Liz wound up with $174,785 in earnings, and three yearlings out of her sold for a total of $495,000.

The point here is one of the most dangerous things you can do in the horse business is get too smart too fast.

Qualities of an Advisor

I hope by now you've decided to get yourself good advisors and that you will check them out before you actually sign with them. Most importantly, you also have to decide you will listen to them once they're on your team.

The next step is to figure out what you want in an advisor. But before going on to list the qualities I feel are important, I'll mention a few agents/advisors you should definitely avoid.

This little section will save you a lot of grief. Avoid, at all costs, the following:

Mr. Know-It-All — This guy knows the name of the Unknown Soldier and, what's worse, will tell you. All talk and no listen. All the trainers are crooks; farm managers are idiots; veterinarians are not only stupid but overpaid; etc. He's the smartest guy in the business — just ask him — and the only reason he hasn't been a success, thus far, is that the business is totally backward and doesn't do things his way.

Do yourself a favor and run like a scalded rat. Even if this guy were right about everything he says — which he isn't — he'd drive you absolutely crazy within the first week.

Bar Trainer — He's charming, witty, fun, but always seems to have time to hang around the clubhouse bar, the turf club bar —

or some other bar. His horses, if he really has any, never seem to run, and the truth of the matter is that he's just trolling for clients. Always trolling, never catching.

Homewrecker with a Catalogue — Okay, okay, I know you don't have to pass any sort of qualifying exam to be a bloodstock agent, but this agent's qualifications are often more apparent to the eye than to any of the other senses.

On a serious note, I don't want anyone to get the wrong impression about my opinion of women in the horse business, particularly in this age of political correctness. Consequently, I would like to reiterate the assertion in the Preface that the horse business is a place where women can and do compete very successfully with their male counterparts, and the vast majority of female bloodstock agents are competent, talented, and honest. Some of them are pretty good looking, too. But all looks and no brains is a recipe for disaster in this business.

You'll have absolutely no problem picking them out, and just one additional word of caution, the horse business is expensive enough without having to add the cost of a divorce.

Pedigree Pundit — Has an encyclopedic memory...can tell you the seventh dam of the winner of the 1958 Albanian Derby, but if you send him to town for a bar of soap, he'll come back with a watermelon every time. As a practical matter, this guy is really not sure which end kicks and which end whinnies, and contrary to most experience, he thinks something that appears in the sixth generation of a pedigree really counts. Worst of all, he'll also bore you to death.

One-Trick Ponies — Has a system of picking out young horses that is absolutely foolproof, not to mention all the others are wrong. In my career of enduring about a thousand of these characters, a few of the systems that I recall are measuring horses, listening to hearts, and checking throat latches. Actually, almost all of these methods have some validity, but they should be used as tools in an overall strategy, not as the solitary indicator of whether a horse will turn out to be a runner.

The single most important component of future success for a young horse cannot be detected or measured in advance: the desire and ability to overcome his defects and win races. If there were a way to ascertain that, the Maktoums would own all the good horses in the world, and the rest of us would be fighting over what's left.

Cell phone and an accent — It's sad but true that it takes more to be successful as a bloodstock agent than possession of a catalogue and a cell phone.

For instance, an accent helps. Contrary to popular opinion, just because someone isn't spicking so good ze Eengleesh don't make him no smarter than anybody else.

Underbidders on John Henry — If all the losers who've told me they were underbidders on John Henry had actually been bidding — and if they had actually bid even $1 apiece — he would have sold for far more than he earned, which was $6,591,860. The same goes for the 1998 sprint champion Reraise, who sold for $8,000 as a yearling and has earned close to seven figures, and 1994 older male champion The Wicked North, a $10,000 yearling and earner of nearly $1.2 million. The only qualification is that the horse must have sold at one time for at or less than $10,000 — which is about ten times what any of these characters could scrape up if they got all their clients to go together on one horse — and the horse should have earned at least $1 million.

Mr. Everybody's a Crook But Me — Like the paranoid walking through the halls of the insane asylum saying "everybody here is crazy except me," this person sees the bad in everybody but himself. Of course, also like the paranoid, he's probably as bad or worse than everyone he's accusing.

From a personal standpoint, I'm just naturally suspicious of the only virgin in the whorehouse.

Now, when you begin to look for this superhuman being who is going to turn you into an instantaneous success, what are the qualities that make for a good advisor?

The following are a few of the criteria that I feel should apply to anyone you hire, whether you decide on a general advisor, a bloodstock agent, a trainer, or some other sort of help.

HONESTY. As much as I hate to admit it, while there are a lot of very good bloodstock agents, over the years the horse business has become a haven for quite a number of charlatans, primarily because so few people know a lot about the business and because luck is such a large element to it. There's an aura of mystery to it, too, that seems to lend itself to people with less-than-sterling character getting hold of new people coming into the business.

As with life, very few guarantees exist in the horse business, but I will provide you with an iron-clad guarantee that if you come around the horse industry looking to get robbed, you'll find somebody to accommodate you in a hurry. Part of the problem is the lack of licensing, peer oversight groups, and ethics procedures for bloodstock advisors or agents. Making it worse is that the shysters seem to get out and spend a lot of time digging up new customers, while the legitimate types are at the office or barn doing their homework. A lot of people do seem to wind up in the wrong hands from the very outset.

Honesty, in this sense, means a lot more than just personal integrity. Your advisor should be willing and even anxious to answer any questions, openly and honestly. And you should ask a lot of questions. Too often people who are successful in other businesses are reluctant to appear stupid by asking a lot of questions about the horse business. Look at it this way: you didn't make a million dollars in the manufacture of widgets without knowing everything there is to know about the widget business. The same thing applies to horses. Beware of someone who has all the answers, though; that's unnatural, too, particularly in today's highly complex horse business (see Mr. Know-It-All, above). Your advisor should try to educate you on the business rather than keeping you in the dark.

INTELLIGENCE. While you don't necessarily need a genius in this business, you also don't want someone who needs to unzip his fly to count to eleven. As mentioned earlier, and as you'll learn as you get further into it, racing is an enormously complex business, with a constant and tremendous flow of information. Your advisor must be able to assimilate that information and interpret it accurately for your benefit. He should be someone who can spot trends and anticipate the market, if not before anyone else, at least early on.

KNOWLEDGE AND EXPERIENCE. While some people tend to think they can impress clients with their encyclopedic knowledge of the minutiae of the business (see Pedigree Pundit, above), there is no substitute for experience.

I would much prefer to have someone who has been around long enough to know where to find the answers to your questions, who knows the ins and outs of the business, rather than to have someone who has spent his entire time in an ivory tower somewhere reading about it.

COMPATIBILITY. If you are going to do things right and your advisor is going to do right by you, you will be spending a lot of time with him. Further, since one of your goals is to make this a pleasant experience, using someone you don't like wouldn't make sense, no matter how good he is. Pick someone with whom you'd like to spend time even if it weren't for your horse business. As a matter of fact, if you have to sacrifice a small quantity of one or two of the other qualities in favor of compatibility, you'll find it works out better that way in the long run.

COMMUNICATION. This ranks right along with compatibility in importance. You don't want to find out your horse is entered in a race by reading it in the *Daily Racing Form* or that something is wrong with your horse by discovering a large number of veterinary charges on your monthly statement. One reason you have all these people working for you is to keep you apprised of what's happening in your business. There are occasional trainers and farm personnel — some of the "best in the business," as a matter of fact — who seem to believe that it's really none of the client's business what's happening with his or her horses, particularly as long as things are going well. That is absolutely not so!

Wayne Lukas, the Great Communicator.

The late Charlie Whittingham operated under the theory that his clients should be treated "like mushrooms…in the dark all the time and up to their necks in manure." Charlie was able to do this because he was one of the best trainers in the history of Thoroughbred racing, so people would put up with that attitude in order to have their horses with him; but you don't want someone with that kind of attitude, especially when you're starting out.

By contrast, there's Wayne Lukas, who has been the leading

trainer in this country for the past two decades. When he accepted the 1998 John W. Galbreath Award, which is given annually by the University of Louisville College of Equine Administration for outstanding entrepreneurship in the equine industry, Lukas said:

"Where do trainers get off thinking that a guy who comes in, buys a yearling for fifty-thousand dollars, or a quarter of a million, or whatever his level is, should have to ask the trainer's permission to see it? That's how this game has been for a hundred years. The owners have to call up to hear their trainers say, 'No, you can't come to the barn, today. You're not allowed.'...I think it's crazy. All the people I've had success with are people I pulled in and got involved. "

He even has staff members whose sole duty it is to communicate with the owners. Which would you prefer to have for a trainer?

You should receive regular reports from your advisor and/or trainer as to how your horses are progressing, all of them. Even if you have a mare who's doing little more than gestating, you should receive periodic reports, because there are critical points in her gestation period when you should know her condition.

Remember, it is you who owns the horse — not the trainer or the farm manager — and you have every right to know what's going on with your horse at all times.

In fact, in addition to Wayne Lukas, a number of the leading trainers and boarding farms also now have an employee who is assigned to communicate with owners about their horses. Some even have web sites on which you can keep up with what's going on around the stable or the farm.

As mentioned, this ranks equally in importance with compatibility and is one of its functions. If you don't really like your associates, and vice versa, you'll be reluctant to call them to find out what's happening, or they will be less likely to call you with the good news, as well as the bad.

Now that you know what qualities to look for in an advisor, it's time to decide what kind of advisor you want. This decision should be based primarily on the extent of your experience, the size of your investment, and the degree of your involvement. You'll have to decide whether you want to retain a general advisor or a bloodstock agent...or both; whether you want to race or breed, in which case you'll need to decide on a trainer or a boarding farm (you should consult with your advisor or bloodstock agent); and whether you want to hire a separate accountant and/or lawyer to work with your horse operation or if you'd prefer to try to convince your present lawyer and accountant to get educated in the horse business.

Here's what you should consider when deciding whether to use a general advisor or a bloodstock agent: First, these are not necessarily mutually exclusive. As a matter of fact, your "general advisor" can, and often will, be someone who functions as a bloodstock agent. The difference is in the function he will serve for you.

A bloodstock agent makes his living buying and selling horses, and many agents feel their responsibility to the client ends with those functions. Others, on the other hand, are very good about giving their clients additional advice about matings, trainers, farms, etc. However, since a pure bloodstock agent makes his money buying and selling — and convincing his owners to buy and sell — he could be more interested in turning over your horses than in meeting your long-term goals.

By contrast, a general advisor is someone who will help you set up a complete program, who will follow you along the steps of that program, and who will look toward achieving your goals. This person will be on a retainer, or if you really want to inspire effort on his behalf, you might want to work out a formula with a moderate retainer and a percentage of your profits or savings.

Further, you might even want to go into partnership with your advisor, if he has sufficient funds to invest at the level of your participation in the business. This, at least in part, insures that you're getting his full attention and full effort, because if you are making money, presumably your partner is making money.

In addition to working with you to set up and oversee your investment plan in the industry, he also can help you pick and coordinate the other people with whom you'll be dealing: the trainer, the farm, sales agents, etc. He can serve as a clearinghouse for your information and bookkeeping, so that you'll have to worry about only one bill per month rather than a lot of them (be careful about this, though); he can make the necessary arrangements for you at the racetrack and/or sales. In short, he can be a personal manager for your equine affairs.

This will, quite obviously, cost you more than having a straight bloodstock agent, trainer, or farm operator handle your business, but the money will be well spent, and like purchasing a fine car, it might be cheaper in the long run than going second class.

If you decide to race, one of the first things you'll want to do is pick a trainer. As with all choices of the people on whom you'll rely, the same qualities you look for in an advisor will be important in your choice of a trainer.

You'll have to make other choices, too. Do you want someone who's up and coming or a "big name" trainer? How big is too big? Where do you want to race: near home, at a major racing center, or abroad? Are you going to be claiming horses or bringing them along?

As you start out, I might suggest an up-and-coming trainer who races somewhere close to your home. This way you can go to the track in the morning to watch your horses train and watch them run in the afternoon, all the time learning more and more of what goes on at a racetrack. You might call the racing secretary at your local racetrack for suggestions. While he won't say "so-and-so will be perfect for you," he should be able to give you the names of several trainers who might be likely candidates for your horses.

Generally, the young up-and-coming trainer will have more time to spend with you, although a number of "big" trainers seem to have a great deal of time to spend with new clients.

It's a matter of organization, really. Some trainers who have a large stable are very well organized and, as a consequence, are able to spend their time with people, while the less-organized ones don't ever seem to have any time, despite having only a couple of horses. Basically, it doesn't really matter how few or how many horses your trainer has; if he doesn't have time to spend with you, it's too many.

Also, it's a matter of how much you're willing to spend. If you start out with a few claiming horses, you're probably not going to get Wayne Lukas or Bob Baffert to train for you. You'll have to find someone on your own level, unless, of course, you're Bill Gates or the Sultan of Brunei. And, it is very important to inquire as to whether he can get stalls for your horses.

As far as your lawyer and accountant go, the size and complexity of your horse business will probably determine whether you use your regular people or hire specialists. Basically, racing and the horse business are pretty attractive to members of both professions, and unless you get into the business pretty deeply, your own lawyer and accountant should be able to learn enough to carry you along. That is, if they consult with some established equine specialists, if they attend one or two of the many seminars that are held each year on equine taxation (most of these seminars qualify for continuing education credits, incidentally), and if they are interested. On the subject of interest, your professionals would find it helpful to accompany you through your indoctrination into the business.

Start by buying each of them a copy of this book. Don't lend them yours; you'll never get it back.

You might encounter other specialists as well, for example pin-hooking and sales preparation experts, but I'll discuss them in more detail in the chapter on sales.

Finally, pay attention to the advice you get.

This may astound you, but some people in the horse business might take advantage of you, given the chance. That is one of the reasons you'll want an advisor who has some experience. He will have a good working knowledge of what you should pay for whatever equine assets you purchase.

And, just like you would do in your other business, if you hire someone to help you make up your mind, listen to him.

This brings to mind another horror story, more recent than the one about the two fellows from Texas, but no less egregious. A fellow, I'll just call him Mr. Beerman, came to Kentucky a while back, and went into the horse business. From what I gather, he had a little bit of good advice and a lot of bad advice, but his goal was to make a big splash in the horse business and teach these rubes around here a lesson.

He bought himself a farm and an interest in a moderately bred Derby winner. Word got around quickly that the guy was spending money like a drunken sailor, paying exorbitant prices for everything he bought.

Word of someone like that gets around fast — particularly when he sent out a letter offering to let long-established breeders buy shares in his Derby winner under terms that were ludicrous for an established and successful sire, much less one who had never set foot in the breeding shed.

Well, not surprisingly it wasn't too long before every charlatan in the Thoroughbred business had him bent over the barrel in order to take advantage of him.

His dream of making a splash in the business quickly deteriorated into the panicked thrashings of a drowning man.

He had to sell off a substantial number of his acquisitions, at drastically reduced prices, I've heard, and while he is still in the business, he has pulled in his horns to the point where he looks more like a stockyard steer than a longhorn bull.

The point is that this guy not only got some bad advice along the way, but when he got good advice, he didn't pay attention.

Fortunately, he seems to be smart enough to have learned his lesson, but it's been a damned expensive lesson at best.

An Indoctrination into the Business

On several occasions in this chapter, I've mentioned an indoctrination into the business. If you've shown enough interest to read this far, you undoubtedly already have a serious interest in Thoroughbreds and, perhaps, a little working knowledge of the business.

If you're really going to get serious and invest a substantial amount of money, though, you also should be willing to invest a little time as well, just as you would if you were going to invest in any other business. This is the reason for the indoctrination course, which you should go through before you invest in the business.

As with the list of "suggested reading" that appears at the end of this book, the course can be altered, rearranged, or parts of it can be postponed, but the various segments of the Thoroughbred business you'll learn about as you go through this are interdependent. Knowing a little bit about each one is helpful, whether you're particularly interested in it or not.

Undoubtedly the best place to start is at one of the New Owners Seminars that the Thoroughbred Owners and Breeders Association holds each year around the country. As the name suggests, these seminars educate people on basic investment in the horse.

These seminars are held three or four times a year, usually in conjunction with some applicable event such as the Kentucky Derby or the Breeders' Cup. The advantages to these seminars are many, but you'll want to attend primarily for these reasons: (a) you'll be matched with other attendees who are of the same interest and approximate knowledge level as you are, so many of them will probably ask the same questions that had you wondering but afraid to ask for fear of being thought an idiot; (b) you'll get to meet a number of participants in the business who are there to teach and to meet prospective clients; and (c) they typically include some sort of access to the attendant event that you might not normally be able to attain.

And, you just may get lucky. One of the new owners seminars is where Bob and Beverly Lewis hooked up with a young bloodstock agent named John Moynihan and began a relationship that

Agent John Moynihan knows how to pick winners for his clients.

has, as mentioned, produced Charismatic and Exploit, among other good horses.

After you've gotten your feet damp at a new owners seminar, or if you're going to go it alone, probably the easiest place to start is at the racetrack, where the entire equation begins, or ends, depending on your perspective. Some tracks have formal programs that are principally designed to teach you how to bet, but you can learn a lot about racing there, too. Or, you may just have to seek out people who know about the business. One thing you will find is that people around the track are very friendly and most of them are very willing to help you out. Be wary, though. Some of the most talkative ones are the ones with the least knowledge…and they'll be the hardest to get rid of once they latch onto you. Go to the general office or the racing secretary's office; they may suggest people who would be good to help you in the business.

While you're hanging around at the track, you'll learn how to read the *Daily Racing Form* and, to the horror of your prospective trainer, possibly a condition book; you'll learn about the classification of races and the concise way that the quality of races puts a value on racehorses. You'll learn how much money and effort it takes to train a horse and how fragile they really are; you'll learn about the training cycle and how many things can go wrong with a horse, especially a good one. You'll want to go out early in the morning during training hours and see how things work behind the scenes (many tracks have special morning programs designed for people who want to learn about training). You'll also learn how hard it is for a horse owner to break even at the track and how you can hit a big lick, à la John Henry and Seattle Slew. In short, you should expand on what you will learn here.

If you intend for your operation to be primarily racing oriented or if you intend to start out racing before going into breeding, I'd strongly recommend that you invest at least a week in this sort of program, less if you're going into breeding or sales right away.

Whether you're going to start out at the races or in breeding, your intermediate stop should probably be at the auctions, and nowadays you'll have plenty of opportunity to attend a sale pretty close to home, no matter where you live. In 2000 alone, there were more than seventy-five auctions in North America, with more than 24,000 horses selling for gross receipts of more than $1 billion (see Chapter 6). Sales took place from Florida to British Columbia, from California to Ontario, and they ran from January 10 to December 28. In short, if you can't find a horse sale, you really aren't looking very hard.

At the sales you'll learn how to read a catalogue; you'll learn something about the value of a horse and the perceived value of a horse; you'll learn about the influence of fashion on the business and about conformation. You'll meet a lot of people, happy ones and discouraged ones, and, most of all, you'll come to the realization that nothing is certain in the horse business. You should probably spend three or four days at the sales, even if you're not ready

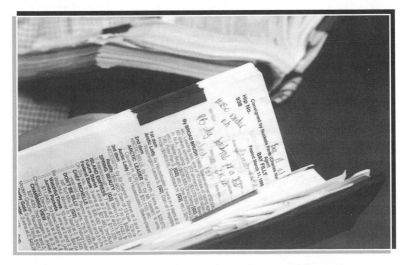

Learning to read a sales catalogue is part of the process.

to buy, just watching and listening to what goes on. You also should make it a point to attend a variety of sales: breeding stock, yearling, and two-year-olds in training.

If you're mostly interested in breeding, you should spend a while at a farm during several seasons of the year. For example, in the winter or spring during the breeding/foaling season, you should spend four or five days watching the foaling operation, observing the activities at the breeding shed, and learning about teasing and the reproductive cycle of the mare. You should spend some time "riding" with the farm veterinarian or with a local veterinarian as he makes his rounds. Then you should come back prior to sales time to spend a day or so learning about sales preparation, spend another day or so at the farm during weaning season, and a couple of days when the yearlings are being broken. In all, it should take a couple of weeks to expand on the contents of Chapter 5.

CHAPTER
FOUR

AT THE RACETRACK

"Keep yourself in the best of company...
and your horses in the worst."

— *An Old Racetrack Saying*

Most horse owners are racing fans whose interest led them beyond the status of mere spectator. As a result, they got into the horse business by buying a claiming horse or two. This avenue of investment offered them immediate action on the racetrack and a good idea of their horse's worth.

But before discussing claiming and other types of races, it would be worthwhile to explain the various types of races and how they rank on the pyramid of quality. In descending order of importance, they are:

Stakes races. Generally these are the highest quality races offered in the business. While the majority of stakes races are characterized by the requirement that owners put up money to enter (stakes money) and by "added money" put up by the tracks, the category of stakes also includes some invitational races. In these races, horse owners do not have to "stake" their horses — the horses are invited based on their performance ability. While stakes races represent only about four percent of all the races run in North America, they carry nearly twenty-four percent of all the purse money. Stakes range in value from $5,000 added (or even lower at some of the smaller tracks in the country) to the $4 million offered in the Breeders' Cup Classic. But the average purse for stakes in North America is about $90,000, which is up significantly from $50,000 in 1983. Stakes can be run under allowance, handicap, or weight-for-age conditions, all of which will be explained below.

Further dividing the category is whether the race qualifies as a graded or group (as they're known in Europe) stakes or just an added-money event. The graded/group stakes concept was created in the early '70s as a guide so that people less familiar with racing would "have a method...for identifying the highest quality black-type[1] events" that appear in sales catalogues, etc. Less than one percent of all races in North America are accorded graded status based on criteria that include the history of the race (principally, what quality of horses have run in it), the purse amount, etc. They are further divided into three subcategories:

> **Grade/Group I.** These classics and championship-quality events represent the most important races in each country, and in North America, account for about one-tenth of one percent of the total races run.
>
> **Grade/Group II.** These represent two-tenths of one percent of all races.
>
> **Grade/Group III.** These represent four-tenths of one percent of all races.

However, I think it's imperative to remind you again of the importance of having experience or an experienced advisor to guide you through the maze of racing statistics. Some countries, for whatever the reason, categorize an extraordinary number of races as graded or group. For instance, in Ireland five percent of all

---

[1] Horses that place first, second or third in a stakes race are assigned bold-face (black) type, which makes them stand out on a catalogue page and look more important than horses who have not won or placed in a stakes.

races are accorded group status, which is more than seven times the allotment of graded stakes in North America. Furthermore, quite a lot of these stakes have very short fields. It's common for four or five horses to go to the post with two or three from the same stable. Consequently, a horse that might be hard pressed to win the second half of the daily double on a Wednesday at Belmont could be group stakes-placed in one of these countries.

As you will see in the next chapter, stakes wins and placings, particularly in graded/group races, are important to the value of a horse as a breeding animal, but you must be careful to assure that the stakes are of real quality.

Handicap races. These are races that provide additional opportunities for the better claiming horses. The owners do not have to pay a fee to enter in these handicaps, but the racing secretary will assign weights to each horse, as he does in some stakes races. The assignments are designed to "handicap" the better horses by making them carry more weight than those deemed of lesser ability, theoretically equalizing all the participants. In its purest form, the handicapper is attempting to make all the horses in the race finish in a dead heat, which, of course, never happens. (Only about twenty triple dead heats have been recorded since the invention of the photo-finish camera. One of those was the 1944 Carter Handicap, considered to be the greatest handicapping feat of all time.) They work very well at minor tracks and/or tracks where there is not an abundance of stakes horses, and they not only provide additional racing opportunities for the better horses and their owners but the bettors like them, too.

Allowance races. These are reverse handicap races of sorts. All the horses start out at a set weight assignment and are given weight off, "allowances," for the things they have failed to do, such as win two races or win one race at a certain minimum class or distance since a specified date. In the general scheme of

TRIPLE DEAD HEAT
CARTER HANDICAP
1944
#5 – Brownie – Jockey – Guerin, E.
#4 – Bossuet – Jockey – Stout, J.
#6 – Wait A Bit – Jockey – Smith, G.L.

DEAD HEAT

PHOTO FOR WIN
BY D&S PHOTO

The 1944 Carter Handicap — a handicapping triumph.

things, allowances and handicaps are about equal, except that handicaps are usually for older, more established horses. In both handicap and allowance races, the class of race is determined by the purse size, and some handicap and allowance races are actually superior to some stakes races.

Maiden races. These are for horses that have never won a race at an official pari-mutuel meeting. There can be maiden allowance races, maiden special weights, maiden claiming, and even maiden stakes races. The one exception is that if a horse becomes a jumper, he will be a maiden in steeplechasing or hurdle races until he wins one of them, no matter how well he raced on the flat.

Claiming races. These are, by definition, races in which every horse entered carries a price tag and can be purchased, irrevocably, by any eligible owner at the meet.

Claiming races make up the bulk of any racing program in America. While they annually represent almost two-thirds of all races run in North America, they account for only thirty-seven percent of the purses. This is a change from 1984 when claiming races accounted for about seventy percent of the races and forty-five percent of purse money. Still, the vast majority of horses at the racetrack ultimately run "for a tag" (as in having a price tag on them) at one time or another during their careers.

The purpose of claiming races is to classify this large population by price. If a horse is worth $20,000, he would generally not be entered in a race where he could be claimed for $10,000. Although he would have a good chance to win such a race, the possibility of having to sell him for half of what he is worth usually prevents

Charismatic, a one-time claimer, winning the 1999 Derby.

people from taking such chances. On the other hand, if he were entered for $30,000, he probably won't be claimed, but he probably won't win, either. A $20,000 horse would most likely be entered in a race with a $15,000 to $25,000 claiming price, depending upon his age and infirmities, and what the owner and trainer felt they could get away with.

In this manner, claiming serves as a great equalizer for the horses that run below the top level of competition.

Some trainers make their living by claiming other people's horses and trying to improve them. They are known as "haltermen." When you visit the paddock, particularly at the smaller tracks, you may see several of the leading trainers marking their program as each horse passes. These marks are for reference in case the trainer finds an owner wanting to claim the horse.

Trainers know that a horse is seldom entered far below his value, and when one drops suddenly in price, there's more than likely a reason. Most of the time the trainer is trying to get rid of an injured horse, but racing is a convoluted game. Trainers occasionally drop a sound horse down in class to win a bet, hoping desperately that the other trainers will think his horse is injured and refrain from claiming it. Then, too, on occasion, a trainer will drop a horse in class in order to get a win under his belt, because, believe it or not, self-confidence is as important to an equine athlete as it is to a human one.

For example, Charismatic, who won the 1999 Kentucky Derby, actually had run in a claiming race earlier in the year. The following appeared in the *Thoroughbred Times* after his Derby victory:

> ...[Bob] Lewis almost did not get to make his second victorious walk to the [Derby] museum. [Trainer D. Wayne] Lukas threw Charismatic, a Summer Squall colt, into a $62,500 claiming race on February 11 at Santa Anita Park. Lukas was looking to get a confidence-building victory into

Charismatic, who was 1-for-9 at the time and had finished last, beaten 13 lengths by General Challenge [who ultimately finished 11th in the Derby], 11 days earlier in the Santa Catalina Stakes (gr. II).
In the 6½-furlong race, Charismatic finished second, beaten a neck by What Say You, but was moved up to first by a disqualification. That was the good news. Then came even better news: no one dropped Charismatic's name into the claiming box.
One trainer who considered it was Mike Mitchell, one of Southern California's best trainers with claiming stock. Mitchell had his eye on the strapping chestnut colt but decided against filling out the claim slip because of one of Bob Lewis's generous impulses. A few days earlier, Lewis had given Mitchell $40 worth of tickets to a drag race in Pomona, California.

Have I mentioned that it pays to be lucky in this business?

Today, almost all racing jurisdictions have what is known as an open claiming rule. This rule provides an opportunity for new owners to claim a horse. Anyone who can establish financial responsibility and has a valid owner's license in the state can claim a horse provided he has deposited the required amount of money (the claiming price, plus sales tax) with the horsemen's bookkeeper by the required time. However, in a few states no one is allowed to claim a horse except an owner who has started at least one horse at the current meeting.

In states where open claiming is not available, you must privately purchase the first horse you race in order to become an owner. If you purchase one horse in order to claim more horses, the horse that you purchase privately is known as a "policeman."

The danger of buying a racehorse by private treaty reminds me of a story Colonel Phil Chinn told years ago. Chinn was a legendary figure — an excellent horseman, heavy gambler, and out-standing raconteur.

It seems the Colonel had an unraced two-year-old of royal line-age, but he couldn't outrun a fat man. He worked diligently with the handsome colt, for which he had paid dearly. But, alas, it looked like the colt was a cropper. The only thing to do was to sell the colt and salvage what he could.

The arrival of spring and the opening of the racing season had brought a raft of wealthy Easterners to Central Kentucky to visit the farms, see the promising two-year-olds, and attend the Keeneland meeting in advance of the Kentucky Derby.

While eating dinner at a local restaurant, the Colonel purported-ly met one of the New York gentry, who was desperately looking for a promising two-year-old. This New Yorker was a great believer in speed, and he offered $50,000 (a mighty sum in those days) for a well-bred two-year-old that could work three furlongs in thirty-five seconds. Now the Colonel knew that his two-year-old couldn't work anywhere near that fast, but he had an idea!

He told the wealthy New Yorker that he had just the horse for him and to be at his barn at six the next morning so he could show him off in a work at Keeneland. Promptly at six, the Colonel's fish arrived ready for the hook. The colt, whose looks complemented his royal pedigree, pranced and showed off as he rounded the barn on the way to the track. Once on the track, he bowed his neck and looked like a world beater. Chinn had instructed the rider to make the colt look like a champion. And that he did. With two quick pops of the whip, he broke the colt off at the three-eighths pole, and the colt worked a very rapid :34⅗! After a hot breakfast in the track kitchen, the deal was made!

Some horsemen commented that the track must have been extremely fast that morning, because more than one two-year-old went three furlongs in :34 and faster, but the next day times were back to normal. No one had even noticed that at midnight, under the cover of darkness, Chinn and his groom had gone out to Keeneland and dug up the three-eighths pole and moved it a hundred feet closer to the finish line!

Buyer beware, *caveat emptor, el comprador se guarda, kunde passen auf,* etc.

If your potential trainer suggests you put money in his own account or the account of one of his other owners in order to claim a horse, be wary! This is against the rules of racing and is dishonest. It is also a poor way to start off in the horse business, but it's not too rare. An unfortunate number of horror stories involve trainers who have convinced neophyte owners to put money in another owner's account to claim a horse. After the claim was made, the trainer refused to give the owner who put up the money his horse. It is difficult to go to the authorities and tell them that you did something dishonest to get in the horse business and then ask them to help you get your money back.

The claim box.

Once a horse is claimed, if he is to be raced he normally must remain at that track until the end of the meeting. This obviously does not mean that if he is injured he cannot go to the farm, but it does mean he cannot run at another racetrack while the meeting during which he was claimed is still in progress.

Most states restrict how claiming horses can be entered after they are claimed. This restriction, known as being "in jail," requires that if the newly claimed horse is entered in a race within thirty days after the claim, he must be entered for a minimum claiming price twenty-five percent higher than the purchase claim price. Thus, someone who claims a horse has to be fairly committed to it and can't just drop it in for a lower price the following week to win a bet.

Claiming varies in different states, so you'll need to check into the specific rules wherever you intend to race. You can get help from the racing secretary's office.

To claim a horse, a slip is filled out, put in a sealed envelope, time stamped, and put in the claim box. To insure privacy, the locked claim box is in an entry booth in the racing secretary's office with a time clock next to it. After the claiming deadline — typically thirty minutes prior to the race — the box is opened and any claim slips are opened. The claim slip must be filled out *perfectly* or the claim will be nullified. Assuming the claim slip is properly filled out (more than one claim has been voided by an incorrect date or misspelling), the racing secretary or his representative, the claims clerk, verifies that the proper amount of money is on deposit with the horsemen's bookkeeper and that the new owner is properly licensed. Once all of that is verified, the claims clerk notifies the stewards of the claim and gives the new owner or, more often, his trainer a delivery order. After the race and with this delivery order in hand, the trainer goes to the unsaddling area near the winner's circle or to the test barn at many tracks where the physical transfer of ownership takes place. The old owner (or his representative) takes the bridle off the horse and the new owner puts on his halter and lead shank and takes the horse to his new barn, thus the term "halterman."

Once you have put in a claim and the starting gate opens, the horse is yours — win, lose, or draw; healthy or sick; dead or alive; even though any purse winnings from that particular race go to the previous owner. More than one claimed horse has broken a leg during the running of the race and has had to be destroyed. Your claim can be insured prior to the race (for seven percent to ten percent of the value of the horse), which may seem expensive at the time, but is less expensive than buying a dead horse.

When more than one claim has been entered for a horse, the new owner is decided by lot. One time several years ago, a filly I bred named Split a Burger (for the record, I would like to state in no uncertain terms that the filly had gone through the yearling sales, and I had absolutely nothing to do with naming her) was entered for a claiming tag of $19,000 in a race in New York. While owners are supposed to claim only for racing purposes and breeders are not supposed to claim at all — at least not for the sole purpose of getting a breeding prospect — the fact that Split a Burger was a half-sister to the multiple graded-stakes winner Taisez Vous may have had something to do with her apparent attractiveness. She certainly was no runner. A few days after the race, the racing secretary of the New York Racing Association described the claim box as having looked "like a ticker-tape parade."

When more than one claim is entered, the claims clerk supervises a "shake" to determine who gets the horse. The shake involves using a "Kelly" bottle with numbered balls, or pills, as they are called. This is the same bottle used by pool players and by racing secretaries to conduct the draw for post positions. If there are five claims, five numbered balls are put in the Kelly bottle. Each claim slip is then numbered on the back so that it corresponds with a number on a pill. The racing secretary draws one of the numbered pills from the Kelly bottle, and the winner is determined. If the horse won easily and came back sound, you may be hoping to win the shake, but if he ran poorly and came back unsound, you will be hoping that you lost.

It can get to be quite a scene if a lot of trainers try to claim a single horse. The record was probably set in 1995, as reported in *The Blood-Horse:*

> On March 15, 25 trainers tried to claim McKenzie's Reef for $20,000 out of the fourth race at Gulfstream Park. Veteran racetrack official Tommy Trotter said, "I've never heard of that many people trying to claim one horse. The racing office must have been awfully crowded."
> It was. With two dozen trainers crowded into the office, clerk of claims Pam Keers had to shake 13 pills, then 12, before a third shake-off of two pills determined Robin Frank the winner.
> "I knew I'd won as soon as the horse lost the race," said Frank.

Like many other aspects of the Thoroughbred business, claiming can be a dangerous game, which is another reason you should choose your advisor carefully.

A claiming horse will not normally change rapidly in value, but occasionally claiming horses become stakes horses.

As mentioned above, Charismatic ran for a price before going on to win the 1999 Kentucky Derby. But, undoubtedly, the greatest claim of all time came in the 1940s when one of the all-time greatest haltermen, a trainer named Hirsch Jacobs, claimed Stymie for $1,500 and went on to win more than $918,485 with him back in the days when a major stakes race carried a purse of $25,000-added.

Not all claiming races are for cheap horses. Races for horses priced at $100,000 and up are not all that uncommon in California and New York, and on Breeders' Cup Day in 1984, Hollywood Park held a race for horses with a claiming price of up to $1 million. None were claimed, incidentally.

However, a number of horses have been claimed for $100,000. One of the most recent was River Keen, who was claimed in December of 1998 even though he had won a grade II stakes the previous year. Since being claimed by Bob Baffert for Hugo Reynolds, he has won three graded stakes, including two grade I races, and $1,338,800 for his new owner.

The more solid claim prospect is often an older horse (age four and up) that has survived the two- and three-year-old "drop-out" years and has displayed ability and competitiveness at a certain price level over time. Most of these old campaigners have infirmities in the form of enlarged ankles or knees, rough tendons, or bad feet, but they run in spite of their aches and pains. They are competitors! They have "heart" — the ingredient that counts most for a racehorse.

The major risk in claiming horses, as it is in any equine investment, is unexpected injury or sickness. In reference to "dropouts," I mean the many horses that get to the races, break their maiden, perhaps win a race or two, and then disappear. They either disappear because the competition overmatches their talent or they "got to hurting" a little and lost their will to compete.

Remember three things if you decide to enter the Thoroughbred business with claiming horses. First, two- and three-year-olds are often overpriced. They have not yet shown that they can't or won't run, so their owners are still high on them. Second, these youngsters do not yet have infirmities that discourage them from running. Two-year-old races generally are the truest run races of all because these horses are eager young athletes bred to race, trying to do what is asked of them. They want to run and haven't learned to "cheat a little" to avoid the aches and pains that come from exhaustion after the total effort expended during a race. With these aches and pains, and with a little experience, racehorses learn sometimes that a ninety percent effort produces fewer after-effects, and those with less heart and desire will give less effort. Third, two- and three-year-olds will normally decline in value as they get closer to being four-year-olds.

For educational purposes, look at the final times for claiming races for four-year-olds and up. Then look at the times for similar races for three-year-olds and two-year-olds. The races for young horses are won in slower times. Sure, the youngsters will mature and run a little faster, but age and conditions of the race restrict competition, too. Keep in mind that when a horse gets to be four, the competition gets tougher.

From the purchase of a claimer or two, owners who become more involved usually do so by moving on to buying younger horses in the form of two-year-olds in training or yearlings.

Naming Your Horse

One of the more interesting and fun exercises you get to do as a new Thoroughbred owner is pick out a name for your potential champion. This is not as easy as it sounds. Any name used for a Thoroughbred during the past seventeen years is not available, and more than a half million names are already taken.

If you want to name your Thoroughbred without incurring extra cost, you must submit your choices prior to February 1 of its two-year-old year.

There are many restrictions on the names that you can use. First, you can't use the names of previous great horses, such as Secretariat, Man o' War, Seabiscuit, etc. If you use the name of a living person, you must secure his or her permission in writing. Names may not have advertising implications or political overtones. There can be a maximum of eighteen characters including spaces. Numbers cannot be used unless spelled out. Obscenities are not allowed (whatever language you might try to pass them off in, and in an attempt to stop this, The Jockey Club requires that you include a translation of any foreign phrase you include in a name). The Jockey Club tries to prevent phonetically similar names, but it is a tough job.

Naming horses has been made a lot less frustrating these days. The Jockey Club has a web site where not only can you look up unavailable names (which used to be the only help you could get), but they publish a list of approximately 50,000 names that have just become available. Further, the site contains all the rules and regulations for naming (and registering a Thoroughbred) and a lot of useful statistics, as well. They have actually reached the point where you can do online registration if you like.

It's at http://home.jockeyclub.com, which, incidentally, is the only place you'll find The Jockey Club without a "The" and without being capitalized.

Name That Horse — All-Time Favorites

Compiled by The Jockey Club. Horse's parentage in parenthesis.

Bed o' Roses (By Rosemont out of Good Thing)
Blondeinamotel (by Bates Motel)
Dirty Old Man (by Tom Fool out of Last Leg)
Find (by Discovery out of Stellar Role)
Flat Fleet Feet (by Afleet out of Czar Dancer)
Heartaquack (by Quack)
Inside Information (by Private Account out of Pure Profit)
Native Dancer (by Polynesian out of Geisha)
Next Move (by Bull Lea out of Now What)
Odor in the Court (by Judge Smells)
Ogle (by Oh Say out of Low Cut)
Prenup (by Smarten out of Homewrecker)
Skip Trial (by Bail Jumper)
Social Outcast (by Shutout out of Pansy)
Sometime Thing (by Discovery out of Now and Again)

Although naming a horse is often difficult, you should work hard at naming yours because it seems that good horses usually have good names. You need one to be proud of when it hits the headlines!

One further suggestion: The Jockey Club is a big place with reams of mail and hundreds of name requests every day. Things do get lost. The best way to establish your communication record with them is by using certified mail, return receipt requested, on all deadline correspondence. For some reason this type of correspondence does not get lost as often.

Gentling and Training

Although this chapter is primarily dedicated to what goes on at the racetrack, the training center is an extension of the racetrack. It is where the horses that run at the track probably received their initial training and where an increasing number of them are stabled.

When I started out in this business, the initial training given to horses was called "breaking," as in breaking their spirit and teaching them to obey. That it is even referred to today as "gentling" is testimony that some elements of training have improved over the years.

Gentling yearlings is highly individualized. There are as many methods as trainers who perform this function. Whatever the method, the trainer will need two things — patience and attention to detail. No two yearlings are the same, and each one requires individual attention, understanding, and patience; just like a child. Without those two basic ingredients, the first lessons will ultimately produce more rogues and outlaws than it will good horses.

The timing and location of yearling gentling is a matter of personal preference and economic judgment. Some yearlings go directly from the yearling sales to begin their schooling, while others may go back to the farm for a while. Most, though, will be sent to a training center to learn the basic manners needed before getting to the actual business of racing.

Wherever a yearling goes, he will have one thing in common with all the other yearlings — he'll have no idea of what a saddle or bridle look like, much less what to do when the bell rings in the gate and the doors open. By virtue of his being a Thoroughbred, he is bred to race, but he is nowhere near that point because he hasn't been trained to race. When you see a horse come from the paddock and parade in front of the grandstand before a race, you take it for granted that the horse is wearing a saddle, accepts the bridle and bit, walks in a straight line, and is responsive to the jockey. But he has to learn all that, and that is what gentling is all about.

When yearlings come to the gentling process, they come with varied backgrounds and temperaments. A homebred from a one-person operation may be pampered and spoiled by a doting owner and will be an overbearing monster, while another may be a terrified introvert as a result of impatience or just plain neglect. Sales yearlings may come to the track or training center well mannered as a result of good sales preparation, but such is not always the case. Many yearlings come away from the sales traumatized by

Getting started in the round pen, a popular training aid.

their experience. This can result in aggressive, overbearing behavior or introverted, "spooky" behavior.

Think about it a minute. A yearling has been raised in a serene farm environment from the time he was born. For fourteen to sixteen months he has done nothing but romp and play. Except for the couple of months of extra attention he received during sales preparation, he did pretty much as he pleased. Then suddenly one day he is loaded onto a van or trailer (he better not hesitate either) and bounced around for anywhere from twenty to a few hundred miles — and if you don't think a trailer or van bounces at forty to fifty miles per hour, you should ride in the back with the horses some time. When the van comes to a stop, he is pushed off by tired attendants who don't give him the opportunity to even think before he is forced to "behave."

He walks into a barn area full of new sights and sounds and is put into a strange stall with strange neighbors. If that isn't enough, the next morning he is paraded back and forth for hours on end in front of all kinds of people who want to poke at him, open his mouth, pick up his legs, and generally perform a panoply of aggravating things on him.

After a couple of days of that, he is led up to a sales ring with glaring lights, people staring at him, and loudspeakers blaring some sort of gibberish that auctioneers call a chant. Then with the drop of the gavel, he has entered a new era. He is led back to his stall where he is allowed to rest a short while before he is loaded onto another van and hauled to a new farm to begin an entirely new life. And people say that horses aren't adaptable!

When training will actually begin depends upon why the yearling is being trained. If he is going to race for an owner who prefers early two-year-old racing, the process may start in August or September. For many big stables, yearlings are gentled in early fall then turned out for the winter. This is particularly common in the northern climates. The horse business generally accepts that this practice will benefit many yearlings in the long run.

Young bones and muscles are susceptible to all manner of injuries, particularly under stress, and as a rule the more time off young horses receive, the better off they are. The disadvantage of this method is cost. When the yearling becomes a two-year-old and re-enters training, at least half of his early education is lost. This is not because he has forgotten it — he has lost the condition, the muscling that he built up during the sixty to seventy-five days of original schooling and galloping.

For economic reasons, more yearlings are being gentled later than was the case years ago. Early two-year-old racing is less prevalent because it has proven so physically damaging. Later gentling means later training, which in turn means later racing. This ultimately has to benefit the young horse by preventing premature stress on immature bodies and bones.

For those yearlings entered in two-year-olds in training sales, the date of the sale and the training requirements for that sale obviously dictate that the gentling process be started in early fall.

Training Centers

While most training centers in the Carolinas, Florida, and Southern California have been around many years, training center construction and use has surged in the past five years throughout the country. Even though racing secretaries complain incessantly about a lack of horses, trainers complain equally vociferously over the inability to obtain stalls at racetracks.

The shortage of stalls is being partially met by more extensive use of training centers, not only for young horses but for older horses, too. Many trainers with large stables maintain a division at the track and another at a neighboring training center.

Several arguments favor training centers over racetracks for training horses. At an operating racetrack, the hours available for training are obviously limited by racing. At a training center, the track may be available full time, except for the minimal time required for actual maintenance. This means that training can proceed at a more leisurely pace (leisurely meaning patient), and more can be done to and for each individual. The well-designed training centers are spacious, more serene, and more attractive than the stable area at most racetracks. They are away from the hustle and bustle of the afternoon racing activity, the crowd, and the noise, all distractions to the horses and the help.

Training centers also may offer several forms of exercise normally unavailable at a racetrack, such as swimming, turn-out paddocks, treadmills, and uphill exercise.

The negatives to a training center (none of which apply to yearling gentling, which should definitely be done at home or at a training center, not at a racetrack) include: (1) the cost and trouble of always shipping to the racetrack for racing; (2) the difficulty of maintaining a training track surface equal to the quality of the racetrack itself; and (3) the cost of stall rental.

Training centers can offer a more relaxed atmosphere.

Many of the new training centers are far different from the old ones, which were mainly private operations only open during the winter for yearling gentling and early two-year-old preparation.

In England and France horses are not stabled at racetracks. Trainers each have their own private "yard" or "stable" where their horses are kept. These private yards are grouped in one area to make use of common gallops (training tracks). On race day, the horses are shipped to the track for their engagement and shipped home that same day.

Since European racing is on grass, the same course cannot be used day in and day out as is done in this country. Race meetings rotate from course to course on a daily or weekly schedule, so Europeans have long been using the training-center concept that is now becoming more popular in North America.

Getting to the Races

After your yearling has been at the training center for about six months and the gentling process has been satisfactorily completed, then, and only then, will your horse be ready to seek his ultimate goal — winning races. By this time he will have learned to accept a rider, be guided, and gallop with other horses. He will have learned to respond to his rider's commands and will have had his basic instructions at the starting gate. Depending on the facilities and his length of time at the training center, he may have been asked to show some of his ability in the form of short, controlled sprints.

When he gets to the racetrack he will probably be as traumatized as he was when he went to the yearling sale. He is faced with a new environment, a new set of rules and regulations — a new way of life. Is it any wonder that many youngsters get the "snots," run a fever, and go off feed? The real wonder is that they don't all go through these maladies. Depending upon the size of the training center where your horse was gentled, he may go to the racetrack the first morning and see ten times as many horses as he has ever seen in his life. With so many distractions, it is not surprising that young Thoroughbreds sometimes forget their manners and their lessons for a few days. But they seem to survive and settle in, and if they were properly gentled, they will be going about their gallops in a businesslike manner in a few days.

How soon your youngster starts his speed work depends upon how much basic legwork (long gallops) he has behind him. The trainer will evaluate his stage of training and decide when he will be asked for his first serious speed work. Trainers like to have a horse under their shedrow for at least a couple of weeks to determine his habits, conditions, and precocity before asking him to display his ability.

From that point, it is a matter of developing his ability and condition until he is fully ready to perform. If he gets ready to race without the onset of ailments and injuries that befall young horses, such as bucked shins, osselets, hot knees, coughs, runny noses,

Training at the track in anticipation of the first race.

etc., he will soon get his final okay from the gate crew and be tattooed by the identifier prior to running.

As mentioned, every horse starts out as a maiden. This puts him in the same category as the seventy percent of his foal crop that will actually make it to the races (see chart below). This means a lot of other horses are probably ready, willing, and able to run in the same maiden race.

Averages for the Breed

Averages for the breed statistics are designed to give the reader a baseline to evaluate the performances of contemporary racehorses, sires, and dams. Statistics shown in the column in the middle below reflect the worldwide performances of all named foals born in North America between 1980-89. Statistics in the column on the right reflect the sale data for foals by the top one percent of all sires by total earnings for the same decade. All statistics are based on data in The Jockey Club Information System's worldwide database. The Jockey Club database includes complete records for racing in North America, England, Ireland, France, Germany, Italy, Puerto Rico, Japan, and United Arab Emirates for some, but not all, of the years covered by these statistics.

Statistics below are designed to give a snapshot of what an average "good" horse should accomplish. (Reprinted with permission of *Thoroughbred Times*)

	Foals of the 1980s	Foals by top 1% of sires
%Starters/foals	69.4%	84.8%
% Winners/foals *(starters)*	44.8% (64.5%)	65.3% (76.9%)
% Repeat winners/foals *(starters)*	31.8% (45.9%)	51.1% (60.2%)
% Stakes winners/foals *(starters)*	3.1% (4.4%)	9% (10.6%)
% Graded SW/foals *(starters)*	0.63% (0.91%)	3.4% (4%)
% Grade I SW/foals *(starters)*	0.20% (0.28%)	1.2% (1.4%)
% Stakes-placed/foals *(starters)*	4.6% (6.6%)	11.5% (13.5%)
% 2-year-old starters/foals	33.7%	46.4%
% 2yo winners/foals *(% 2yo starters)*	11.2% (33.1%)	18.5% (39.8%)
% 2yo SW/foals *(% 2yo starters)*	0.94% (2.8%)	2.48% (2.92%)
% 3-year-old starters/foals	60%	76.8%
% 4-year-old starters/foals	45%	57.3%
% 5-year-old and up starters/foals	26.9%	36.3%
Average career starts/foal	15.6	21
Average career starts/starter	22.5	24.8
Average win distance in furlongs	6.78	7.18
Average win distance on turf	8.60	8.75
Average earnings/starter	$23,572	$56,447
Average earnings/starter male *(female)*	$27,489 ($19,440)	$67,947 ($43,962)
Average earnings/start	$1,050	$2,277
Average earnings/start male *(female)*	$1,061 ($1,033)	$2,241 ($2,338)
Average Racing Index	1.15	2.56

One of the difficulties facing an owner today is limited opportunity for maidens. A racing secretary would describe this situation not in terms of limited racing opportunity but as "too many maidens." The racing secretary, of course, has a different point of view than the owner of a prospective champion that still happens to be a maiden.

The Racing Secretary

Every track has a racing secretary whose job it is to design a program to accommodate the horses available for racing at his track.

However, the racing secretary also must be the tightrope walker, the Great Wallenda of the track management team, because in order to design his program successfully, he must not only accommodate the horsemen (who, believe me, are very hard to please), but also provide entertainment for racing fans — the people who come to the track and bet their money, which is where the purses come from.

Horse people frequently forget that aspect of a racing secretary's job. Remember, the racing secretary works for the track, and without an attractive, competitive racing program, people will not bet. And, if they don't bet, there will be no purses. Ultimately, then there will be no racing. So when you have difficulty running your maiden when and where you want, try to understand the racing secretary's problem, too.

A racing secretary must design his racing program in two parts.

Before a race meet starts, he will put together a stakes program for the entire meeting. This program is fairly permanent; normally only minor changes are made from year to year for realignment or expansion. Stakes are scheduled on Saturdays, Sundays, and holidays for a long meeting, or more often for various categories of horses. The purpose of these stakes is to give the best horses at the track an opportunity to race for an attractive purse and to earn

2000 Fall Stakes Schedule

Date	Race	Purse / Closing
Oct. 7	**Shadwell Keeneland Mile (Gr. II)**	$400,000-added
	3yo & up, 8 furlongs (turf)	Closes Sept. 27
Oct. 7	**Fayette Breeders' Cup (Gr. III)**	$200,000 ($150,000-added
	3yo & up, 9 1/2 furlongs	plus $50,000 Breeders Cup Fund)
		Closes Sept. 27
Oct. 8	**Queen Elizabeth II Challenge Cup (Gr. I)**	$500,000
	3yo fillies, 9 furlongs (turf)	By Invitation
Oct. 8	**Lane's End Breeders' Futurity (Gr. II)**	$400,000-added
	2yo, 8 1/2 furlongs	Closes Sept. 27
Oct. 8	**A.P. Indy**	$75,000-added (includes $10,000 KTDF)
	f&m, 3yo & up, 5 1/2 furlongs (turf)	Closes Sept. 27
Oct. 11	**Raven Run**	$75,000-added (includes $10,000 KTDF)
	3yo fillies, 7 furlongs	Closes Sept. 27
Oct. 12	**Perryville**	$75,000-added (includes $10,000 KTDF)
	3yo, 7 furlongs, 184 feet	Closes Oct. 4
Oct. 13	**WinStar Galaxy (Gr. III)**	$500,000-added
	f&m, 3yo & up, 9 1/2 furlongs (turf)	Closes Oct. 4
Oct. 13	**Warfield**	$75,000-added (includes $10,000 KTDF)
	3yo & up, NWGSAAMOV, 8 1/2 furlongs	Closes Oct. 4
Oct. 14	**Three Chimneys Spinster (Gr. I)**	$500,000-added
	f&m, 3yo & up, 9 furlongs	Closes Oct. 4
Oct. 14	**Phoenix Breeders' Cup (Gr. III)**	$250,000 ($150,000 added
	3yo & up, 6 furlongs	plus $100,000 Breeders' Cup Fund)
		Closes Oct. 4
Oct. 14	**Seattle Slew**	$75,000-added (includes $10,000 KTDF)
	3yo, 8 furlongs (turf)	Closes Oct. 4
Oct. 15	**Walmac Int'l Alcibiades (Gr. II)**	$400,000-added
	2yo fillies, 8 1/2 furlongs	Closes Oct. 4
Oct. 15	**Thoroughbred Club of America Stakes (Gr. III)**	$100,000
	f&m, 3yo & up, 6 furlongs	Closes Oct. 4
Oct. 15	**Nureyev**	$75,000-added (includes $10,000 KTDF)
	3yo & up, 5 1/2 furlongs (turf)	Closes Oct. 4
Oct. 18	**Bryan Station**	$75,000-added (includes $10,000 KTDF))
	f&m, 3yo & up, 8 furlongs (turf)	Closes Oct. 4
Oct. 19	**Indian Summer**	$75,000-added (includes $10,000 KTDF)
	2yo fillies, 6 furlongs	Closes Oct. 11
Oct. 20	**Fort Springs**	$75,000-added (includes $10,000 KTDF)
	2yo, 6 furlongs	Closes Oct. 11
Oct. 21	**Valley View (Gr. III)**	$100,000-added
	3yo fillies, 8 1/2 furlongs (turf)	Closes Oct. 11
Oct. 22	**Sycamore**	$75,000-added (includes $10,000 KTDF)
	3yo & up, 13 furlongs (turf)	Closes Oct. 11
Oct. 25	**McConnell Springs**	$75,000-added (includes $10,000 KTDF)
	3yo, NWSSOAM, 8 1/2 furlongs	Closes Oct. 11
Oct. 26	**Green River**	$75,000-added (includes $10,000 KTDF)
	2yo fillies, 8 1/2 furlongs (turf)	Closes Oct. 18
Oct. 27	**Hopemont**	$75,000-added (includes $10,000 KTDF)
	2yo, 8 1/2 furlongs (turf)	Closes Oct. 18
Oct. 28	**Dowager (Listed)**	$100,000-added
	f&m, 3yo & up, 12 furlongs (turf)	Closes Oct. 18

Keeneland's fall stakes schedule.

black type. A racing secretary usually schedules his best stakes during the latter part of the race meeting so horses that are being trained up to these races will be running throughout the meeting and so that the climax comes with the closing.

Take a look at the stakes schedule from the 2000 Keeneland Fall meet on the previous page. Before going too much further, let me make one important point with respect to this schedule, and, for that matter, with respect to racing in general at Keeneland. Because Keeneland is a not-for-profit organization and principally because the highly successful sales operation is able to subsidize racing at Keeneland, this is not a typical stakes schedule. Despite having only two short race meetings and a moderate pari-mutuel handle, Keeneland ranks among the leading tracks in the world for daily purse distribution and average purse per race. Most tracks will have a single stakes race on Saturdays, Sundays, and holidays, but you'll notice here that Keeneland is able to card three stakes on October 8, 14, and 15 — the latter two days in particular because those were exceptionally good days to have prep races for the Breeders' Cup, which was held at Churchill Downs three weeks later.

Now, on to the nuts and bolts of the condition book (your trainer is going to hate me for this).

The second and more difficult part of the racing secretary's job is to design a daily racing program. While every owner wishes he could run a horse in one of the big stakes races, most enter their horses in the supporting races on Saturday and the nine or ten daily races during the week. These races are what keep all tracks going, be it New York, California, New Mexico, or Arizona. And it is the betting on these races that provides the money for the big races. But make no mistake, big purses and good horses bring out the fans!

The racing secretary keeps his racing program in the form of a condition book. Before each race meeting starts, the horsemen applying for stalls need to know the quality of racing offered, what type of racing will be held (whether the emphasis will be on younger horses or older horses, distance racing, turf racing, etc.), the purses being offered, minimum claiming price, etc., so he can determine whether his stable fits and if his horses will have the opportunity to pay their way. The condition book is the bible that contains all this information.

The purse size is dictated by the mutuel handle, but the meet emphasis can be, at least partially, the preference of the racing secretary, tempered by his knowledge about what kind of horses raced at this particular meeting in the past. At most tracks, the condition book is issued in ten- or twelve-racing-day segments, providing the racing secretary with flexibility as the meeting progresses, and conditions and horses change.[2]

Normally the first condition book is written before the racing secretary has allocated stalls, and is a statement of purpose. For instance, Keeneland is known as a breeders' track because it is run by and for breeders. Consequently, you will see an abnormally high percentage of races for maiden fillies in the condition book. Keeneland offers more opportunity for future broodmares to break their maiden than other tracks because if all other factors are roughly even, foals out of mares that have won at least one race are more valuable than foals out of mares that could not break their maiden.

Truth is, bettors don't seem to like maiden races very much. In a typical maiden race there might be three or four first-time starters, mixed in with a few horses that have one, maybe two starts, and a few more that have made a number of starts without winning. So it's hard to pick maiden races at most tracks, and the fans have a

---

[2] Once again, Keeneland is different. Since they only have a sixteen-day meet in the fall, they can include the entire meeting in one condition book and because the sales are so successful they can offer purses which have little actual relation to the parimutuel handle.

hard enough time picking winners among the best horses in the world (as evidenced by the 2000 Breeders' Cup), much less a field that they can't really get a handle on.

Once the race meeting starts, subsequent condition books will normally reflect a realistic appraisal of the horses available and an effort to give all the horsemen who have been granted stalls an opportunity to race their horses and earn purse money.

The condition book can vary in form and substance from track to track, but the basic ingredients are the same. As mentioned above, it will include the stakes schedule; local rules of racing, including entry time and scratch time; post time; stakes nomination blanks; entry preference rules and regulations; stable area regulations; eligibility rules; and a variety of other facts pertinent to a racing operation. (For more information on these rules, pick up a condition book at any racetrack. Keeneland's condition book, for instance, contains several pages on the rules of racing.) While it is your trainer's responsibility to know these rules, I think it's also important for you to read them at least once, particularly the first time you intend to race at a track. You don't want your horse to get excluded from a race because of some clerical error.

The meat of the condition book is in the pages describing the proposed races. Most racing days will include one maiden race or more, several claiming races, and when the horses are available, an allowance race or two to support the feature. The more quality races the secretary is able to conduct, the bigger the crowd and the higher the mutuel handle.

In many cases races do not fill, i.e., they don't receive sufficient entries to justify inclusion on the racing card. Most racetracks do not like to include on their program races with less than eight separate betting entries. In fact, the rules of racing in Kentucky provide that any non-claiming race with six or more entries cannot be called off and any claiming race with eight or more entries must be run. The public likes to bet on horses with reasonable odds, and short fields with a small number of entries do not provide the kind of odds that would entice people to wager.

The racing secretary will normally offer three or four substitute races each day to be used in case the originally prescribed races don't fill. At most tracks, one or two of these substitute races might be included in the condition book, but most are published on a daily basis. At some racetracks, substitute races are included in the condition book, although their inclusion does not prevent the racing secretary from offering even more substitute races (or, as they are called, "extras"), should it become necessary to provide races with full fields.

The size of individual purses is determined by the racing secretary based on his assessment of the quality of competition in the race — better horses, of course, running for better purses. The overall amount of purses awarded at a racetrack during the meeting is determined in some states by law and in some states by contract with its horsemen's association. Normally, though, it is about half of the racetrack's share of the pari-mutuel commission.

The major portion of operating funds for racetracks comes from the mutuel commission. The rest comes from admission and parking fees, program sales, and concession income. Although the laws vary from state to state, a commission ("take-out") of approximately fifteen percent (usually on win-place-show betting) up to an astronomical thirty-five percent (on doubles, exactas, trifectas, etc.) is deducted from each dollar bet, before the payoff to the bettors is determined. State law also determines how the commission is split between state taxes, track operating funds, and purses.

As an example, let's look at individual conditions for several races from Keeneland's opening day of the 2000 fall meet. Keep in mind that this is a high-quality operation. On this particular card, there is only one claiming race (as opposed to approximately five or six on a normal racing card at most tracks), two maiden races, four allowance races, and two stakes.

The most inferior races are traditionally stacked at the beginning of the day. This is because the daily double, which lets bettors choose the winners of usually the first two races, makes up for, at least in part, the distaste for cheaper races among the hoi polloi (those who are actually there to gamble, for those of you who have not been sufficiently ingrained to the social structure of racing to look down on the fans).

---

1   **The Kayrawan**   **Claiming**
Purse $11,000 For fillies and mares, three years old and upward.
     Three year old fillies ....120 lbs.
     Older fillies and mares...122 lbs.
Non-winners of two races since August 19 allowed ....2 lbs.
     a race since then ....4 lbs.
     two races since July 4.. 6 lbs.
Claiming price $10,000.
(Races where entered for $8,000 or less not considered).
Julep cup - Shadwell Farm
                                                        Six furlongs

---

As you can see from the conditions, the first race is a six-furlong claiming event on the main track for fillies and mares, three years old and older. You'll note that the three-year-old fillies get to carry two pounds less than the older mares. As I'll discuss later, this should make a difference of about half or three-quarters of a length at six furlongs, and that allowance is given because the older mares are presumably more mature and better seasoned than their younger counterparts.

Also, there are other allowances for fillies that haven't won in a certain amount of time. So, if a three-year-old filly that hadn't won since July 4 was entered in the race, she would be able to get in with 114 pounds.

The claiming price is $10,000, so there will be no weight

allowances for lowered claiming prices. (There's another interesting sidelight in this race. Here's a group of horses that are presumably worth about $10,000, and they're running for a purse of $11,000. Keeneland is one of the few places that you'll see horses running in races where the purses are worth more than the actual horses.)

Finally, you'll note that the winner also gets a silver julep cup courtesy of Shadwell Farm, which has sponsored the major stakes of the day. As you'll also note, the races on the undercard (the support races for the stakes) are all named after Shadwell horses, which is a lot classier than having the races named after some group that is attending the races that afternoon, e.g., "The Beer-Guzzling Dart Throwers Club From Ralph's Bar Purse."

3 **The Dayjur** **Maiden**
Purse $50,000 (includes $7,500 KTDF). For maiden two year olds. ....120 lbs.
Julep cup - Shadwell Farm
Seven furlongs

The third race, named the Dayjur, is open to two-year-olds, both colts and fillies, but since it is the fall fillies are not given a sex allowance (normally three pounds). The symbol under the number of the race indicates that the purse contains a supplement from the Kentucky Thoroughbred Development Fund, which, in this case, is $7,500.

The fifth race, "the Swain" (see conditions on following page), is an allowance race that, as you can see, also gives weight off of certain horses in an attempt to equalize the field. For instance, three-year-olds get four pounds from older horses, and horses that haven't won $18,000 twice over the turf since January 8 get six pounds. So, if you had a three-year-old that had only won an $18,000 race since January 8, you could get in with 113 pounds,

> **5**
>
> **The Swain**   **Allowance**
> **Purse $65,000 (includes $9,750 KTDF). For three year olds and upward which have not won three races other than maiden, claiming or starter , or four races.**
> Three year olds ....119 lbs.
> Older ....123 lbs.
> Non-winners of $35,000 twice over nine furlongs
> on the turf in 2000 allowed ....2 lbs.
> $26,000 twice over nine furlongs on the turf
> since April 28..4 lbs.
> $18,000 twice over a mile on the turf since January 8........ 6 lbs.
> (Races where entered for $50,000 or less not considered in allowances).
> Preference by condition eligibility
> Julep cup - Shadwell Farm
>   **Twelve furlongs (on the turf)**

which should theoretically move your horse nearly ten lengths closer to a consistent older horse that had to carry 123.

The sixth race is the first of two stakes on the card, and as you'll notice from the conditions on the following page, the owners of horses that ran in this race had to "stake" their horses by putting up $200 on September 27 when the entries closed and an additional $2,000 on the Thursday prior to the race in order to start. The track has put up $150,000 that is money "added" to the money put up by the horse owners, and the Breeders' Cup also has sweetened the pot by an additional $50,000.

This stakes is run under allowance conditions, which are fully set out along with the division of the purse and how the field will be limited if too many horses are entered. These provisions limiting the size of the field are relatively new and basically stem from the 100th running of the Kentucky Derby, when nearly everyone in the horse business wanted to have a runner. In the case of an overabundance of entries, many stakes are run in two divisions, but in races that are considered to have more significance, this is not practical. The exclusion rules caused considerable consternation when they were being developed, but they are pretty much accepted these days. The controversy was better than having, say, Fusaichi Pegasus, winner of

100

6 **Forty-second running of**
Grade III
$200,000 added*
($150,000 added plus $50,000 Breeders' Cup Fund)
The Fayette Breeders' Cup **Stakes**

For three year olds and upward. By subscription of $200 each, which should accompany the nomination; $2,000 to enter and start. $150,000 added and an additional $50,000 from the Breeders' Cup for cup eligible only. Keeneland Association added monies and all fees to be divided 62% to the owner of the winner, 20% to second, 10% to third, 5% to fourth and 3% to fifth. Breeders' Cup fund monies also correspondingly divided providing a Breeders' Cup nominee has finished in an awarded position.

Three year olds ....122 lbs.
Older ....125 lbs.
Non-winners of a Grade I stakes over a mile in 2000 allowed ....3 lbs.
a Grade II stakes over a mile in 2000..5 lbs.
a Grade III stakes at a mile or over in 2000...................................7 lbs.

The maximum number of starters for the Fayette Breeders' Cup will be limited to fourteen. In the event that more than fourteen horses pass the entry box, the fourteen starters will be determined at that time with preference to those nominees that have won a graded or group stakes; next, highest earnings in 2000. Breeders' Cup nominees given first preference only in equal quality situations. Same owner entry cannot start to the exclusions of a single entry. Starters to be named through the entry box by the usual time of closing. A Breeders' Cup trophy and a Gold Julep Cup will be presented to the owner of the winner.
Nominations close Wednesday, September 27, 2000
Nine and one half furlongs

the Kentucky Derby (gr. I, 2nd div.). You'll notice, too, that while it's sort of stated in a negative manner, Breeders' Cup eligibles will get a preference, all other things being equal.[3]

Preference for horses that are eligible for a subsequent race is an adaptation from Quarter Horse racing. This practice is found mainly in the Southwest in races that have big entry fees followed by periodic sustaining payments, which owners must make to keep their horses eligible. This results in huge purses without the track having to put up much money. For example, the All-American Futurity, a $2-

---

[3] Starting preferences are also given to the highest weighted horses in handicap races.

million race for Quarter Horses, only carries $50,000 in added money. That means that $1.95 million of the purse has been put up by the owners in the form of entry fees and supplemental and sustaining payments!

Nominations for a stakes race may close a week or two before the race, four months before the race, as is the case with the Triple Crown, or as much as two years before the race, as is the case with some futurities in which the foal is nominated in utero.

There's also another little anachronism here. At most racetracks, this distance would be stated as one and three-sixteenth miles. From the Old English, a furlong is an eighth of a mile, and most racetracks state distances under a mile in terms of furlongs and over a mile in terms of miles. But Keeneland often does things its own way...for instance, in the spring they run a lot of two-year-old races on the Headley Course, which is four furlongs and 152 feet around a half of a turn, and in the fall it runs races on the Beard Course, which is seven furlongs plus 184 feet. Both are named for famous leaders in the history of the track, who, for various reasons, designed races at odd distances. Makes you wonder why they don't have a Chinn Course — three furlongs minus 100 or so feet.

The feature race of the day is the Shadwell Keeneland Turf Mile, a grade II event run at eight furlongs (see following page). Note a number of interesting things about this race, and the first one is the name.

Twenty years ago, it was unthinkable to include the name of a sponsor in a race for fear of (a) appearing to be something less than the Sport of Kings, and (b) having to run something like the GalleryFurniture.com Stakes, which replaced the Jim Beam Stakes at Turfway Park in March of 1999. Jim "Mattress Mac" McIngvale, the owner of Gallery Furniture store in Houston, jumped on the chance to market his new web site sales program when Jim Beam Brands' sponsorship ended in 1998. It's a sign of the times.

8 Fifteenth running of
Grade II
$400,000 added
The Shadwell Keeneland Turf Mile

For three year olds and upward. By subscription of $400 each, which should accompany the nomination; $4,000 to enter and start. $400,000 added of which 62% of all monies to the owner of the winner, 20% to second, 10% to third, 5% to fourth and 3% to fifth. Weights: Three year olds 123 lbs.; Older, 126 lbs. The maximum number of starters for the Shadwell Keeneland Turf Mile will be limited to ten. In the event that more than ten horses pass the entry box, the ten starters will be determined at that time with preference to those nominees that have won a graded or group turf stakes; next, graded stakes winners, then highest turf earnings in 2000. Same owner entry cannot start to the exclusions of a single entry. Starters to be named through the entry box by the usual time of closing. A gold julep cup will be presented to the owner of the winner.
Nomination close Wednesday, September 27, 2000
Eight furlongs (on the turf)

It just makes sense. Purses are what makes the game go, and the attitude of many track managers today is any way you can improve purses (short, of course, of being nice to the fans) is a good thing.

As you might also note, the field in this race was restricted to ten, whereas the field in the Fayette was fourteen. That is because the turf course was added as an afterthought in 1985 and is narrower than the main track. Also the turns are tighter, so the field is kept smaller in the interest of safety...both for the riders and for your horse. In fact the Kentucky rules of racing provide that a field will be limited to ten starters on any course where the circumference is less than a mile. (Churchill Downs had to get a variance on this rule to have the Breeders' Cup there.)

If the field is full, and, say, twenty-five horses had been entered originally, your horse could earn $279,000, which is not a bad payday for him and should get him an extra carrot with his oats. It'll be a pretty nice payday for you, too, but, unlike your horse, you won't get credit for the full winner's share (see next section).

Fees, Etc.

Although you pay no entry fee to run your horse (except in stakes races), you must pay a jockey fee. Jockey fees are normally established and regulated by an agreement between the horsemen's association and the jockeys' association, although in some states they are established by the racing commission.

You must put these fees on deposit with the horsemen's bookkeeper before you race. The horsemen's bookkeeper, as his name implies, keeps the financial accounts of all owners. His office is normally adjacent to the racing secretary's office. His job is to credit purse money to winning owners; make appropriate charges to each owner's account for jockey fees, pony fees, stakes engagements, etc.; and disburse funds when requested.

He will also handle the collection of fees and disbursement to the jockeys. Should you require a lead pony to help get your horse to the gate, as 99.99 percent of horses seem to do these days, you also will be assessed a fee by the horsemen's bookkeeper as a contribution to the local horsemen's association. This is not the fee you actually pay the pony person, who will be paid by your trainer and billed to you, but an additional fee.

As an owner, you are entitled to your purse earnings as soon as the post-race test clears the state lab, but not before. As a protection to you, your horse, and the betting public, post-race drug tests are performed on several horses following each race — usually the winner, the second horse, a horse chosen at random, and any horse that runs inconsistently with expectations (for example a heavy favorite that finishes far out of contention) — to determine whether any prohibited substances have been administered to the horse. Also, today's tests are intended to determine that the horses run on the medications that they are supposed to be running on.

Finally, the custom of the trade is now that the jockey will get ten percent of the winning purse; the trainer will get ten percent (many trainers will subtract an additional one percent of the winning purse for the groom); and you'll be expected to give a generous tip to everyone at the track from the guy who parked your car to the guy who handed you a towel in the mens' room. Basically, though, you'll probably wind up with about seventy-five percent of the money, which isn't bad…and think of the fun you've had and the amount the breeding rights to your horse have increased.

Weights and Weight Allowances

As discussed above, weight is a critical variable in horse racing, and one of increasing importance as races lengthen. Over the years, the following rule of thumb has evolved in international ratings of horses for weight to make a one-length difference in a horse's performance at varying distances:

> 6 furlongs — 3 pounds
> 6 to 7 furlongs — 2½ pounds
> 8 to 9 furlongs — 2 pounds
> 8½ to 10½ furlongs — 1¾ pounds
> 11 to 12 furlongs — 1½ pounds
> 13 furlongs and up — 1 pound.

For example, if one horse beats another by two lengths at one and one-eighth miles (nine furlongs) with each carrying 121 pounds, rematching them with the winner carrying 121 pounds and his rival carrying 119 pounds should produce a dead heat. It won't, of course, because of all the other variables, but that is the basis for weight allowances.

In the majority of races, horses are given "allowances," or weight off, for meeting certain conditions. For instance, a colt may be required to carry 121 pounds, but may get a three-pound "allowance" if he hasn't won since a certain date and possibly a five-pound allowance if he hasn't won since an even earlier date.

Further, fillies and mares get a sex allowance, which varies from, say, five pounds in the spring (breeding season) when they are considered to be at a bigger disadvantage, until September 1, when they get only a three-pound sex allowance.

In a claiming race, the horses may also get weight off for a lower claiming price. For instance, in a $25,000 claiming race, a horse might get three pounds off for each $2,500 his claiming price is reduced, until his claiming price is $20,000. So, if the basic weight to be carried was, say, 121 pounds, your horse could get in with 115 pounds. Like dropping a horse down in class, this is a dangerous temptation, because a trainer has to weigh the benefits of getting weight off against the probability of getting his horse claimed.

An apprentice weight allowance also is available. When a jockey first starts riding he is known as an apprentice jockey. To make up for the lack of experience and to give trainers incentive to use an

A jockey weighing in.

apprentice, such jockeys are given weight concessions. This allowance is in addition to any other weight allowance for which a horse is eligible. Although the apprentice allowance has some variations (from three to seven pounds), in most cases it is five pounds.

This means your apprentice fully clothed, helmet, boots, saddle, and all, should weigh 105 to 110 pounds, which is mighty light. Theoretically, say you are running a filly in the spring at the minimum claiming price with an apprentice rider. The filly could conceivably get weight allowances of up to twenty pounds, which means she would have a seven and a half- to an eight-length advantage over the horse carrying 121 pounds at one and one-sixteenth miles.

As with everything else, there is a catch to all this — youngsters coming into the jockey ranks today are bigger, better nourished, and larger than their counterparts of twenty years ago. The current scale of weights used in this country was established in the 1850s and creates an impossible situation for jockeys, who may be required to make weights as light as 100 pounds. That is one reason you see so many foreign riders.

Overweight is a common condition in racing today. Riders can't stay thin enough to make the weight, and many undergo torturous daily regimens to do so, often causing danger to themselves and other riders. This is another anachronism in racing that needs to be changed, but, of course, raising the scale of weights is opposed by a lot of people who subscribe to the fallacy that weight causes horses to break down more than speed.

The jockey, with his saddle and other equipment, is weighed before he leaves the jockeys' quarters — this is called weighing out. If the horse's assigned weight is more than the jockey's normal weight he either uses a heavier saddle (most jockeys have two or three different weight saddles) or has lead weight pads added to his tack.

The weight pads are called "dead weight" and are less desirable than the weight of a jockey, which moves in concert with the horse in most cases. At some tracks, if the rider is underweight the horse will carry a more ergonomic weight pad, which is healthier for the horse. For instance, a Kentucky veterinarian, Philip Shrimpton, has invented something called the Best Pad, designed to distribute weight more evenly and thus protect the horse's back. The Best Pad is gaining wide acceptance at major racetracks.

After the race, the jockeys are weighed again ("weigh in") on a scale at the finish line to determine whether they carried the correct weight. It is the trainer's responsibility to calculate the proper weight allowances and claim them at the time of entry.

Preference Systems

Stakes are not the only class of races where an overflow field may necessitate excluding some horses — in fact, it seems to be an increasing problem in cheaper races, indicating a glut of lesser-quality animals.

This brings up the question of what happens in an overnight (non-stakes) event in the condition book that draws an overflow

This entry blank allows an excluded horse to get on a preferred list.

number of entries. At some racetracks, the number of maidens entered in one race may go as high as 100, so this becomes a very important question.

Two methods are widely used in North America. The oldest is known as the "star" system. Under this system, when a horse is entered to run but is excluded, he receives a star by his name and is put on what is known as the preferred list. The more stars he has, the higher he goes on the list until he gets into a race.

There is one catch to this, however. The "stars" apply only to races of the same distance with the same conditions. For instance, if a maiden enters a maiden claiming race at six furlongs and is excluded, this preference star does not apply to maiden special weight races or maiden races at a different distance. Preference stars that are granted to fillies entered in a race exclusively for fillies and mares do not apply to races with no sex restriction.

The star program can be cumbersome, difficult to manage, and sometimes works to the disadvantage of a horse that may have been excluded several times from different types of races but does not have the necessary number of stars for the upcoming race that fits him. I think the star system is pretty much on the way out.

Most racetracks have replaced it with a date preference system, in which every horse is assigned a date the first time he is entered, and horses with the earliest dates are given preference. Once a horse starts in a race, that becomes his preference date. This works well by allowing a trainer to get a horse ready for a particular race. By watching the overnight entries, he can determine the approximate date his horse will become valid for entry.

The preference system has the further advantage of eliminating the crossover from one type of race to another and simply gives horses that have had the longest lapse of time since their last start the most preference.

At the Secretary's Office

The racing secretary's office is the nerve center of the racetrack. When your horse is ready to run, this is where the trainer or his agent will go to enter him. From 7:30 a.m. until 11 a.m. on entry day, this office is a beehive of activity. It is a world unto itself where the nuts and bolts of the racing card come together. Spend some time there and watch what goes on.

Almost all racetracks in America today operate under the forty-eight-hour rule (a few opt for seventy-two hours), under which entries are taken two days before the actual running of the race. In the old days, entries were made the day before the race (which is why non-stakes races are still called "overnights"), but in order to allow time for promotion and publicity, the entries are now made two days before the race. Closing time for entries at most race-tracks is 10 or 10:30 a.m., and while some tracks adhere closely to this rule, the majority hold the entries open until the racing secretary is satisfied that he has sufficient entries in his feature races to make an attractive race card.

One of the racing secretary's most difficult jobs is convincing trainers that their horses have a chance in one of the feature races with a short field. Like any other business, cooperation and help are needed from both sides. A trainer who helps a racing secretary fill a race may find it easier later to request a race with conditions to fit one of his horses.

At a few tracks private entry booths are set up so that other trainers cannot determine who is being entered in a race while at many other tracks most entries are made over the phone. The trainers specify the particular race from the condition book, the weight that the horse is to carry under the conditions of the race, and who the jockey will be, if he knows.

At tracks that use the star system, the entry form has a place for the number of stars being claimed. The trainer is responsible for the correctness of the entry form, even if he delegates filling it out to an agent. A trainer who enters an ineligible horse or miscalculates the weight the horse is to carry may be subject to a fine and/or disqualification of his horse.

As the entries begin to come in around 9:30 a.m., the racing secretary starts to have an idea of which races have sufficient entries, which are borderline, and which ones are obviously not going to fill for the day. He then announces a "rundown" to the trainers and agents who are assembled in the office and his assistants call trainers whose horses might help fill out the day's program. This rundown allows trainers of horses that are in called-off races to make alternate plans where possible. If there are other races with similar conditions, the rundown will allow the racing secretary to start hustling the trainers of eligible horses. A little later, as entries continue to come in, the racing secretary may call off more races with few entries in an effort to encourage entries in the remaining races. At that time, the racing secretary will solicit horses for the borderline races. When he is finally satisfied that he has done all he can — that he has developed the best possible racing card for the day — he will close the entries.

During the morning hours as entries are being taken, the assistants in the racing secretary's office will also verify the eligibility of horses for the particular races. They also will check the entries for possible errors and check the preference claims and entry dates where the date preference system is used. All these assistants are making an effort to verify what the trainer has stated on the entry blank. Keep in mind, though, your trainer is ultimately responsible for what is on the entry blank, not the racing secretary or his assistants.

Drawing for Position

Once the entries are closed and a final check is made to reconfirm the eligibility of the entered horses, it is time to draw for post positions. All of the entry blanks for a particular race are placed in a box facing away from the outside of the counter so that the only thing the horsemen who do the drawing can see is the back of an entry form. (There is always a crowd of horsemen around the drawing eager to find out if their horses are "in.")

At the same time these entry blanks are placed in the box, balls or pills with post positions corresponding to the number of entries for the race are placed in a Kelly bottle, just like the one described earlier.

A horseman or a track representative takes the Kelly bottle and draws out one of the pills. At the same time the pill is drawn, an entry blank is pulled from the box by another designated horseman — two people are involved to eliminate any possible collusion. One by one, the pills and entry blanks are matched. In the event that more than twelve horses are entered (or whatever number constitutes a maximum field at a particular racetrack), the first twelve drawn comprise the field.

In addition, four or six more entry blanks are drawn and these horses are called "also eligibles." This means that should one of the original entrants in the race scratch (that is drop out of the race by the designated scratch time), one of the horses on the also-eligible list may "draw in" to the race. At tracks where the date system is used, the horse with the earliest preference date will draw in, but will be assigned the outside available post position.

Should more than one horse scratch from the race, then more than one horse will be drawn in from the also-eligible list. The also-eligibles that don't get to run and the horses that were not selected for the field are the ones known as excluded and will be given a subsequent preference for future races.

After the post positions are drawn, the assistant racing secretaries check once more for errors and corrections and the jockeys are named for each horse. The racing department will make up the "overnight sheet," which is a list of the entries for the day's card. As explained above, it's still called "overnight" even though it now comes out two days before the race.

The number of the race in the condition book will not normally correspond to its position on the racing program. The racing secretary wants continuity in his racing program so that he can draw the largest crowd and betting handle possible. The "overnight" is the same information sent to the *Daily Racing Form,* the local paper, and whoever prints the racing programs

Scratches

Racetrack scratch times are found in each racetrack's condition books, but normally it is the day before the race. Scratch time used to be the morning of the race, but tracks have moved it up to allow more time to print the program, get the proper entries with the scratches included in the morning newspapers, and help the publicity department promote the day's program.

Trainers of horses that have gotten sick or injured since entry time, or trainers who do not want to run their horses because of a change in track conditions or because they don't like the competition, turn in scratch cards prior to the prescribed scratch time. These scratch cards are reviewed by the stewards. If the racing field will not fall below a certain minimum size, there is usually no problem and no reason is necessary. This is normally the case in races that have also-eligibles and races with full fields. However, if the scratch of a horse causes the field to fall below a certain minimum (which at most racetracks is eight horses), the trainer must have a legitimate reason, such as sickness or injury.

When the field is reduced below the acceptable minimum, the stewards may order the trainer to run his horse anyway. This horse is called "stuck," in that he is stuck in the race and will not be excused without a good reason. They will not order an ill or injured horse to run, so often the trainer will claim the horse is "not right." In cases like that, the stewards will usually order the state veterinarian to examine the horse and determine the legitimacy of the trainer's complaint. If this occurs, the horse is placed on the veterinarian's list and cannot be re-entered until he has been taken off the list, normally a minimum of five to seven days.

Emergencies after scratch time, such as cases of sickness or injury, again must be verified by the state veterinarian and approved by the stewards. The veterinarian's list restriction also applies. The only exception is in a stakes race. Since the owner must pay to start his horse, he is entitled to scratch in most states right up to the afternoon of the race.

Track Condition

Having brought up track conditions, this is probably as good a place as any to describe and explain them.

The normal condition is "fast." This is when the track is in good shape and does not contain an abnormal amount of moisture.

When a quick, hard rain falls, the track usually goes from fast to "sloppy," which means the track has a great deal of water standing on the surface but is still firm underneath. A sloppy racetrack gives the appearance of a pond. Race times on a sloppy racetrack will be very close to those on a fast track.

If the rain persists or comes more slowly over a longer period, the water soaks into the whole cushion of the racetrack, making it "muddy." A muddy racetrack is very difficult for horses to run through. Some horses, though, seem to have a preference for mud, either because of infirmities that don't hurt them as much on it or a way of going that favors a holding type of surface.

The worst track of all is described as "heavy." This is merely the culmination of a soaking rain, which results in a very tiring surface to run on for a horse as the mud sticks to his hooves...and everything else.

As the track begins to dry out after a rain, it becomes "slow." This is essentially equivalent to muddy except it is drying. It is not yet really good but nevertheless better than heavy. Most tracks have dropped this designation in recent years. Who knows why?

As the track continues to dry and is getting close to its optimum condition, it is described as "good."

One other track condition perhaps should be mentioned now that winter racing has picked up around the country, and that is "frozen." It occurs, as one might suspect, when rain is followed by a drastic drop in temperature and the water in the track freezes. The condition is dangerous, not so much because it is slippery, but because the frozen moisture forms rock-like clods that can injure a horse, as well as the rider.

Turf tracks have five conditions. The normal turf condition is "firm," which means the track is in good shape and horses should run at their optimum.

Tractors working the surface during winter racing.

The next condition, like dirt tracks, is "good"; it has rained recently, and the course is either drying out or is on its way to a softer condition. On "good" courses, horses usually run to form without being unduly hampered.

After rain, many races are taken off the turf, but when the turf is not firm but nevertheless good enough to race over, it is termed "yielding." As the name implies, it means soft, tiring, and more difficult to run over.

The worst condition of a turf course is "soft." This means the horses will sink into the turf, throwing up big clods of grass and dirt. Very few racetracks will keep races on the turf under such conditions, with the exception of stakes races.

The other condition, which occurs in periods of drought, is called "hard." This is an adverse condition, particularly when a horse has some infirmity with the foot or lower limb, because his legs will sting when he runs on a very firm surface.

Before going on to race day, two other items should be discussed: getting licensed and designing your silks.

Getting Your License

Racing is the best policed sport in the world. Everybody from the lowliest hotwalker to the president of the track must be licensed by the state racing commission. This includes you.

At the racetrack, you will fill out a form, get fingerprinted, and be photographed. The license fee ranges from $10 in some states to $200 in California. After your application is approved by the state racing commission, you will get your owner's license and be issued a badge with your picture, much like your driver's license. This will allow you access to the backstretch so you can watch your horses going through their morning exercise.

If you're going to race in more than one state, you may have to go through this procedure more than once. Most of the state racing commissions are so possessive of their authority that they have not been able to come up with a universal license, despite years of effort. Things have improved substantially, though. Just as this book was going to press, I received a letter containing the wonderful news that a total of seventeen states had agreed to accept a national owner's license that is hoped will be in effect as of July 1, 2001. Other states are expected to sign on by July 1, 2002. The license will be available for owners only and will cost $150 for three years (plus the normal fee charged for a license in whatever state you want to race). It still will be cheap at twice the price if you don't have to fill out a separate application and get a separate set of fingerprints for every state where you want to race, as is the case, today. (For more information, call the Racing Compact at 859-224-2538.)

Selecting Your Colors

One of the really fun things you can do as an owner is design your own colors for your jockeys to wear, or silks, as they're often called (another carryover from the early days of the sport when they were actually made of silk). In most places your design can be just about anything you want, from solid white to a multicolor rainbow, so long as someone else isn't already using that scheme and you've registered it with your state racing commission.

If you race in New York, New Jersey, or Florida, however, you will have to register your colors with The Jockey Club. The Jockey Club registers colors on a ten-year or lifetime basis. Once colors are registered in an owner's name, no other owner can have the same combination. In addition, The Jockey Club has some restrictions on what is acceptable in the way of special markings on colors. Even if you don't plan on racing in New York initially, get your colors approved and registered there for the day when you ship to the Big Apple for the Belmont Stakes. The Jockey Club will be happy to send you the necessary forms and instructions if you request them.

A few suggestions: Use bright colors, they are easier to see. Stay away from the basic colors as much as you can; everyone else is using them. Use one color for the jacket and a different color for the sleeves or special markings on sleeves — such as hoops or chevrons — that are easy to see. Even though you may like your initials or the logo of your company, any symbol on the front or back of the jacket is not visible when the jockey is hunched down, whipping and driving, so it will not help you pick out your horse. The place for your initials or symbol is on blinkers; you can spot them there.

Allow plenty of lead time; don't wait until your horse is ready to run to order your silks. It takes four to eight weeks to have silks made after they are registered.

One last thing, the people who make the silks will be more than happy to help design them. The leading silk manufacturer in the country, Silks Unlimited, has its office right down the hall from me. Two very nice ladies, Pat and Linda Green, run the place and can be an enormous help. Tell them I sent you, and they'll give you a peppermint, if they can steal one from me.

Race Day

Finally, the big day arrives, and your excitement is almost uncontrollable. You can barely eat breakfast in your hurry to get to the barn to be sure everything is okay. Your young horse knows something is up, too! He didn't go to the track this morning and perhaps his hay was taken away (this is known as "drawing" a horse, and many trainers do it before a race). He gets a little extra attention and encouragement from his groom.

Later, the call comes through the backstretch on the loudspeakers, "Get your horses ready for the second race." This is it! The groom gives your youngster a final brushing, checks his mane and tail for any unwanted straw or snags, cleans out his feet one more time, and slips on the bridle. A few minutes go by and the big call comes, "bring your horses to the paddock for the second race."

In the paddock, your prancing youngster is all eyes. What's this all about? Who are all these people? Why are they here staring at me?

What a shock the paddock must be to a green two-year-old the first time he sees it! As a matter of fact, most youngsters are really too curious to be upset the first time they are there. They spend their time wondering what it is all about.

Some tracks are particularly traumatic for young horses, and they're generally where many, if not most, of the high-quality two-year-olds make their first start, i.e., Keeneland and Saratoga. Both have very attractive saddling areas under the trees adjacent to the paddock, which is just lovely in that it permits the patrons to get a close-up view of the horses, but they also crowd the horses. It's testimony to the intelligence of the horses that some idiot hasn't gotten killed by a fractious two-year-old, because the crowds do walk right up behind the horses at both of those tracks as they are being

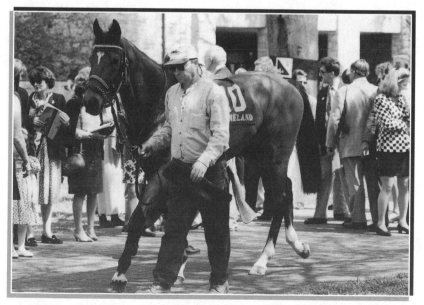

After years of preparation, race day has arrived.

led from the saddling rings into the paddock.

If they are fractious and nervous, the second trip to the paddock is often the worst, especially if they had a bad experience in their first race. Keep that in mind. For a lot of horses the second start is likely to be the most traumatic and may be the most disappointing. In the second start your youngster knows enough that he may be too worried to perform well. Very few horses win their first start, and many run poorly in their second start.

Your youngster, however, gets saddled, behaves well, and you are relieved. Here comes the jockey in your new silks. How splendid he looks!

Your trainer gives the jockey his instructions: "Break sharply. This colt is good from the gate. Lay third or fourth down the backstretch. Don't go four horses wide and lose a lot of ground on the turn. Tap him turning for home and let him go to the front. Don't abuse him; just let him win by a couple."

Of course, eight or nine other trainers are giving their jockeys the exact same instructions! Remember, the best jockey in the world can't get off your horse and carry him home, which brings me to another old story that is usually attributed to Bill Shoemaker, but could apply to almost any rider in the country:

Before the race, the trainer gives his rider very explicit instructions on how to rate the horse. "Drop in behind the leaders leaving the gate; tuck in along the rail, fourth down the backstretch; move up to third going into the far turn; move him up to second turning for home; take the lead at the eighth pole; and draw away from there home."

As the race developed, the horse was first leaving the gate, second down the backstretch, third going into the far turn, fourth turning for home, fifth at the eighth pole — and nowhere to be found at the finish.

The enraged trainer dashed down to the unsaddling area to

meet his errant rider, where he screamed for everyone to hear, "You didn't follow my instructions. I told you to lay back early and go to the front at the eighth pole."

"I would have done that," the jockey replied, "but I thought I'd stay with your horse."

An old saying has it that there are a million ways to lose a race and only one way to win — get to the finish line first! It's true. In team sports there is one winner and one loser. In racing there is one winner and as many as eleven losers or more, so you will probably have more downs than ups no matter how successful you are. But what ups! Take it from me, they are worth the downs. It would take a whole book to write about what can and does go wrong in a horse race. Take what you hear and see, and analyze it for yourself. The racetrack is the greatest rumor mill and gossip center in the world. Don't accept what you hear as fact unless you can verify it — but do listen and learn from your experiences!

Good horses make good jockeys and good trainers. A good jockey and a good trainer get the most out of a horse but can do no more. A bad trainer or a bad jockey can ruin your chances.

Jockeys

Pound for pound, jockeys are among the finest athletes in the world, and they are a very important part of the horse business. I can guarantee that you'll get mad at your rider from time to time (show me the person who hasn't made a crack about a size five shoe and a size three hat, and I'll show you someone who hasn't been around the track for long). But if you think it's easy work, try living on 700 to 800 calories and riding five or six races a day, in addition to working a few horses in the morning. Another thing you can try: Turn on a televised race, get about halfway down in a deep knee bend, lean forward, and support your weight on the balls of your feet. Now rock back and forth like that for the duration of a race, imagining all the while that you're trying to urge a thousand-pound horse to go places he really doesn't want to go, faster than he wants to go there. It's an enlightening exercise, and, believe me, it is exercise.[4]

Your trainer should be the one to select a rider who fits your horse. Most trainers have developed a relationship with a few jockeys whom they prefer to have riding for them. It is even better if the jockey has been on your horse before the race in a morning workout so he will be comfortable and have some knowledge about your horse.

Remember, the selection of a jockey is your trainer's responsibility and where and when your horse races is his responsibility. You have hired a professional. You can talk to him about his selection, but you should probably let him do his job to the best of his ability.

Spend a lot of time with your trainer, both before and during the races. Ask lots of questions. But, by the same token, don't second guess him too much. The purpose of this book is to help you understand the business you are in and to understand your trainer's problems better, not to encourage you to go around with a condition book in your pocket, looking over his shoulder. If you are going to do that, you are doomed to failure and my advice has gone for naught. Training horses is his business, and he is a professional. When you hire a plant manager for your business, you give him the authority to do a job. Consider your horse business as another plant, your trainer as a plant manager, and give him the authority and support to do his job.

---

4 Don't let your spouse or significant other find you doing this or she'll think you're crazy. Oh, what the hell, she probably already thinks you're crazy anyway.

The Edge

Racing is so competitive, so dependent on luck as well as skill that trainers are inclined to seize on any little thing that they think will give them "the edge" over other trainers or, more likely, help them to keep up with other trainers.

One recent example is aerodynamic silks, which became popular a few years ago when some genius postulated that the drag from the original looser silks was probably costing horses races. Well, they started making tight-fitting silks in an attempt to eliminate that costly factor, but I don't notice many sets today.

I remember when Bobby Frankel was having a particularly successful meeting at Hollywood Park and the rumor went around that he was having his farrier only use three nails on each shoe to save weight. Notwithstanding the fact that Frankel has been one of the most successful trainers in the country for the past three decades — largely through the dint of hard work, a good eye for a horse, and attention to detail — a lot of trainers began to mimic that ridiculous behavior. I don't know whether it helped their bottom line any, but it helped the bottom line of the farriers who got a lot more business replacing thrown shoes.

Medication is the same way. Of all the things that have gotten out of hand on the backstretch recently, perhaps "controlled" medication is the farthest out in left field. When the proponents of pre-race medication were making their case back in the '60s and '70s, the reason they cited for permitting the administration of, say, butazolidin, an analgesic that alleviates soreness, was that it would permit horses to race more often and alleviate short fields. Well, the exact opposite has happened — from 1960 to now the average number of starts per year for Thoroughbreds racing in North America has declined about thirty-six percent from 11.31 to 7.29, and despite a large increase in foal crops, the average field size has declined almost nine percent. Still, it is not unusual to see 100 percent of the horses on a given race day racing on butazolidin and another seventy-five percent racing on furosemide (Lasix), which is supposed to permit horses to breathe up to capacity. While I do believe that the occasional horse needs butazolidin or furosemide, or both, to race up to capacity, I truly believe that the prevalence of these medications is primarily triggered by trainers' suspicions that other trainers' horses will have an edge.

Finally, nose strips. Last year, several trainers, Wayne Lukas in particular, began to race horses with nasal strips similar to those worn by human athletes. Then, of course, a few jockeys began to wear them. In fact, Lukas did win a couple of Breeders' Cup races in 1999, but I don't see this trend taking off like some of the others. Most of the competition realized that Lukas' success came because he had the best horses, not because of some silly nose strips.

The bottom line is this (although not always): the trainer who does the best job and has the best horses will win most of the time, whether those horses are racing on butazolidin and furosemide, have three or six nails in their shoes, wear nose strips, and carry a jockey who wears aerodynamic silks and a nose strip himself.

CHAPTER
FIVE

ON THE FARM

"I often say we are in the dream business."

— Michael Osborne, founding chairman, Dubai World Cup Committee

The drama and thrills we experience at the racetrack or at the sales don't just happen. Those yearlings standing wide-eyed in the sales ring, those ten prancing two-year-olds on their way to the post for the first time, are the product of a multibillion-dollar industry, a huge agricultural enterprise extending from Florida to Oregon, from New York to Southern California, and with tendrils in most civilized countries of the world.

On their first trip to a Thoroughbred farm, most people are not only awed and thrilled by the beauty of the horses, but they are amazed at the complexity of the operation. By the same token, most racing fans have no idea of how much effort has gone into getting a field of horses to the post; and I mean before the horses have even gone near a racetrack.

Horses, like people, come from a variety of backgrounds. Each one arrives at the racetrack or sales grounds from differing circumstances and methods of being raised. At the racetrack, you will find many homebreds racing for their breeders. They spent their first couple of years on one farm, from foaling through gentling, until readied to go to the track. On the other hand, since nearly a quarter of all yearlings are offered at public auction, many will be racing for their second owners. Still others may have changed hands two or three times, having been pinhooked as weanlings or yearlings and resold as yearlings or two-year-olds. Some will have been purchased privately. Some will have been broken by loving hands at "Mom and Pop" operations, while others will have been schooled at large training centers by professionals. Regardless of background, most of each youngster's life took place amidst the beauty and serenity of a farm. And this chapter is about what takes place on the farm.

Breeding as an Investment

Many newcomers to the Thoroughbred business have started out as racing fans and bettors. As their fascination for the sport grew, those who could afford it bought a racehorse or two, either by claiming or privately.

First thing they knew, a filly they owned broke down and, bingo , the race fan/owner found himself with a broodmare prospect. Not everyone followed this path, but a great many of today's breeders got where they are today that way.

One of the most significant changes in the Thoroughbred business the past few decades is the number of newcomers who have become involved in the sport strictly as a business investment rather than as an outgrowth of being a racing fan.

Several factors have established and bolstered this trend. First, as I alluded in Chapter 4 and as will be discussed in more detail in Chapter 7, while the costs of owning a racehorse have risen substantially — coupled, of course, with the inherently greater risks of racing — purses, although rising, have failed to keep pace with the escalating cost of bloodstock and of training. Secondly, if you look at overall trends, despite our problems of the late '80s and early

'90s, the value of breeding stock has risen exponentially the last two decades. The world-record syndication price for a stallion more than doubled during the past decade, from $28 million for Storm Bird to a reported $60 million to $70 million for Fusaichi Pegasus. From 1992 to 2000, both the average and the median prices for broodmares have risen steadily every year, which, as discussed in Chapter 2, is largely the result of an extraordinarily healthy yearling market.

Racing a colt for a year to earn $1 million in purses makes no economic sense when keeping him in training costs so much and when he could be earning $10 million to $15 million in the breeding shed. (If you don't see how it can cost $1 million to keep a horse in training for a year, consider this: If the horse is worth $10 million as a stud prospect, the insurance alone on that horse will run you around $750,000. Then add shipping, security, ten percent of purse money each to the trainer and the rider, stakes payments, and tips to everybody from the groom to the parking attendant when he wins, and you're probably actually losing money when your horse wins "only" $1 million in a year.)

In short, the cost of doing business today is so high that even those involved in the horse business for many years have had to seek outside capital to compete. This explosion of prices has also attracted new investors to the breeding and pinhooking segments of the business while bypassing the racing game.

Considering that it can be nearly as big of a thrill to watch a foal being born or to send a prospective high-priced yearling into the auction ring, breeding has become an increasingly popular avenue of investment, particularly since it is considered somewhat safer than other segments of the Thoroughbred business. Still, even in the breeding business investors today are forced to rely on the "home run" to break even or make money, just like owners at the racetrack.

At the Farm

If you are human, or at least have what I consider to be a human soul, when you drive onto a well-managed Thoroughbred farm on a sunny afternoon, you will be overwhelmed by its beauty and tranquility. The mares are fat and dappled as they graze peacefully in lush green pastures while their foals romp about, pictures of health. The grass is mowed and the fences painted. The barns are neat and clean. Everything is beautiful and serene.

It all looks very natural, but, take it from me, it takes a well-oiled, hard-working organization seven days a week, fifty-two weeks a year to make it look that way. Horses have no holidays — no Christmases, no Thanksgivings, no New Year's Eves, no Sundays. Horses eat every day and need care every day. Contrary to what a lot of people may think, horse farming is not seasonal — the only thing that changes is which phase of the operation needs the most attention during a particular time of year.

To familiarize you with the basics of farm operation, though, it makes sense to look at it over the course of a year. No matter where you start, what happens often is the result of what has gone on before, so I'll start with January 1.

A Kentucky Thoroughbred farm — no simple operation.

The Year Begins

This is a good place to start since all

Thoroughbreds born in the Northern Hemisphere share January 1 as a birthday. No matter what date a Thoroughbred is born, even December 31, no matter what the IRS says, he becomes a year older on January 1. This is another anachronism that we endure from the early days of Thoroughbred racing in England. Since the racing season ended in late fall and did not resume until spring, the logical time to change the age of all horses was during the lull in racing. Today, year-round racing in the United States (racing is still seasonal in Europe except for some minor race meetings in Southern Europe) has made January 1 merely an arbitrary and problematic day for change of age.

The primary difficulty is that it is out of tune with nature. The Thoroughbred, both stallions and mares, are seasonal animals; a stallion is generally more fertile and a mare will have her best heat cycles from April until August, so that the resulting foal after a 342-day gestation will be born in the spring or early summer, when the weather is right. Many mares actually go anestrus (do not come in heat) for a varying length of time during the winter months. However, many people feel that an early foaling date is essential to the precocity of youngsters both for racing and sales.[1] This puts pressure on the breeders to have early foals, which, in turn, puts pressure on the breeding farms to develop methods that encourage early conception in the broodmare band. All of which go against the laws of nature.

Colonel Phil Chinn, whom I discussed earlier, was fond of saying that his biggest Christmas present arrived on New Year's Day when he went out to the tobacco barn on the back of the farm (tobacco barns in many cases in Kentucky are used as a combination tobacco and horse barn) and saw all of the big, good-looking foals that had been born there the night before.

---

[1] I don't believe this has been statistically proven, however.

The obvious implication of this story that the Colonel had foals born before the first of January has always elicited a nervous reaction from breeders. There is no question that he is not the only breeder who has had foals born by accident before the first of January (a gestation period that is three weeks short is unusual but not rare).

Take it from me, a foal born in late December is a disaster. If two people know something, it is no secret, and if you try to hide a December foal, the chances of getting caught are almost 100 percent. Consequently, your foal will become a yearling when it's only a day or several days old. As a result, it will be almost a year less mature than its "contemporaries," which is an insurmountable obstacle at the yearling sales and through the sophomore season on the racetrack.

The truth, though, is that December foals are very rare because most breeding sheds don't open until the middle of February and most mares are difficult to get in foal in early and mid-winter because it is not nature's time.

Artificial Lighting

Modern science and research have proven a mare can be fooled into thinking it is spring, thus ovulating earlier, by using artificial lighting. Over the years, research has established that a horse's conception of the time of year is a direct response to photoperiod — the length of the day. For years, chickens have been kept under lights twenty-four hours a day to encourage growth and egg production.

Most well-managed commercial farms today put their barren mares and their stallions "under lights" around December 1. Some farms bring the mares into a stall, while others keep them in small pens under strong uniform lighting. The hours vary, but typically the length of the day is extended to around seventeen hours. The

The use of artificial lights is widespread.

use of lights and hormones can usually give the farm a three- to four-week jump on the normal spring cycle of the mare and is particularly useful in maiden (first-year) mares. They can be bred before the breeding shed gets too busy,[2] thus affording them a chance to get in foal earlier and giving them more time before they "fall off the calendar," which will be explained further below. This doesn't guarantee conception, but the farm and the farm veterinarian have more time to work on getting her in foal. Similarly, a stallion's sperm is seasonal, and some farms use lights with stallions to produce similar results, although this practice seems to be waning.

Fertility

Over time the percentage of foals registered with The Jockey Club has bounced between fifty-five percent and sixty percent of the

---

[2] Because of the use of lights and hormones, many farms are getting to the point where the breeding shed is often as busy in early February serving those early-cycling mares as it is at the height of the breeding season.

mares reported bred the previous year. This is staggering when you consider that good commercial farms need to maintain a seventy-five percent to eighty percent live-foal rate in order to survive economically. Even in Kentucky where we feel we have the top management in the world, the rate is under seventy percent. This means that some breeders are getting very few of their mares in foal. Horses, incidentally, have the lowest reproduction rate of all domestic animals, and Thoroughbreds in particular have among the lowest reproduction rates among horses. No doubt, selective breeding for speed rather than reproductive ability has contributed.

At least part of the fertility problem can be attributed to the unnatural breeding season. Part of it can also be ascribed to the previously mentioned explosion in bloodstock values, which has made it economically feasible to keep breeding mares that had extremely poor production records. This trend was somewhat reversed in the doldrums, but the astounding recovery of the bloodstock market has now made problem mares feasible again.

Years ago the accepted breeding season would extend from February 15 to June 15. The February 15 opening date is estab-

Many mares are bred again soon after foaling.

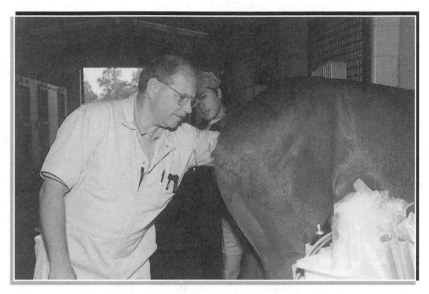

Palpating a mare to see if she is ready to be bred.

lished both by weather and to avoid having December foals. With the use of artificial lights in recent years, some breeding centers open a week or ten days earlier. The practical closing date was June 15 because most breeders felt if a mare was not in foal by that time, her yearling with a resulting late foaling date would not sell well. Again, because of the explosion in bloodstock prices because of the prevalence of no-guarantee seasons and because of rising prices at the September sales, breeders in recent years have felt that a late foal from an expensive mare was better than no foal at all, and the breeding season was extended to June 30, and in some cases July 15. In addition, many popular stallions are standing dual hemisphere seasons, but I'll discuss that in more detail below.

With the normal gestation period for a Thoroughbred mare being 342 days, a mare has difficulty producing a foal each year. Breeding a mare back on the foal heat period, called by many the nine-day period, has many advocates and detractors. At any rate, it brings the number of days from conception to first possible breeding date to about 351. If for any reason the foal heat is not used for breeding, the next normal heat period is at 372 days, so even assuming that everything goes perfectly each year — and your mare does not carry longer than the normal 342 days; and she cycles promptly; and she conceives the first time she is rebred — the foaling date gets a little later each year.

I can guarantee you, even with a "perfect" mare things will not go right every year. We are not dealing with machines, and if the mare does not conceive on her first cover, she will foal as much as a month or more later the next year.[3] As this continues for several years, most mares will inevitably "fall off the calendar," and your mare will need to be given a year off sometime along the way (although some breeders will even breed a mare on Southern Hemisphere time, rather than to "waste" a year). If you don't, she might just take one on her own, which may not be a totally bad thing. If you notice, as I have over many years, a lot of stakes winners seem to be first foals or foals that were born in a year after the mare had gone without producing a foal.

When all is said and done, the majority of Thoroughbred foals are born in February and March in the major breeding areas, and April and May in many other areas, which means their dams conceived in May and June. The best heat period produced by mares ("best" meaning the most predictable, the shortest, the most obvious in terms of the mare's interest, and the most breedable follicle) normally comes at that time of year, which is the one nature intended. By the time a horse is a three year old, any advantage of a two- or three-month earlier foaling date has evaporated.

Even the veterinarians will tell you, working with nature can be a lot more productive than working against it.

---

3 The use of prostaglandins to induce heat in mares in recent years has helped with the problem.

Foaling Time

In the fall after their foals have been weaned, mares are rechecked for their pregnancy status and are normally divided into groups according to their anticipated foaling date. Almost every commercial farm has a foaling barn[4] with a foaling crew, which can range from one experienced night watchman on most farms to a four- or five-person team in larger operations. Most foaling barns contain one or more extra-large stalls to allow the mare more room to foal naturally if everything goes well, and if things don't go well, to allow room for emergency procedures, which may include medications, oxygen, and heat for stalls.

Normally around December 1, as the foaling date for the first group of mares approaches, these mares are moved to an area near the foaling barn.

Each mare's vulva is checked for sutures, and a notation is made whether she will need to be properly opened just prior to foaling.

It is a common practice today for a mare's vulva to be sewn shut, either on the racetrack or after breeding, to prevent "wind sucking" — drawing air and attendant debris into the vagina — which can cause infection and resultant abortion. The reasons for what is known as a Caslick's procedure are twofold. First, in breeding horses for speed, we have developed a rear end (anus and vulva) that is slanted forward more than was evident in the first Thoroughbreds, and the placement of the anus above the vulva in this condition has tended to cause uterine infections. Secondly, as a mare ages and has more foals, her anus tends to sink forward and her vulva loses its muscular tone, allowing wind sucking.

---

[4] In Kentucky these days, a number of the larger farms maintain several foaling barns, and instead of rotating the mares through one foaling barn as their dates near, they rotate their primary foaling operation from barn to barn. It's another attempt to prevent the spread of sickness or disease during the foaling process.

Suturing is required on most older mares, regardless of their original conformation.

Some farms have their mares foal outside, particularly those in the southern climates. There are strong arguments in favor of foaling outside — this is where the mares would naturally foal and disease tends to be less concentrated in open areas. Even in states like Kentucky, foaling outside during the winter is probably as healthy or healthier than in a foaling barn, but because it is so unwieldy, uncomfortable, and inconvenient for the farm personnel, it is not done very often.

I cannot emphasize enough that an experienced night watchman or night crew can easily be the difference between life and death of the foal and the mare when a difficult delivery occurs. In cases of abnormal presentation of a foal, some mares may panic and actually push out their insides trying to get rid of the pain. Every farm has a veterinarian on call, but the time it takes him to get to the foaling barn can be critical, and an experienced foaling crew can well make the difference in the outcome.

Once the foal is born, he will be checked to ascertain whether he has absorbed sufficient antibodies from his mother's milk (colostrum), and he'll get an enema. If nothing appears wrong and a veterinarian did not attend the foaling, the foal will be allowed to wait until the next morning before receiving a veterinary examination. The foal will be standing and nursing in an hour or so, but the first three days are critical to the foal's long-term health. Prenatal and perinatal infections may show themselves at this time, and the trauma of coming into the world will expose malfunctions or malformations of limbs and organs, plus any latent weakness. A few days after foaling, the mare is resutured and is ready to be teased in preparation for being bred again.

Teasing

Teasing is the method used for determining when a mare is in heat (receptive to a stallion). It is one of the most time-consuming and vital functions carried out at any breeding farm. Teasing can be done in many ways — in the open field or in the confinement of a stall — but it must be thoroughly supervised by a competent, experienced, and interested member of the farm's staff, a person who takes pride in getting mares in foal.

Unlike humans, horses will normally accept mating only on or about the time conception is possible. Rather than expose the valuable stallion to the frustrations and the danger of determining which mares are ready to be bred, a "teaser" is used, and it's one of the worst jobs in the animal kingdom. This teaser can be a male horse or pony, a gelding full of male hormones, or it can be a stallion whose lack of popularity has made him available for lesser duties. In any case, the job is very frustrating for the teaser, because he is normally equipped with a shield or some other device to prevent him from breeding a mare by accident. As a

The teaser's job is frustrating for him, but important.

matter of routine, seventy-five percent to eighty percent of the mares he teases are going to be diestrus (not in heat) and therefore highly likely to kick him, bite him, or attack him in other ways too numerous to mention, which is why I have empathy with the teaser. A good teaser is worth his weight in gold. Many farms tease on an every-other-day schedule, which when coupled with veterinary assistance, is normally adequate. There are exceptions, especially during the height of the breeding season when most farms opt for a daily teasing schedule.

Record keeping is the name of the game, just like in any other business. As the breeding season progresses mares will develop a pattern of behavior. This pattern along with the teasing person's experience and observation, and a veterinary examination, will be the overriding determinant in decisions about when to breed a mare. Although each mare is different, each one has traits and patterns of behavior that are particular to her and are relatively constant. Mares have a tendency to retain the same patterns year in and year out, so that old teasing charts from previous years can be invaluable to getting a mare in foal. If your mare is moved from one farm to another, the teasing charts, along with her other health records, should accompany her.

Stallions

Stallions can be the most lucrative part of the breeding business, but standing them is one of the more highly specialized and labor-intensive aspects of the business. While, if you're lucky, you get one foal per year out of a broodmare, a stallion can be bred to upward of 100 mares. In fact, The Jockey Club's report of mares bred for the year 2000 listed eighty-two stallions that had books of 100 or more mares, led by Tale of the Cat with 175. Sixty-three of those lucky guys stood in Kentucky, followed by nine in Florida, six in California, and one each in Maryland, New York, Oklahoma, and

Washington. In all, early reports show that 3,681 stallions serviced 59,785 mares in 2000,[5] an average of 16.2 mares per stallion, although several hundred of those stallions only bred one mare. In Kentucky, 399 stallions covered 20,807 mares, an average of 52.2 mares per stallion, which is the highest ratio in the country.

Let's consider a few little multiplication exercises here:

Storm Cat: 118 mares X $300,000 X 78% fertility = $27,612,000

A.P. Indy: 130 mares X $150,000 X 81% fertility = $15,795,000

Tale of the Cat: 175 mares X $30,000 X 78% fertility = $4,095,000

Then, when you consider that nearly seventy stallions are doing dual-hemisphere seasons, which probably adds another forty percent to their income, the stallion business is not really all that bad. The fact is, even an "average" stallion can generate $1 million to $2 million a year for his connections.

Stallion management is a highly specialized aspect of the business, and I wouldn't advise it for just anybody. The competition to get a top horse is fierce, even among the leading stallion farms. You have very little hope of competing with the top five or ten farms to get a top horse, which is necessary to attract additional stallions to your operation.

In today's market, successful stallion management also requires spending additional money to construct a stud barn, breeding shed, etc., and to hire a lot of extra help — from experienced handlers to booking staff in the office — and requires several areas of additional expertise that are learned over years of hard lessons.

For instance, in my mind, the most important factor in successful stallion management is pricing his seasons and shares to obtain maximum revenues for the stallion owner (whether it is a syndicate or a single person) without pricing him so high that he becomes too expensive for mare owners. This is an art, and experi-

---

[5] Because Thoroughbred breeders are not among the best in the world at paperwork, these are preliminary numbers and will change substantially over the next couple of years.

enced stallion managers are experts at striking this delicate balance. Also, from a strictly personal standpoint, I believe it is worse for a horse to be overpriced than to be underpriced — particularly with a young stallion — because in the latter case the stallion will generally have an overabundance of applications to breed to him, and the stallion manager can pick and choose in an attempt to make the stallion. Additionally, you can always raise the price a little bit, while it's the kiss of death to have to discount fees.

In recent years, advertising stallions has become an art in and of itself. It once was a relatively simple thing — you would just set aside the cost of a season — and run a few ads in the trade journals to say what his foals were doing and how his yearlings were selling . Nowadays, with the competition to attract broodmares as fierce as getting the stallion to the farm in the first place, most farms have elaborate advertising budgets. They include money for ads in trade publications, but also also allow for expensive and fancy brochures extolling the horse's virtues, television ads on racing programs, videotapes of the stallion's career and his foals (which, despite a long career in the print media, I think are often much more revealing than print ads, because, after all, the horse is not a static animal). Before the 2000 breeding season began, Walmac Farm even sent out a compact disc for your computer that not only included information on its stallions, but allowed a breeder to plug in proposed matings of his mares with those stallions to look at how the offspring would catalogue.

Booking Mares

The term "book" in the Thoroughbred business applies to all the mares the stallion is contracted to serve during a particular breeding season. The syndicate manager or stallion manager is responsible for filling the stallion's book. Depending upon the popularity of the stallion, the farm where he is located, and the stud fee, booking may consist of an extremely tight selection of mares in terms of quality or the stallion manager having to go out and hustle as many mares as he can.

Syndicated stallions have an obvious advantage because many of the shareholders are inclined to use their seasons. This is particularly true if the outside demand is insufficient to allow the shareholders to sell their season or if the stallion is doing well. In either case, the syndicate manager starts out with a reasonable number of mares in the stallion's book, which makes filling it much less difficult. Stallions standing as the property of a single owner are sometimes more demanding of a stallion manager since he has to find a great number of people to submit mares.

You will hear of a stallion "having a full book." Since most syndicates, even today, are made up of forty shares, a full book usually means about fifty to sixty mares, but, as mentioned above, many stallions will be bred to books in excess of 100. Another factor to remember is Thoroughbreds must be bred by "natural cover," which means artificial insemination is not allowed. In the case of Standardbreds and Quarter Horses, where artificial insemination is allowed, a book may consist of 250 or 300 mares.

This may be a good thing for some of the stallion owners — and, in fact, can be a boon to mare owners if they are breeding strictly to race. Stud fees will generally be lower with an unlimited book, and they will normally be able to breed to a better stallion than they might have been able to otherwise because of artificial insemination — but other economic considerations must be thought out as well. Even without artificial insemination, Thoroughbred breeders, who are far more market oriented than many other breeders, are becoming increasingly disturbed when they breed to one of those stallions with a book in excess of 100 mares and then enter their yearling in the sales only to discover thirty to forty other yearlings by the same sire are in the sale. In short, their yearling must be absolutely perfect or he won't draw much interest.

Then again, there will be a lot of runners by those stallions and, barring some catastrophic occurrence, a lot of runners often means a lot of winners, which sometimes but not always means success as a stallion.

Another concomitance of success is the quality of a stallion's book. When a stallion is referred to as having "a high-quality book," it means the mares that are contracted to be bred to him are of high-quality pedigree and race record. While a lot of people think I'm nuts — and I do realize that a foal gets half its genetics from the stallion and half from the mare — I truly believe that the success of a stallion is probably seventy-five percent to eighty percent a function of the mares to which he's bred.

Until a stallion is established, syndicate managers often, justifiably, go to prodigious lengths to obtain high-quality mares for him. For example, to attract U.S. mares to its beautifully bred champion Dubai Millennium, who stands in England, Darley Stud will pay air fare for accepted mares, board them free, and return them to the United States as more incentive to breed to its stallion.

So, a high-quality book is very important in my book (no pun intended).

In fact, back in the days of *The Thoroughbred Record*, Bill Robertson and I developed what has now evolved into the Sire Production Index or the Mare Production Index, depending on who's talking about it. In short, it measures the quality of a stallion's offspring with all the other offspring of all the mares to which he's been bred, by all the sires to which they have been bred, and tells you whether a stallion is moving up his mares in quality or they are moving him up. It is now a number easily available on the computer and regularly published among the myriad of statistics about every stallion in the breeding pool. However, when I did the first version of it by hand, it took me almost eight weeks to work out three stallions. Of course, by the time I got through with the study, the numbers were already out of date. Let's hear it for computerized horse records.

Selecting a stallion for your mare is one of the most complex and daunting tasks you'll face as a breeder.

Most breeders think almost all year long about the selection process, which varies depending upon whether you're breeding for the market (in which case a stallion's yearling average and median and the ratio of those figures to his stud fee are important) or breeding to race (in which case his percentages of starters, winners, stakes winners, etc., becomes more important). Then, of course, you always have to consider the possibility that your yearling may not bring what you want and you might wind up racing it yourself, so you may need to strike a balance somewhere.

As I will point out in Chapter 8, in either case it doesn't make much economic sense to over- or under-breed your mare. For years, the rule of thumb was that you should breed to a stallion whose stud fee is approximately a quarter to a third of the value of your mare. Today, that guideline probably tends more toward the higher side — and, of course, can go higher than that if you're not realistic about valuing your mare.

Nowadays, in addition to the magazines and stallion registers that used to be about all we had to work with to make these critical decisions, there are all manner of newsletters, computer programs, web sites, mating services, advisors who specialize in matings, etc., etc., etc., to assist you in selecting a stallion for your mare.

One bit of advice: If you're not in it full time, get some help. Otherwise, you could very well drive yourself crazy with all the information that is available.

After having studied the various sources and conferred with your various consultants, you will select the stallion you want for your mare (if she is of sufficient quality) either from your home state or some other.

Next, you have to enter into a contract, which is pretty much standard. The stringency of a stallion contract in terms of payment is usually determined by the popularity of the stallion, i.e., how much abuse the mare owner is willing to endure to get to him. If he is very, very popular, such as A.P. Indy or Storm Cat, or if you purchased your season at an auction, such as Stallion Access (or these days, on-line), you might be required to pay the entire stud fee "up front" with no guarantee.

While the term "no guarantee" is freely used in the marketplace, it generally means there's no guarantee that your mare will get in foal, but it does carry the guarantee that the stallion will be breeding sound when your mare is ready. However, be careful...some no-guarantee contracts (particularly those sold at auction or on-line) mean exactly what they say...you're not even guaranteed the stallion will be alive when your mare is due to be bred.

If the stallion is pretty popular but not outrageously so, the stud fee might be due on a fifty-fifty basis, meaning that half the stud fee is due up front on a no-guarantee (the traditional kind) basis and the second half is due on a live-foal basis. Still others are due on a sixty- or ninety-day pregnancy check, the reasoning being that if she loses the foal after that, the stallion has done his part and any loss is the mare's fault. Finally, other stud fees are "live foal" but are due September 1 or October 1 of the year the mare is bred. This is merely a method for the stallion manager or share owner to use your money for six months. For most stallions, though, the fee is due when the foal stands and nurses.

I really think that unless you have no other way to get to a particular stallion or you are breeding at the very top of the market and have a lot of money to spend, a no-guarantee contract has little justification. There are times when a no-guarantee season may be so "inexpensive" that you can afford to pay for it (plus live-foal insurance), but those instances are very rare. Too many things can go wrong, and you ought to have at least some element or percentage of a live-foal guarantee in your contract. You wouldn't pay for a car and not expect to get it, so there is no reason to pay for a foal and not expect to get it.

If you sign a contract to breed to a stallion, honor that contract. It is very difficult for a stallion manager to plan the stallion's breeding season if people don't honor their commitments. There have been instances in recent years where people book a mare to a stallion and then just didn't show. Obviously, you have no financial commitment, but you certainly have a moral commitment to fulfill your contract, unless your mare is dead, unbreedable, or you have sold her. Should one of these occasions arise, notify the stallion manager promptly — don't just fail to show, particularly if you are going to stay in the business for a while and if you ever want to breed at that farm again. (Some stallion contracts today contain a provision that half the stud fee is due anyway for "no shows.")

Breeding Your Mare

The term booking a mare is used interchangeably for signing a stallion service contract, as discussed above, and for making the appointment when the mare is ready to be covered. Almost all large commercial breeding farms in Kentucky have too many stallions to allow all the mares being served to board at their farm. As a matter of fact, the majority of mares bred at large commercial farms in Kentucky are boarded at smaller farms nearby.

When your mare comes in heat, the veterinarian will determine the approximate day and time she should be covered through a combination of ovarian palpations, speculum examination, and ultrasonic examination. The manager of the farm where your mare is being boarded will then call the farm manager where the stallion stands and book your mare.

Depending upon the popularity of the stallion, how well he is "stopping" his mares (getting them in foal), and the time of year, your mare may get the exact day and time requested. This is a very tricky part of the business since the optimum time to service a mare is within twenty-four hours before ovulation. While sperm have been known to live several days under ideal conditions, the chances of your mare conceiving when covered more than forty-eight hours prior to actual ovulation are greatly diminished. On the other hand, if your mare is covered after she ovulates, your chances decrease rapidly and are nearly zero twelve hours after ovulation. Since heat periods and follicular development vary widely from mare to mare, you can see that familiarity with your mare and attention to detail are vital if you are to exceed the national average of fifty-five percent live-foal rate.

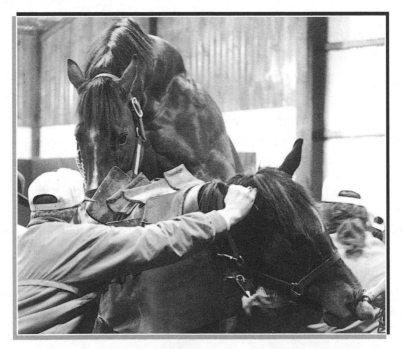

The business of the breeding shed is not for the amateur.

Depending upon the farm where you board, the mare will be either vanned by the farm itself or a local vanning service will be used. The mare will be delivered to the farm where the stallion stands and will begin further preparations attendant to being bred.

When a stallion and a mare get together in real life, it's not a romantic interlude. The stallion and the mare aren't turned out in a tree-lined paddock with a small creek bubbling through it and a big tub of sweet feed for them to eat before they get down to it. It's a business...very clinical and, in most cases, highly efficient.

There are several attendants (generally two for the stallion and another one, sometimes two, for the mare) with an attending veterinarian and one or two onlookers. The mare has been thoroughly teased (at most good stallion operations, she has been teased one last time just to make certain she's in heat) and prepared for being introduced to the stallion. The person in charge of the breeding shed will have thoroughly checked your mare's paperwork; he will have checked to see if she's sutured and if so, will have had the sutures removed; her genital area will then be washed, another health precaution for both the mare and the stallion; the mare's tail will be wrapped with gauze (it's amazing the accidents that can happen in the breeding shed; for instance, a tail hair can cut a stallion's penis and cause the horse to be out of action during the most critical part of the breeding season); and she will be restrained either with hobbles or a leg strap to prevent her from kicking the stallion in a moment of fear or excitement.

The actual mating is not an amateur's business, and many a stallion, mare, or attending hand has been seriously injured during the process. Remember, these are a pair of 1,500-pound animals that can literally kill a person with a well-placed kick, and they are in a stressful situation in the breeding shed.

Speaking of stress, the mare's foal usually stays back at the farm, squealing and complaining bitterly that he has been deserted in a dark stall. Believe it or not, by the time the mare is fifteen minutes down the road, she has forgotten, at least temporarily, her foal and, except in rare instances, will be much better behaved in visiting the stallion than she would be if the foal was there within hearing distance to remind her of his presence. Leaving the foal behind is much safer for everybody.

Many stallion managers will allow two covers per heat season. The second cover is in instances where the mare was bred early with the first cover or the follicle did not mature and ovulate as rapidly as the veterinarian anticipated. "Doubles" are normally allowed forty-eight hours after the original cover, but you can get a double only if you are not squeezing out another mare that has not been covered during her current heat period.

Finally, it is customary for matings today to be videotaped for insurance purposes and for potential future legal problems.

Pregnancy

Your mare has been covered, and you hope she is in foal, so what happens now? The normal cycle of a mare is eighteen to twenty-one days. If your mare didn't conceive on her first cover, she should be back in heat fifteen to eighteen days after she went out of heat. Assuming she does not come back in heat, you have approximately an eighty percent chance that she has conceived. On a speculum examination her cervix will be closed with no color and on palpation, her uterus will have good tone.

The introduction of ultrasound in the early '80s as a method of examining mares for pregnancy at fourteen to twenty-two days after service has proven to be a great boon to the breeding process, particularly for early detection of pregnancy and immediate detection of a twin pregnancy. Ultrasound consists of going into the mare rectally with a probe, which in turn takes a picture of her uterine horns and actually shows the forming fetus on a television screen. Your veterinarian will let you look at the screen, which is a fascinating and awe-inspiring experience, because as early as twenty-six to thirty days you actually see a heartbeat and know the fetus is alive. It is not foolproof, however, and even an ultrasound picture with a single fetus is no guarantee that your mare is going to have a live foal next spring. Assuming that the ultrasound does show a single live fetus, she will need to be checked again several times prior to foaling, both by ultrasound and by manual palpation by your veterinarian to confirm this presence and the "feel" of the uterus to determine both the health and the growth of the fetus. More than five percent of mares that conceive will lose their developing fetus between thirty and ninety days. This is known as early embryonic death, abortion, or resorption, but whatever you call it, it is a real loss. Fetal development requires regular monitoring, even after a mare's original pregnancy confirmation.[6] You can't just have your mare shipped home after a thirty-five-day pregnancy examination, turn her out in the field, and feel confident that she is going to foal when she is scheduled to next spring.

Even after the breeding season your mare should be rechecked periodically to determine her pregnancy status. (Many are rechecked by ultrasound two to three times a year. There are various appropriate times in the season, for instance in September or October when the stud fee is due.) That way, if you should be greeted by an unpleasant surprise, at least you have a jump on doing something about it for the next year.

Yearling Sale Selection

While all the foaling and breeding is taking place on the farm, the select and open yearling sales are drawing closer. As early as

---

6 Incidentally, in a sales catalogue, production record, or a veterinary certificate, a mare is described as "pregnant" only if she's carrying a foal forty-two or more days following her last breeding.

February, nominations are made for the select sales at Keeneland, Saratoga, Fasig-Tipton Kentucky, and Del Mar, and computers begin spitting out pedigrees to selection committees.

Sales are discussed in Chapter 6 from the buyer's point of view, but in this chapter I am talking about the breeder who is hoping his yearling will be chosen for one of the select summer sales and bring a big price. After the computers are finished, the sales committees go to work reading and grading the pedigrees, and then they fan out across the country for on-site field inspection. These inspections are done by experts on conformation. During the spring, yearlings are undergoing rapid changes in size, physique, and temperament, which makes judging what they are going to look like four months later an arduous, difficult, and tricky procedure. After the physical inspection, the committee makes its final decisions and the breeders are notified.

The yearlings that have not been selected will be sold in the fall

An inspection team sizing up a potential sales yearling.

in the larger open yearling sales. Those that are going to the select summer sales often begin a regimen of sales preparation that includes hours of hand walking, intensive grooming, and customized feed programs so they will grow rapidly and turn into big, shiny sales prospects. However, the practice of treating sales yearlings like hot-house plants is coming into growing disrepute as consignors and buyers alike realize the practice may be harmful to the ultimate careers of the yearlings.

Those that were rejected may be more fortunate because they are allowed to exercise longer, retain their freedom, and grow naturally. They will be picked up and put in stalls a little later, but not on the same arduous crash program as any of those destined for the select summer sales.

The homebreds (those who will be raced by the people who bred them) are perhaps the most fortunate of all because they are allowed to grow up naturally until breaking time. They may well inherit an advantage later because of the unrestrained, natural growth (assuming that they receive the same attention, nutrition, and health programs as the sales yearlings).

While the select summer sales are wonderful, even top breeders do not get more than a small percentage of their yearlings in them. Further, some top breeders are choosing to hold even their best yearlings until September to let them benefit from the additional time to mature. For instance, Lane's End Farm, one of the world's leading consignors of yearlings, did not send any of its yearlings to the 2000 Keeneland July sale or the Saratoga August sale, electing to sell them all at Keeneland in September. The result was so successful that there was some talk around the sale that this might be the beginning of the end for the select summer sales (see Chapter 6). I doubt it. As long as there's a Thoroughbred business, there will be dreamers, and as long as there are dreamers, there will be those of us who want to sell at the summer sales.

For the rest of us, select yearling sales are a hope and a dream for the future. Marketing is not a dream, though, and spring brings with it a necessary time for realistic reappraisal of your yearling crop and how the individuals have grown and changed over the winter. Some may have not done as well as hoped; others may have done better. Realistic appraisal at this time and selection of the right market for each yearling can be critical to the price you achieve. Your advisor should play a strong part in what must be an objective decision. I feel very strongly that being among the top twenty-five percent of any sale is much better than being in the bottom twenty-five percent. It's the old adage about it being better to be a big fish in a little pond than vice versa, but it's true.

June Is Fun

As the foaling season winds down, the final phase of the breeding season becomes more hectic. You hope that the mares that "didn't do right" earlier are producing good, breedable follicles and are getting covered — it's better late than never. The mares that foaled in May are being bred back for the first time. June is a desperately busy month on the farm. All the foals are born, and foals, like young children, are likely to get sick, very sick, very quickly. If there is trouble to be found, a way to get hurt, they'll find it…and I can promise you, the more prized a foal is, the more likely it is to get hurt. They need a lot of care and attention over and above routine mare management.

The mares you're still working with that haven't conceived are the problem mares, which makes teasing more arduous and time consuming. Because all the other farms are having the same problems you are, in many cases booking mares to stallions at this time of year is sometimes more difficult than it was earlier in the season. Grass and weeds from spring rains are growing like crazy and trying to get ahead of you. On top of all that, it's time to start sales prep for the yearlings that will be in open yearling sales around Labor Day, and those yearlings in the select summer sales are already receiving constant attention.

Your herd health program requires a lot more attention now, too — your foals need deworming and vaccinations, and all this is time consuming. A good commercial farm has an extensive herd health program, including deworming every eight weeks, a variety of vaccinations, and monthly hoof trimming. The introduction of farm management software programs for home computers has made herd health more manageable. There are several programs available that will remind you when to vaccinate, when to deworm, when to trim or shoe, along with keeping track of the breeding and billing.

Yearling Sales Prep

As the breeding season comes to an end, the farm crew's attention is turned more and more toward preparation for the yearling sales. Over the past ten to fifteen years, sales preparation for yearlings has changed considerably to include more exercise and less hot housing, but some of the latter still exists. You have to think of it from an economic standpoint; one little scratch or minor injury to a sales yearling can literally cost hundreds of thousands of dollars. It's a nerve-wracking time.

There are arguments for and against the various methods of yearling preparation. Determinants include personal preference, costs, labor intensity, and potential value of the yearlings. Exercise does help muscle up yearlings and make them more attractive for sale, but it also costs money and can result in injury. Increasingly, breeders, even some very large ones, are leaving the sales prep up to sales agents who specialize in that aspect of the business. I'll discuss them more in Chapter 6, but, again, it can be money well spent.

Sales Time

Finally the big day arrives and your yearlings are shipped off to the sale. This is probably one of the only businesses in which your entire marketing effort is concentrated in one or two weeks a year. Three whole years of work can go down the drain if a yearling gets hurt or sick within a week or two of the sale. On the other hand, your profit for the year can be doubled if a close relative to one of your yearlings wins a grade I or group I stakes just before the sale.

Think about it — the commercial breeder is marketing on one day what essentially is the product of three years of work. In year one, he purchased a broodmare because of her race record, pedi-

For breeders, three years of hard work culminate in the yearling sales.

gree, and conformation. He selected a stallion that he thought fitted well with his mare. In the second year, if everything went well, she produced a correct, attractive foal, and the stallion continued as a successful sire. In the third year, assuming the foal didn't get sick, hurt himself, or grow crooked, the breeder has a product to sell that he hopes will provide a satisfactory return on his money. And then, when the time to sell actually comes, he is given perhaps a minute or two to attract bids and attain the right price. Is it any wonder that commercial breeders have ulcers?

Foal Registration

Keep this date in mind: August 31. That is the deadline for registering your newborn foal with The Jockey Club. The price for registration goes up steeply after this date. Completing the forms takes time and effort, so don't wait until the deadline.

Some state breeders' organizations assist you with registration, and some even do the job for you — for a fee. Independent operators in major breeding areas specialize in registering foals for a fee, and The Jockey Club now includes instructions and the forms for registering foals on its web site. Once again, if you have a smallish operation, hiring a professional is money well spent.

If you do the job yourself, do it very meticulously. A properly filled-out registration form flows through The Jockey Club relatively smoothly. An improperly filled-out form with incorrect or incomplete information goes into a red flag department and may stay there indefinitely while seemingly endless correspondence and phone calls add up to a lot of needless frustration.

Get the proper forms early, fill them out carefully, and get many clear photographs. Don't be afraid to take extra close-ups of any unusual markings. The Jockey Club won't turn down your application for having too many photographs or ones that are too clear — only for too few or unclear photographs.

Remember that any mare having her first foal must be blood typed before a foal can be registered. Get the blood typing done before she foals. Why? Suppose she dies foaling and you haven't done it — you have a real problem on your hands. If you buy a mare that has already had a foal, finish the paperwork and photographs for ownership transfer before foaling for the same reason. Save yourself some grief.

Weaning

When your foals are four or five months old, it is time to separate them from their mothers. Even today, there are as many varying opinions on when and how to wean foals as there are breeders, but almost everyone I can think of now uses interval weaning, a process in which one or two mares are removed from a field of foals every day or so until all the mares are gone.

The normal procedure is to start with mares with the older foals, and mares that are not doing well as a result of the stress of nursing a foal. You pull out a mare or two at a time from a field of ten or twelve mares and foals right at afternoon feeding time to distract the newly motherless foals. The foals have been eating sweet feed and pellets since they were just two or three days old and most of them don't really notice their mother leaving. Even though they can't find her, they are convinced that she is there somewhere. Except for a few squeals, the foals just go on about their business. The mares take it a little harder because they are aware that they have lost their foals, but usually settle down soon, too.

This is a lot less stressful than stall weaning, which is now almost nonexistent. Stall weaning takes a foal out of his natural environment and may lead to accident and sickness. Furthermore, if two foals are stall weaned together, they often become attached to each other and have to be weaned from each other later.

Some breeders still use the "sign" of the zodiac to wean by and

The Blood-Horse and *Thoroughbred Times* still publish them, but I have never set much store by astrological signs, even though my wife, my ex-wife, and a wonderful person with whom I had a long-term relationship in between are all Capricorns.

Weaning time is as good as any to reappraise your foals that have physical problems. You may want to separate some foals from others because of overeating, aggressiveness, epiphysis (enlargement of the joints), or because they require dietary control.

You may want to sell some of your weanlings early, particularly if they have growing faults. It is almost a sure bet that if they have conformation faults as weanlings, the faults will grow worse as they get older. By selling them as weanlings you can minimize your expense, both in upkeep and sales preparation. You have to decide whether you think the yearling value of the foal is going to justify the expense of keeping it another nine months or longer.

Weanlings require daily attention and handling to keep them gentle and to allow close physical inspection. Some farms separate weanlings by sex at weaning time, while others wait until January or February. In no case should weanlings of the opposite sex run together much after Christmas. Although puberty is not anticipated in horses until fifteen months, there have been cases where it came a lot earlier, and accidents do occur. Even more important, colts tend to play rougher than fillies.

So, as the year winds down, it's time to assess what has happened in the previous year and begin to think about what to do differently (and the same) in the next year.

By December 1 the barren mares are being teased regularly, with those coming in heat being cultured and those that need it being treated for uterine infection. In the meantime, barn repair, fence repair, road repair, and future construction, if any, are proceeding at a rapid clip. Before you know it Christmas arrives — the year is over and it is time to go back to day one and start again.

CHAPTER
SIX

AT THE SALES

"Everything has its price —
there is no horse born that is priceless."

— *Sheikh Mohammed*

I f you enjoy the adrenaline rush of watching a field of good horses blazing out of the turn into the homestretch, you'll probably get a pretty good charge out of bidding for horses at the sales.

In this chapter, I'll tell you a little about what to expect, what to look for, and what to avoid at the sales. I'll explain the different types of sales and the advantages and disadvantages of each. I'll teach you how to work over a sales catalogue and will include a little bit about conformation, your responsibilities and those of the sales company, how to bid, and what to do after you've purchased your horse.

While the title of this chapter is "At The Sales," it also covers what you should do before you even go to the sales. Those preparations are, I think, more important than most of the things you'll actually do at the sales. As part of your preparation, take a look at the Keeneland web site, which has a helpful section for new buyers and prospective buyers.

Before you begin your pre-sales preparation, though, I recommend, once again, that you have a written plan for your participation in the Thoroughbred business. As part of that plan, you, along with your advisor and accountant, will have to decide what kind of horse or horses you want to buy and how much you want to spend. If you haven't taken that step, it doesn't make any sense to spend time working over a sales catalogue. As you'll see in the section on sales catalogues, when I say "work over" a sales catalogue, I do mean work. For instance, if you have $100,000 to spend, you can scan the catalogue for the Keeneland July yearling sale and drool all you want, but don't waste a lot of your time poring over it, or for that matter even going to the sale, when you know the average price is going to be around $500,000 to $600,000.

So, now that you've decided whether to race or breed, your price range, and that you are going the auction route rather than through private sales, here are your choices:

Types of Sales

Yearling sales are the most prevalent type of sales, making them a good place for us to start. In 2000, there were fifteen major yearling sales conducted in North America and about forty others that would have to be considered minor. In all, a total of 12,642 yearlings were catalogued (which represented slightly less than a third of the entire foal crop) and 9,530 of them (twenty-six percent of the foal crop and seventy-five percent of the yearlings that were catalogued) were sold for $519,443,808, an average of $54,506, the all-time record, and a median of $11,500, down $500 (four percent) from 1998 and 1999. They ranged in price from $200 to $6.8 million for a colt by Storm Cat, which was sold at Keeneland and represented the highest yearling price since 1985. While this may not seem like much of a change from 1984 when 9,268 yearlings (twenty percent of the foal crop) sold for an average of $41,396, its significance is that the 2000 sales set all-time records for the percentage of the foal crop that was sold, the gross revenues, and average price. Unfortunately, it also set a record — twenty-five percent — for yearlings that were not sold.

If you're going to the yearling sales, you'll have to choose whether to go to a select sale or an open sale. The select sales — the Keeneland July sale, the Fasig-Tipton Saratoga sale, the Fasig-Tipton Kentucky July sale, and the opening sessions of the Keeneland September sale — traditionally are the premier yearling sales in the world. The Tattersalls Houghton yearling sale in Newmarket, England, also falls into that category. They are the most desirable for consignors because they attract the world's leading buyers, and they are the most desirable for buyers because the yearlings are the choicest.

When a horse is nominated to a select sale, a team goes over his pedigree and rates it, generally from A+ to C. Yearlings that are A+ have the best, most commercial pedigrees. They'll probably make it into the sale even if they have a few conformational defects. Yearlings assigned a C have less-glamorous pedigrees but are promoted as strong physical specimens. In most cases, C yearlings also have a top salesman making a case for them for admittance.

This is a good place to put in a little aside about sales agents. In recent years, they have become increasingly influential on the sales scene. If you are not boarding at a major farm — particularly one that takes a major consignment to most sales — you really can't hope to succeed in today's competitive sales environment without using a sales agent.

While the sales companies make a concerted effort to be fair to everyone, I can assure you that your one- or two-horse consignment will receive better placement in the catalogue and on the grounds if a sales professional is handling it. These agents have developed a degree of trust with the sales company and can go to the director of sales and say, "Look, I've got confidence in this yearling…he'll sell better than you might think just from looking at his catalogue page. You really ought to move him up a day or two in the sale." And if you don't think that's important, hang around Keeneland on day twelve or fourteen of the September or November sales. Agents also can advise you on whether your horse might be better off at a sale in, say, Maryland, Texas, or California than in Kentucky. If they don't have a consignment going to those sales, they'll be able to recommend someone local who is competent and honest.

Sales agents are highly knowledgeable students of the horse market and can help you to put a realistic reserve on your horse. It's only human nature that you will think your horse is more valuable than anyone else does. This affliction occasionally befalls even the most professional horseman, and an arms-length evaluation is useful before deciding on the reserve price.

Further, you can probably benefit from the promotional effort a good sales agent will undertake — something you might not be able to afford (or think of). People will try almost any sort of promotion to draw attention to a top sales horse. I remember a few years ago at Keeneland, a plane circled overhead towing a banner promoting some yearling or other.

Finally, like stallion managers, these specialists have spent many years developing a good reputation with buyers, who often rely on the agents to pare down their large consignments to horses that fit the buyers' tastes. Many a yearling, weanling, or mare that would have been overlooked has been well sold because an alert sales agent directed a buyer in his or her direction.

Like any other agent, the qualities you'll look for in your sales agent are honesty, knowledge and ability, and communication skills. Compatibility isn't so important here, but it doesn't hurt. Your advisor probably will have developed a relationship with one or two of these specialists — if he isn't already one of them himself — or if he hasn't, the *Thoroughbred Times* publishes an annual listing of the top sales agent in the country. You can always start there.

Let me get back to the yearling selection process. If a yearling's pedigree warrants consideration, a team of conformation experts will conduct a physical examination. Afterward, the pedigree and conformation teams will decide which yearlings are accepted. At that time, a few with excellent pedigrees are thrown out for conformational reasons, while others with less attractive pedigrees make the cut because of exceptional conformation. The benefit of select sales, most people believe, is that two teams of experts have already completed part of the selection process for them. Prospective buyers don't have to pore over thousands of pedigrees and look at hundreds of horses to find candidates. The reverse side of the coin is that buyers are obviously going to have to pay more for yearlings in select sales.

Escalating yearling prices have coincided with increasing selectivity on the part of the sales companies trying to maintain the averages that they trumpet so proudly. For instance, Keeneland's 2000 July yearling sale included only 180 yearlings, which were sold in three sessions as opposed to the traditional four sessions.

Reducing the number of horses in a sale to maintain or increase the sale's average is walking a dangerous tightrope, though, because consignors and buyers may decide there aren't enough horses and move on to other sales. Carried to its illogical conclusion, one could speculate that one day Keeneland could hold a July sale that would average $10 million, but only three yearlings would be in it.

Recognizing that fact, the major sales companies have begun to offer selected sessions — typically the first two days — even at their "open" sales. Because of that and several other reasons, an increasing number of consignors are opting to place their yearlings in Keeneland's September yearling sale, giving those yearlings nearly two more months to mature.

For example in 2000, Lane's End Farm, one of the industry's leaders in sales as well as breeding, decided to sell all of its yearlings at the Keeneland September sale rather than dividing them between July and September as it had in the past. The majority of Lane's End's offering went in the September select sessions. The result was a ripper of a sale, both for Keeneland and for Lane's End, which obtained a gross of $45,697,000 and an astounding average of $1,015,489 for the forty-five yearlings sold during the select sessions. Overall, Lane's End grossed $53,874,300 at the sale, selling some of those yearlings as agent.

"Open" sales are for yearlings that do not necessarily qualify for select sales or whose owners did not enter them in a select sale. In either case, the only qualifications for an open auction are that the yearling be a Thoroughbred and that his breeder pays an entry fee.

A lot of excellent racehorses are sold at open sales every year, but then again, a lot of horses are sold at open sales.

Several companies have attempted to become more selective and reduce the size of their open sales by increasing the entry fees to the point where entering low-class yearlings wouldn't make economic sense. For example, the entry fee for the Keeneland September sale, which is "open," is $1,000 and there is no five-percent commission on sales below $20,000. This was done on the theory it wouldn't make sense to enter a yearling unless it was worth at least $20,000. That seemed to work for a little while, but the 2000 Keeneland sales with 4,652 yearlings catalogued over thirteen days in September, and 5,111 mares and weanlings catalogued over fourteen days in November, show that they may have to consider further steps to reduce the size of their open sales. (Keeneland has announced it will lower its commission to 4.75 percent beginning in 2001, but, for the life of me, I don't see how that's going to help the situation of too many horses.)

This has resulted in an interesting phenomenon with respect to timing — both in the placement of your sales horses and in trying to buy horses at auction.

If you'll pardon another reference to my love of scuba diving, there are basically two types of life in the ocean: diurnal and nocturnal. With the increasing size of open sales, I have noticed two distinct populations over the past several years: the Euronal and the Westernal. The Euronal, recognized by quilted jackets, those little go-to-hell caps, corduroys, croup boots, the occasional ascot, and foreign accents, is usually around for the first four or five days of the sale when prices are their highest. On the last four or five days of the sale, you'll see a lot of jeans, cowboy hats, boots, big belt buckles, and pickups pulling gooseneck trailers, which are the identifying characteristics of the Westernals. While the averages may be a lot lower than during the first few days, considering the value of the horses on offer, prices can be almost as strong as they are at the beginning of the sale.

Just as the ocean has transition periods when a lot of the diurnal fish get eaten by the nocturnal ones, and vice versa, I believe the sales also have transitional periods when the Euronals have left and the Westernals haven't arrived that offer substantial opportunities for buyers. Sellers might not want their horses to sell on those particular days because the only buyers left are the "hardboots," a euphemism for a hard-boiled, hard-eyed Kentucky horseman, who really doesn't want to spend what a horse is worth.

Let's get back to the basic message. The advantage of purchasing yearlings is the wide selection. With almost a quarter of the foal crop going through the ring each year, you can find just about anything you want. The disadvantage, if you're looking for excitement, is that you're normally about six to nine months away from seeing your horse under silks. It also can be a fairly expensive period because, as you'll learn in Chapter 8, yearling breaking and training up to a race is costly.

If you're not as patient as some (and you don't want to incur the expense of yearling breaking), you might try one of the sales of two-year-olds in training that are usually held during the first few months of the year in warmer climes.

At these sales, the horses are usually sixty to ninety days away from a race. Your lead-time will be less, but you'll also normally pay for the training that the young horses have received; in other words, you'll have to pay more for a two-year-old in training than a comparable yearling. As a matter of fact, a number of people make a pretty good living by "pinhooking" yearlings then reselling them at the two-year-olds in training sales. Since such a large percentage of the two-year-olds sold at auction are a result of pinhooking, you have the additional advantage of being able to find out what they brought as a yearling and adjusting your thinking accordingly.

There are other advantages and disadvantages, of course. The Europeans call these "breeze-up" sales, and, as the name implies, a lot of sales companies require these two-year-olds to breeze.

A two-year-old breezing before a sale.

This allows your trainer to get a better idea of the young horse by watching him breezing or galloping on the track.

However, some people seem to think that owners selling at a two-year-olds in training sale have already had a look at what the horse can do and don't like what they've seen (or at least will raise the reserves on ones that show significant potential).

The principal criticism of two-year-old sales is the incentive to breeze very young horses — most of which have not even reached their actual second birthday — in very fast times. At most of these sales, the highest-priced horses have breezed a furlong in ten and change, which is probably faster than they'll ever have to run in their lives. As a point of reference, the world record for six furlongs is 1:06.35, which is a little over :11 per furlong. The world record for a mile on the main track is Dr. Fager's 1:32⅕, which equates to about :11⅘ for a furlong. A generally accepted rule of thumb is that if you have a horse that can do quarters in :24 (therefore, eighths in :12), you have a horse that can win the Kentucky Derby. So the criticism goes — and I must agree — that to attain a high sales price, consignors are forcing very young horses to breeze at excessive speeds and are putting excessive stress on an immature bone and muscle structure. According to an analysis in the *Thoroughbred Times*, the statistical results obtained on the track for horses sold in the major two-year-old sales from 1995-99 are quite similar to those sold in the major yearling sales during the same period and a little bit better than those for the breed:

	Sold as Yearlings	Sold as Two-Year-Olds	Averages for the Breed
Average Sales Price	$53,707	$54,503	$39,639
Starters	82.4%	76.6%	69.4%
Winners	52.9%	59.2%	44.8%
Stakes Winners	4.9%	5.4%	3.1%
Graded Stakes Winners	1.6%	1.5%	0.6%

NOTE: It is logical to expect a certain amount of precocity in horses that went through the sales.

However, with certain notable exceptions — Unbridled's Song comes to mind — I don't notice a lot of horses that worked in ten and change at a two-year-old sale still around in the classics or as older horses.

Two lessons can be learned here. First, try to find out about the person who is selling a horse at auction, any auction. This can tell you quite a lot. For example, if a person has a history of making a living by pinhooking yearlings for the two-year-old sales and he doesn't race, you can feel pretty safe about buying from him. However, if the consignor is someone who generally races home-breds and he's selling one two-year-old, this should raise a red flag.

The second lesson is very important: nobody, *nobody*, can tell you what a horse is actually going to do on the racetrack until the gate has opened in an actual race. Generally, you can't tell until it's opened a couple of times. You can get a clue about ability, but a horse has so many indefinable qualities that contribute to success that there's absolutely no way to tell how he will turn out. And anybody who says he can is a liar.

Major racing centers around the country also hold regular sales for older horses in training. In contrast to the sales for two-year-olds, these sales often contain culls — horses that can't stand the competition where their owners race and don't particularly have the pedigree to make them saleable as breeding prospects. Remember, though, one man's ceiling is another man's floor. A horse that's a cull in New York or California can be a very useful racehorse elsewhere.

The final type of sales you might want to attend is a breeding stock or a "mixed" sale. At these sales, you'll find yearlings, weanlings, broodmares, broodmare prospects, stallions, stallion prospects, and about any kind of horse you want to see. Obviously, if you're going into breeding, you'll attend this type of sale.

In 2000, broodmares ranked second only to yearlings in number sold and volume of sales, as 5,490 were sold for gross receipts of $311,141,964, an average of $56,674, and a median of $9,000.

While I'm on the subject, some of the sales companies are now offering "select" — or, as they are more commonly called, "preferred" — sessions at the breeding stock sales, just as they do at the select yearling sales. Even at Keeneland where they don't admit to having preferred sessions, they make the consignors divide up their sale offerings, putting the better quality horses in the first couple of days and the lesser quality animals later in the sale.

When you buy a broodmare in foal, you're usually about two years away from seeing any return on your investment. However, you can look forward to a very exciting and beautiful event, the birth of her foal, normally within three to five months if you buy her in November when most mares are sold. There are also large breeding stock sales in January, in which case you won't have to wait so long for your foal to arrive. As a matter of fact, mares occa-

When you buy a broodmare, a foal usually is part of the package.

sionally have been known to foal at the sale.

The mixed and breeding stock sales also contain a large number of weanlings, which are normally a little cheaper than a comparable yearling because the owner doesn't have as much money invested in them. You'll find only a few select sale quality horses being sold as weanlings, but during the past several years as weanling pinhookers have become a more active and important part of the market, the quality of weanlings offered at breeding stock sales has improved substantially.

There are, of course, other reasons why weanlings are cheaper than comparable yearlings, but most relate to the amount of investment. Sales preparation, for instance, is much less complicated and costly for weanlings than for yearlings, although that, too, is changing as a result of pinhookers. Whereas yearlings have sixty to ninety days of specialized care and training, weanlings today are given considerably less sales prep. Also, there's a lot of attrition between weaning time and yearling sales time, because horses are just like

Weanlings usually cost less than comparable yearlings.

children — they love to play and often get hurt.

It is probably more important at breeding stock sales than at any other type of sale to attempt to ascertain why the animals are being offered, as well as the other things I'll discuss shortly about the catalogue.

For instance, a breeder who is in the business for the long term will be very reluctant to sell a decent broodmare unless he's in a tremendous cash flow bind (broke). So, if he's not broke, he might be selling her because she's got some problems, because he's had her for a while and doesn't believe she's going to turn out well as a producer, or because he's seen some of her foals and they're as crooked as a West Virginia highway. For that reason, try to look at some of her foals, too. Good broodmares are almost irreplaceable at any sort of cost-effective price, so let me say once again that if an established outfit is selling a broodmare, especially one that looks pretty good on paper, it would behoove you to find out why she's being sold.

The same goes for weanlings. While a few people specialize in the sale of weanlings, most of the ones you'll find in the November sales are there for some other reason. Again, it's often a cash flow problem, but occasionally a breeder who usually sells his stock as yearlings might believe that his weanling's pedigree is particularly hot (fashionable) at that time and doesn't have faith that the fashionability will last. It's also pretty tough to tell how a weanling is going to turn out. You'd be amazed at the amount a young horse can change, for better or worse, between the time he's weaned and the time he's a yearling (more often than not, it's for the worse). There are a few, a very few, really good pinhookers who seem to be able to pick out a weanling that'll develop into a profitable yearling, but even those experts will tell you it doesn't always work out as planned for them, either.

Before the Sales

Once you've decided what you want to do and which sales you want to attend, you'll have to take care of a few other things beforehand.

The first is to establish some sort of identity with the sales company. You'll need to write or call to receive the catalogues for the sale you wish to attend. You should have to do this only once, because once you get on the sales company's list, you'll normally find you get just about all the catalogues they publish. In the front of the catalogue you'll find a credit application, which you should fill out, take to your bank for verification, have notarized, and send to the sales company. You should do this well in advance so you won't get lost in the rush. You can also find the applications on the web sites of most sales companies.

A week or so after you've done that, you might want to call the sales director and see whether the credit application is in order. This is an introductory call, really, and it'll give you an opportunity to ask any other questions you might have about the sale and the area where it's being held — what are the nearby motels, what are the good restaurants, etc. Also, if you've ignored my repeated advice about choice of advisors, the sales director can possibly point you toward some trainers or veterinarians who can assist you at the sales. Of course, he won't give you any specific recommendations, but he'll give you a list of people from which you can choose. You also can inquire about state sales taxes and, if it's appropriate, send in the sales-tax exemption form that is also included with almost every sales catalogue.

The bottom line is getting acquainted with someone at the sales company. While he won't have much time for socializing at the sales, if you get into a problem it's nice to know someone who can possibly help you out, someone whose name you know and who knows your name.

If you're planning to attend the sale in person, you probably should check on seating. While many sales companies will just let buyers sit anywhere, others have reserved seating, which is at a premium at the more important sales. If you're sending an agent, you'll need to fill out (and have notarized) the Agent Authorization form that also is in the catalogue.

There's one more thing I'd like to urge you to do before you begin to work over the sales catalogue — read the conditions of sale.

Conditions of Sale

While this section of the catalogue has been written by sales company lawyers who are primarily concerned with the company's protection, the conditions of sale also afford buyers some protection. At the very least, the conditions of sale set forth the rules and regulations under which you'll be operating. The conditions of sale are printed in the front of the catalogues or at the front of each session — that's how important they are. Also, a final admonition: take a few minutes at least to skim through the conditions before any sale at which you plan to participate. While major sales companies have moved toward standard conditions of sale over the past two decades, variations still exist. If you take twenty minutes or so to read the conditions of the sale, you may someday wind up saving a lot of time, trouble, embarrassment, and, most importantly, money.

Sales conditions are so important that I strongly advise you to read them in their entirety before any sale you plan to attend.

As you'll see when you read them, some conditions are binding. They are set out in capital letters in some catalogues, boldface capitals in others. Here are a few of the more important ones you're likely to find:

"**LIMITATION OF WARRANTIES**: THERE IS NO WARRANTY, EXPRESS OR IMPLIED, BY AUCTIONEER, OWNER, CONSIGNOR OR THEIR REPRESENTATIVES, AS TO THE RACING SOUNDNESS,

MERCHANTABILITY OR FITNESS FOR ANY PARTICULAR PUR-
POSE OF ANY HORSE OFFERED IN THIS SALE. ALL HORSES ARE
SOLD "AS IS" WITH ALL EXISTING CONDITIONS AND
DEFECTS..."

Basically, you're on your own. You had better do your full "due
diligence" — veterinary inspections, etc. — prior to bidding on any
horse in the sale. There are a few little bits of wiggle room, though.

"LIMITED WARRANTIES AS TO DESCRIPTION: UNLESS OTH-
ERWISE ANNOUNCED OR DESCRIBED BY AUCTIONEER THERE
IS NO REPRESENTATION OR WARRANTY AS TO THE BREEDING
QUALITIES OF ANY HORSE WHICH AT THE TIME OF SALE IS
OFFERED IN ITS YEAR OF FOALING, OR ITS YEARLING OR TWO-
YEAR-OLD YEAR, OR IS DESCRIBED AT TIME OF SALE AS A
HORSE OF RACING AGE."

 If a horse that is sold as a colt turns out to be a ridgeling (i.e., he
has one or more undescended testicles after July 1 of his yearling
year) or a gelding (or vice versa), he can be returned to his consignor, provided you get a veterinary certificate to that effect and
return him within forty-eight hours of the sale.

"LIMITED WARRANTIES AS TO SOUNDNESS: UNLESS
EXPRESSLY ANNOUNCED FROM THE AUCTION STAND, OR BY
OFFICIAL PUBLICATION OF AUCTIONEER OR AS HEREINAFTER
PROVIDED, THERE IS NO WARRANTY OR GUARANTEE OF ANY
KIND AS TO THE SOUNDNESS OR CONDITION OR OTHER
QUALITY OF ANY HORSE SOLD IN THE SALE."

If a horse is a "cribber" (i.e., he sucks air), suffers from impaired
vision, is a "wobbler" (a locomotor disease), is two years old or less
and has undergone joint or abdominal surgery, or is unsound of
wind, an announcement must be made at the sales, unless the
horse is being sold as a breeding prospect, in which case it must
be announced that he is being sold as a breeding prospect. In
addition, if a horse is sold in a sale of two-year-olds or other hors-

es in training and it has an injury or other problem that would impair its racing ability, that must be announced at the sale. In the past several years, sales companies have provided buyers with a repository of veterinary information about the horses in the sale. Having a veterinary certificate in the repository that reveals these conditions can be construed as providing the required notice. I'll put in more about the repository later.

With the exception of cribbers and bleeders (in which case, you'll have seven and fifteen days, respectively, to return the horse), if you are going to try to return a horse bought at auction, you will have to notify the sales company in writing (a) within forty-eight hours of the sale, (b) before you remove the horse from the sales grounds, or (c) if it is a horse in training, before you work it or run it in a race:

"...WITHIN FORTY-EIGHT (48) HOURS AFTER TIME OF SALE THE AUCTIONEER RECEIVES WRITTEN NOTICE FROM THE BUYER AND A WRITTEN VETERINARY CERTIFICATE, BASED ON EXAMINATION BY THE CERTIFYING VETERINARIAN, STATING THAT SUCH A CONDITION EXISTS, AND THE SAME EXISTED AT TIME OF SALE. AS TO ANY HORSE SOLD AS A TWO-YEAR-OLD IN TRAINING, THE VETERINARY CERTIFICATE MUST ALSO STATE THAT THE INJURY TO OR DISEASE OF THE BONE STRUC-TURE MATERIALLY AFFECTS THE HORSE'S SUITABILITY FOR RACING AND SUCH CONDITION WAS NOT REVEALED BY RADI-OGRAPHS PLACED IN THE REPOSITORY BY THE CONSIGNOR. ALL WARRANTIES TERMINATE UPON THE EARLIER OF (1) EXPI-RATION OF FORTY-EIGHT (48) HOURS FROM THE TIME OF SALE, OR (2) REMOVAL OF THE HORSE FROM SALES GROUNDS, AFTER WHICH THERE SHALL BE NO RIGHT OF RETURN HERE-UNDER; PROVIDED, HOWEVER, BUYER SHALL HAVE SEVEN DAYS FROM THE TIME OF SALE TO PROVIDE AUCTIONEER WITH THE REQUIREMENTS OF CONDITION THIRTEENTH TO

ESTABLISH ANY RIGHT OF RETURN AS TO CRIBBERS AND FIF-
TEEN DAYS FROM THE TIME OF SALE TO PROVIDE AUCTION-
EER WITH THE REQUIREMENTS OF CONDITION THIRTEENTH
TO ESTABLISH ANY RIGHT OF RETURN AS TO HORSES ON AN
OFFICIAL "BLEEDER'S LIST". NOTWITHSTANDING THE FORE-
GOING, ALL WARRANTIES ON A HORSE OF RACING AGE TERMI-
NATE IMMEDIATELY WHEN SUCH HORSE STARTS IN A RACE."

Normally, horses that are found to be not as announced at the
time of sale may be returned, along with a veterinary certificate
stating what's wrong. Each sale is videotaped these days, so in case
of a dispute or ensuing lawsuit, there is a record of exactly what
was said while the horse was in the ring.

Breeding Status. At breeding stock sales, a buyer should know
whether the mare he's trying to buy is pregnant.

As the prices obtained for broodmares escalated exponentially
in the '80s and '90s, more and more lawyers began to get involved
in the business of breeding stock sales, and things got more and
more complicated.

Now, at breeding stock sales a Certificate of Reproductive Status
must be on file for each mare or breeding prospect. Instead of "In
Foal," "Barren," and "Not Bred," which were the categories you
were likely to encounter for a mare in the early '80s, today the certificate is likely to categorize the mare in one of five basic ways:

(1) That said mare is pregnant.

(2) That said mare is not carrying twins, but this cannot be deter
mined with absolute certainty by the examination performed by
me.

(3) That said mare is not pregnant.

(4) That said mare has aborted.

(5) That said mare is suitable for mating.

Within each of the categories are a number of subtle and important distinctions. For instance, in a sales catalogue, production record, or a veterinary certificate, a mare is described as "pregnant" only if she's carrying a foal forty-two or more days following her last breeding date; she is "barren" if she has failed to get in foal or has lost her foal prior to forty-two days after her last breeding date; and she has "aborted" if she lost her foal after forty-two days. These definitions are so crucial that I have included them in the glossary at the end of this book.

Further, this condition of sale more than any other might illustrate the necessity of listening to the auctioneer's announcements. They take precedence over the pregnancy status as published in the catalogue. (Going from "pregnant" to "not pregnant" will probably be the most frequent change of breeding status you'll hear at the sales.) If the catalogue says the mare is in foal, and you don't listen to the announcements that say she's barren or has slipped, you're responsible for the price you paid. The company will play the videotape of the announcement back to you, and say "sorry about that."

It is important to know that **buyers must have mares checked by their own veterinarian within twenty-four hours after the sale and before the mares have been removed from the sales grounds for any notice of rejection to be valid.**

Buyers also should remember that stallion service fees become payable by the seller at any time a mare is sold, and the contract does not follow the sale of the mare. What that means is if a mare has been bred on a "live foal" contract or a "return" contract, those rights do not follow the mare, and if she slips or fails to produce a live foal, there'll normally be no refund or return from the stallion or share owner. As will be discussed in Chapter 8, you can get insurance for the foal.

Title. When the auctioneer bangs the gavel and says "sold," title passes to the new owner, along with all the risks and responsibility of ownership. If the auctioneer pronounced a horse as sold to you and then someone were to shoot it in the ring, the loss would be yours. Most insurance companies offer "fall of the hammer" insurance to protect you from the instant the horse is sold, and that, too, is something you should arrange prior to the sale (you don't have to tell them what horses you'll be bidding on in order to be protected, incidentally). Also, as a practical matter, even though the horse becomes your responsibility at the moment it's sold, most sales companies require that consignors care for it until the next day.

One other important point: effective title to a Thoroughbred is carried by The Jockey Club registration certificate — nothing else. When you buy a horse at the sale, you'll get a release certificate, which permits you to take the horse off the grounds, but you will not receive the registration certificate until the horse has been paid for and the check has cleared. Unlike other businesses, possession is not eleven points of the law in the Thoroughbred business.

Other conditions of sale state that the auctioneer is the final authority in the adjudication of most disputes that might arise as a result of the sale (although if the dispute is over a veterinary matter, most sales companies will have a veterinarian or panel of veterinarians that will mediate it). The sales company also has jurisdiction in instances of default by the buyer and in cases of late payment (they charge you 1½ percent interest a month, generally).

Working over the Sales Catalogue

Now you should be ready to begin tackling the pedigree pages, the meat of the sales catalogue.

The most important thing to remember about a sales catalogue is that each pedigree page is an advertisement. A trained expert, often with years of experience, has prepared each page to emphasize the most attractive portion of the horse's pedigree and minimize the least attractive parts. As a consequence, *what doesn't appear on the catalogue page is often more important than what does appear.*

Also, as the result of lawsuits over the years, sales catalogues are now more specific than they used to be in certain areas, especially the produce records of broodmares that are being sold and first dams of yearlings, weanlings, etc., but you still need to further check the information on the catalogue page.

This has become much easier than in the past, but I'll discuss that in more detail later.

When studying pedigrees in your sales catalogue, first scan the entire catalogue and eliminate anything that doesn't fit in with your plans and/or is obviously out of your price range. At the same time, you can mark the ones that interest you. This shouldn't take too long once you've done it a couple of times and you've got an idea of price ranges. Then you really get down to work.

You can refer to a number of sources to get catalogue updates and supplemental information, but the best two are the *Thoroughbred Times' Buyer's Guides* and *Catalogue Updates*, the latter of which is published by the excellent newsletter, *Racing Update*. Apropos of newsletters and their being germane to the sales I highly recommend two — *Racing Update*, as alluded above, and *MarketWatch*, published by *The Blood-Horse*. Both of these provide in-depth analyses before and after major sales and over time have proven to be remarkably accurate in their analyses and predictions. Prior to the sale, they will include stallion statistics for horses with offspring in the sales. They also will have looked in depth at the catalogue so they can better anticipate what to expect than someone who has not really studied it. After the sale, they will publish how stallions did and include further analyses.

For instance, while sales summaries in the trade press almost always include histories of the average and median for major sales, and while these measures are a good guide to trends in the business, the actual quality of horses in a particular sale can vary widely from year to year. That variance is not taken into account in the strict reporting of average and median, so if you want a true representation of the trends, you should read these newsletters.

If you are even moderately computer literate, Bloodstock Research Information Services and Equibase can provide up-to-date and complete catalogue-style pedigrees that are *not* edited to accentuate the positive and eliminate the negative. So, you can now check the pedigree pages of the horses you're most interested in on the computer, or in a sales guide, without having to spend hours looking up each horse, as used to be the case.

A little later in the chapter I'll include a single catalogue page and identify some of its essential elements, followed by portions of some catalogue pages, both good and bad, that I have selected at random from recent sales. Then I'll explain what additional information you should be able to derive from looking at the sales guide or a computer printout on the horse.

Throughout, I'll try to give you some hints on what makes a pedigree good or bad and what I think you should look for in a pedigree.

About Black Type

First you should know some basics about pedigrees in catalogues. In 1957, Fasig-Tipton Company, the world's second-largest sales company, adopted a system of highlighting the better horses in a pedigree by setting them out in what is called in the industry today "black type." The names of stakes winners are printed in boldface type and all capital letters, while the names of stakes-placed horses appear in boldface type, with capital and lower-case letters. While this practice has continued and is likely to remain in force in perpetuity, reformers began to argue that the use of black type without further qualification — especially with respect to cheap stakes at small tracks — wasn't a true indicator of class. In the early '70s, racing authorities in England, Ireland, and France got together and came up with a system of identifying their leading stakes as "pattern races" and later changed the name to group races. As discussed in Chapter 4, they are subdivided into group I, group II, and group III, according to importance, with the group I being the most important. The United States followed the next year with the same system, except that the stakes were called graded stakes instead of group stakes.

Recognizing the large variance in the quality of stakes races around the world, over the past twenty years or so the International Cataloguing Standards Committee of the Society of International Thoroughbred Auctioneers (SITA) has attempted to standardize the worldwide system of cataloguing.

However, once again, I must include a little warning. Some sales companies are not members of SITA, so if the company conducting a sale is not a SITA member, you might be particularly wary as you peruse its catalogue. Also, on occasion a single farm or a couple of farms might get together and have a sale on their own and write their own sales catalogue. Just be a little more careful when you read those catalogues.

You can look for the SITA symbol that appears in the catalogues of its members. If that symbol appears, you can be assured that horses whose names are printed in black type have either won or placed in a stakes that fits the following criteria:

(1) The race must close at least seventy-two hours in advance of its running;

(2) The conditions of the race must include a fee paid by the owner of each horse that is entered; and

(3) It must have a purse value of at least $15,000.

The minimum purse value has been raised periodically over time, until now a race must carry a minimum purse of $25,000-

added or $35,000-guaranteed in order to qualify as a stakes. The standards apply for the year in which the race was run, though if a horse won a stakes in 1987, which is before the bar was raised, it still qualifies for black type.

In addition, stakes have been divided into three categories: graded or group stakes (as explained above), listed stakes (non-graded stakes with $50,000 or more in added money that have not yet received graded status), and "Other added money black type races" ($15,000 to $49,999 in added money, plus a lot of other qualifications).

Further, a lot of stakes races are now restricted in various ways, most often by stipulating that the runners must have been foaled in a particular state or sired by a horse that stands in a particular state. While they do qualify for black type, they carry the designation "R" to indicate that they are restricted.

Finally, on occasion you might encounter a horse's name in black type with a "Q" designation. This is the result of an abortive attempt in 1985 to include horses that had won an "open" (non-restricted) allowance or handicap race with a purse of $30,000 or more. The fact that it applies only for 1985 indicates its success.

While I don't want to waste too much of your time with all the minor ramifications and qualifications surrounding this system, it is pretty important, so I've included the full explanation in the appendix along with the conditions of sale.

Also, if you'd like, you can get a copy of *International Cataloguing Standards*, which is an annual publication of the International Pattern Race Committee, from the Thoroughbred Owners and Breeders Association, The Jockey Club, or a horse-oriented book store.

Now, on to the pedigrees. Reproduced on the next page is a pretty nice yearling pedigree, a colt by Mr. Prospector—Angel Fever, by Danzig, that brought a final bid of $4 million to top the 1998

Keeneland July sale. If you read Chapter 1, you'll recognize it as the pedigree of Fusaichi Pegasus, who is perhaps one of the most successful yearling purchases in history. His pedigree is included here just to explain the elements of a catalogue page and to show how fancy a pedigree can get.

Fusaichi Pegasus' page differs from a pedigree for a breeding stock sale with its emphasis on the immediate pedigree rather than the produce record, which would be considered more important in a breeding stock sale. Also, in a sale of horses of racing age, a race record for the horse being sold would be included and backed up by an insert featuring the latest past performances of the horse in question. I'll discuss those elements further on.

(A) **Consignor Line**. This identifies the person who is selling the horse whose pedigree is on the page. You would think this would be fairly simple, and it used to be. This line used to say either "Property of," which meant it was being sold by its owners, or "Consigned by," which meant it was not being sold by its owners but by someone who is acting as agent for the real owners. Today, with the prevalence of sales agents, they all say "Consigned by." If the horse is not being sold by its owner or breeder, some pages will come right out and include the name of the actual owner — "Consigned by Veryimportant Farm, Agent for John Littleguy" — while others will not.

Most of today's yearling sales catalogues will include an index of breeders, so you can look up who actually bred the horse.

Finally, thanks to our friends in the legal profession, you will see a lot of the consignments for the major sales agents divided into "BigAgent, Agent XXXIV," with Roman numerals to designate various sectors of their consignments. This separates the consignment of one owner or breeder from another who is selling with the same agent so if there is a lien or some other obligation on one owner, a lawyer can't tie up the revenue from one agent's entire consignment.

(A)

Consigned by Stone Farm, Agent

(B) Hip No.
228

(D) **BAY COLT**
Foaled April 12, 1997

Barn
17 (C)

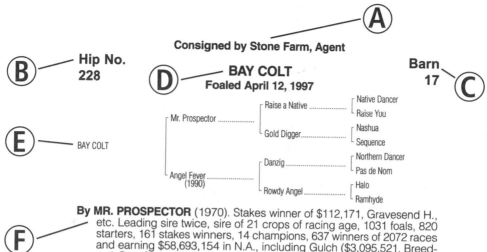

(E) BAY COLT

			Native Dancer
		Raise a Native	Raise You
	Mr. Prospector		Nashua
		Gold Digger	Sequence
		Danzig	Northern Dancer
			Pas de Nom
	Angel Fever (1990)		Halo
		Rowdy Angel	Ramhyde

(F) By **MR. PROSPECTOR** (1970). Stakes winner of $112,171, Gravesend H.,
etc. Leading sire twice, sire of 21 crops of racing age, 1031 foals, 820
starters, 161 stakes winners, 14 champions, 637 winners of 2072 races
and earning $58,693,154 in N.A., including Gulch ($3,095,521, Breeders' Cup Sprint **[G1]**, etc.), Forty Niner ($2,726,000, Travers S. **[G1]**,
etc.), Rhythm ($1,592,532, Breeders' Cup Juvenile **[G1]**, etc.), Afleet
($995,235, Jerome H. **[G1]**, etc.), Golden Attraction **[G1]** ($911,508).

1st dam

(G) **Angel Fever**, by Danzig. Winner in 2 starts at 2, $25,665, 2nd Colleen S. [L]
(MTH, $10,000). Sister to **PINE BLUFF**. Dam of 3 other registered
foals, 3 of racing age, including a 2-year-old of 1998, 1 to race--
Minersville (g. by Forty Niner). Winner at 3, 1997 in England.

2nd dam

ROWDY ANGEL, by Halo. Placed at 3, $16,395. Dam of 7 winners, incl.--

(H) **PINE BLUFF** (c. by Danzig). 6 wins at 2 and 3, $2,255,884, Preakness
S. **[G1]**, Arkansas Derby **[G2]**, Remsen S. **[G2]**, Nashua S. **[G3]**, Reb-
el S. **[G3]**, 2nd Southwest S. [L] (OP, $20,000), 3rd Belmont S. **[G1]**,
Champagne S. **[G1]**, Futurity S. **[G1]**. Sire.
DEMONS BEGONE (c. by Elocutionist). 7 wins in 14 starts, 2 to 4, $609,-
944, Arkansas Derby **[G1]**, Rebel S. [L] (OP, $86,520), Southwest S.
[L] (OP, $35,940), Ahoy S. (MTH, $19,980), 2nd Champagne S. **[G1]**,
Futurity S. **[G1]**, 3rd Razorback H. **[G2]**. Sire.
Angel Fever (f. by Danzig). Stakes-placed winner, above.

3rd dam

RAMHYDE, by Rambunctious. 7 wins, 2 to 4, $78,108, Virginia Belle S., 3rd
Open Fire S.-**G3**, Free State S., Politely S., Cameo S. Dam of--
RAMTEN. 16 wins, $185,998, Pennsylvania Futurity-R, 2nd Iroquois H.
[OR], Iroquois H.-R (PHA, $5,749), 3rd Nick Shuk Memorial H. [OR].
Rambitony. 3 wins at 2 and 3, $40,668, 3rd Blue Mountain Futurity-R.
Dam of 2 foals, both winners, including--
Perfect Habit. Winner at 3, $36,914, 3rd Heritage S. [L] (PHA, $5,929).

4th dam

(I) CASTLE HYDE, by *Tulyar. Unraced. Half-sister to **THE IRISHMAN** ($105,-
375), **KNOCKLOFTY**, **Leix**, **Shenanigans**. Dam of 4 winners, incl.--
RAMHYDE. Stakes winner, above.
Castle Star. Winner at 3, $15,450. Dam of 7 foals, 5 winners, including--
FLATHORN. 6 wins, 2 to 5, $142,757, Week of Fame Life Derby [L]
(FG, $60,000), 3rd Nashua S. **[G3]**.

(J) Vaccinated for influenza.
Engagements: Breeders' Cup.

(K) Foaled in Kentucky. (KTDF).

183

(B) **Hip Number**. This is an identification number assigned to every horse in a sale. It is cleverly named hip number because it is pasted on the horse's hip before it is sold. The only thing you really need to know about hip numbers is that they are assigned in the order that the horses are to be sold and that is determined alphabetically according to first dams at yearling sales (the letter of the alphabet is chosen by lot for each sale to prevent anyone from gaining any perceived advantage of position).

(C) **Barn Number**. The barn is where the horse is stabled on the sales ground. The only comment here is that you can save yourself a lot of time and effort by organizing the horses in which you're interested according to barn number before you get to the sales.

(D) **Brief Identification**. This little blurb identifies the color and sex of yearlings and weanlings or the name, color, and year of birth of other horses. Further, you'll note it includes the actual birth date of yearlings and weanlings, as opposed to the year of birth for older horses. This, believe it or not, is very important in yearling and weanling sales. Since young horses grow at a phenomenal rate (up to three and a half pounds a day in certain phases of growth), a few weeks — and especially a couple of months — can make a great deal of difference in the size and maturity of yearlings or weanlings at the sales. You can't expect a May foal to be as big as a January or February foal, and this must be taken into account when you're looking at yearlings.

(E) **Schematic Pedigree**. This is just a standard three-cross pedigree of the horse being sold, and it shows, in addition to much of the information that's carried further down the page, how the sire is bred. Note here the age of the mare at the time the yearling was born. Also, I find it's a good place to make notes on the pedigree, such as the sire's yearling average, what the mare's previous foals have brought, etc.

(F) **Sire Summary/Blurb**. This merely highlights the stallion's race record (if he's a young stallion) and record at stud (if he's older). This will be discussed in further detail later.

(G) **First Dam**. This is undoubtedly the most important part of the pedigree. Like the stallion summary, it highlights the mare's race and production record. It will also be discussed in further detail later.

(H) **Second Dam**. The second dam is obviously less important than the first dam and the summary is usually shorter — at least it should be. All yearling pedigrees have at least something about the second dam. A "decent" pedigree on a yearling will have something about the third dam, too; if you have to get into the fourth dam or, on rare occasion, the fifth dam, the pedigree is considered to be pretty weak on the female side.

(I) **Health/Inoculation Record**. While this is stuck down at the bottom of the page, it's vital for transportation and herd health at the farm where your purchase may be headed. Occasional influenza outbreaks, for example, have been devastating at racetracks around the country, so most tracks won't allow a horse on the grounds without an influenza vaccination. Also, if your yearling hasn't been vaccinated, you really don't want him to be put in with a lot of others that have received their shots. Health requirements differ from state to state and from farm to farm. Most consignors today will provide all the health records for the horse to the new owner. If they don't, you should ask for them.

(J) **Engagements**. This is significant because it lists the stakes and futurities to which a yearling has been nominated. It also tells you whether the horse is nominated for the Breeders' Cup, the European Breeders Fund (E.B.F), or possibly one of the various state breeders funds (with some, a foal is eligible simply by virtue of having been born in that state, but others require registration). Keep this in mind because many of the programs will require you as the new owner to make the subsequent nomination payments, or your horse will be dropped from eligibility. If that happens and the horse turns out as well as you hope, you might find yourself making a substantial supplementary payment at the time of the race. Also, with the Breeders' Cup, there's an optional series payment, so you should find out whether the horse is nominated in full or just partially.

(K) **State Where Foaled**. This is important because of the many lucrative state breeding programs that offer purse supplements and owner and breeder awards for state-bred horses.

The Stallion Summary

The stallion summary tells you a little bit about the sire of the horse you intend to purchase, so pay attention to it:

By **STORM CAT** (1983) Stakes winner of $570,610, Young America S. **[G1]**, etc. Leading sire, sire of 10 crops of racing age, 632 foals, 452 starters, 79 stakes winners, 338 winners of 1142 races and earning $43,250,889 in N.A., including champion Silken Cat [L] (3 wins in 4 starts, $102,120), and of Mistle Cat (hwt. at 6 in Italy, Premio Vittorio di Capua **[G1]**, etc.), Catrail **[G2]** (hwt. 3 times in Europe and England), Munaaji **[G2]** (hwt. in Germany), Cat Thief ($3,951,012, Breeders' Cup Classic **[G1]**, etc.).

These blurbs used to be a lot less specific than they are today. For instance, in today's catalogues the stallion blurb will start out with a very brief synopsis of his racing record, then follow with the essential numbers from his overall breeding record: "sire of 10 crops of racing age, 632 foals, 452 starters, 79 stakes winners of 1142 races and earning $43,250,889 in N.A.". If you'll remember the "Averages For The Breed" from Chapter 4, these numbers should give you a rough idea if he gets sound horses (indicated by high percentages of runners from foals) and if he gets high-quality horses (indicated by percentage of stakes horses and earnings per runner). You can expand on this information by going to the stallion registers that are published by *The Blood-Horse* and *Thoroughbred*

Times, or delve into the matter even further with BRIS or Equine Line to find more information on soundness (a high number of average years raced and/or a high number of average starts per year), quality (average earnings per runner and per start, does he have a lot of superior runners), or are they too slow to break down?

If you'll look up this horse in the buyer's guides, you'll also discover that Storm Cat's stud fee is climbing — from $200,000 in 1999 (which is the probable stud fee that the seller has in this weanling) to $300,000 in 2000 (which is the stud fee that consignors who are selling mares will have paid to breed to him). Is he popular? You bet...his stud fee has gone to $400,000 for 2001.

2000 Stud Fee: $300,000; 1999 Stud Fee: $200,000. Dosage: (7-4-16-1-0); DI: 2.11; CD: 0.61

2000 Sales Yrlgs: 32 offered, 25 sold, $1,253,468 avg., $650,000 med., $6,800,000 high, $53,000 low.

1999 Sales Wnlgs: 6 offered, 4 sold, $662,500 avg., $700,000 med., $900,000 high, $350,000 low.

You'll also see that his offspring are excellent commercial prospects, as well. He had thirty-two yearlings catalogued for the sales in 2000, and the twenty-five that sold averaged $1,253,468, with a median of $650,000, a high of $6,800,000, and a low of $53,000. You can also see how his weanlings sold in 1999.

While I'm on the subject, note that the sires of horses at a breeding stock sale are just as important as they are at a yearling sale because statistics show that while there is a definite sex bias among stallions (i.e., some sires are better producers of fillies than colts, and vice versa), in general, good sires make good broodmare sires.

The sire you pick also depends, like everything else you do, on your goals. If you intend to race, you'll take one tack, another if you intend to breed. For example, if you're looking to race on a moderate scale, you want a horse with a high percentage of starters and a high percentage of winners, while average earnings per runner and average per start may be a little less important.

This is probably as good a place as any to put in another thought about commercial stallions. The horse business today is something of a slave to fashion, which leaves a lot of good sires that produce excellent runners (but not the top ones) whose offspring can be bought at moderate prices.

If you intend to race, you can come up with these stallions by studying stallion registers, computer printouts, etc., and you don't have to pay an arm and a leg for breeding potential of the foal. Incidentally, at breeding stock sales, similar stallion summaries at the bottom of the page tell you about the sire to which the mare was bred, if she's in foal. It will be a little briefer than the summary of the sire of the horse that is being sold, but you can find out more in the sales catalogue's general sire index. The other major difference you'll find is that the sire summary of a mare selling in a breeding stock sale will generally mention stakes winners produced by his daughters.

In general, here are some things to look for in a sire summary:

• If a stallion has a good race record or is old enough to have several crops racing, the sire summary shouldn't have to go too deeply into his family to fill out space. He should be making it on his own, not because he's a son of a good sire or a half-brother to a stakes winner. This one is not so bad because his first crop is two-year-olds, but I, for one, would prefer a horse with a race record

By A.P. JET (1989), in Japan, Keisei Hai, 3rd Lord Derby Challenge Trophy, Asahi Hai Sansai, Keidei Hai Sansai S. Brother to Tappiano [G1] ($1,305,522), half-brother to black type winner My Earl. His first foals are 2-year-olds of 2000. Sire of winners Crispy Jet ($46,080, Finger Lakes Juvenile S.), Tequestas ($41,400), etc.

sufficiently strong that you really don't have to go into his family:

• By the same token, if he's producing at stud, the summary shouldn't have to go into great detail about his race record, denoting that he was third in some minor stakes somewhere. That indicates that the person writing the sire summary is having trouble filling up the space rather than cutting the performances to fit. The same applies to his offspring.

By **SPEEDY PROSPECT** (1977), black type winner of 12 races, $167,877, Sunny Isle H., Saul Silberman H., Broward H., 2nd Sunny Isle H., 3rd Palmetto H. Sire of Speedy Rasputin (Premio Hipodromo de San Felipe **[G3]**, etc. in Peru), Finer Prospect (Premio Manuel Checa Solari, etc.), black type-placed Automatic Speed ($154,582), Onlis **[G3]**.

Mare Summaries

Just as with the stallion side of the pedigree, the dam side will contain desirable elements and others you want to avoid.

Since a mare produces one foal a year as opposed to fifty to more than a hundred for a stallion, you should expect the mare summary to be more explicit than a successful sire summary, and they generally are, especially in the information included about the first dam. Her produce record on a catalogue page must state the number of foals she's had, the number that have reached racing age, and the number of winners. However, looks can still be deceiving.

This mare looks like a pretty hot producer, and, indeed, she did

Sharp Call, by Sharpen Up (GB). 2 wins at 3, $44,651, 2nd Ontario Colleen S.-R (WO, $10,630). Dam of 8 registered foals, 7 of racing age, 5 to race, 3 winners, including—
FLAG DOWN (c. by Deputy Minister). 4 wins to 4 in France, La Coupe **[G3]**, Prix Edmond Blanc **[G3]**; 7 wins, $1,572,208, in N.A., Pan American H. **[G2]**, Gulfstream Park Breeders' Cup H. **[G2]**, Bowling Green H. **[G2]**, W. L. McKnight H. **[G2]**- ncr, 1 1/2 mi. in 2:24, Red Smith H. **[G2]**, 2nd Turf Classic Invitational S. **[G1]**, Man o' War S. **[G1]**, Early Times Manhattan S. **[G1]**, Manhattan H. **[G1]**, Gulfstream Park Breeders' Cup H. **[G2]**, Bowling Green H. **[G2]**, Hialeah Turf Cup H. **[G3]** twice, Knickerbocker H. **[G3]**, 3rd Breeders' Cup Turf **[G1]**, Jockey Club Gold Cup **[G1]**, Hollywood Turf Cup S. **[G1]**, Caesars International H. **[G1]**, Sword Dancer Invitational H. **[G1]**, Crown Royal Pan American H. **[G2]**, etc.

produce a graded stakes winner of $1.5 million. However, remember this is an advertisement, even if it is a very good one. If you'll look at the computer produce record of Sharp Call, you'll see that Flag Down earned his money the hard way, racing through the age of eight...all over the world. Further, the pedigree writer had to include all his seconds and thirds to fill out the space for this mare. When they start including all the stakes placings, it should send up a red flag. Further, if you look at the rest of this mare's produce record, you can see that her other winners (which weren't mentioned in this summary) were Call for Change who didn't win until he was seven and West an Wewaxation[1] who didn't win until the age of five.

```
1991 slipped.
1992 Exit Strategy, g (Vice Regent). Unraced.
     KEESEP 1993 Yearling Sale, $60,000, Buyer: WYGOD, PAM AND MARTIN
1993 Call For Change, c (Time For A Change). 2 wins at 7 $13,366 in 5 starts
     in NA.    (SSI=1.61)(AWD=7.25)
     2000 In NA 5 2 1 1 $13,366  01-Apr-2000 TP 08 Allowance Fin:7th
     Owner: Bearden Wayne & England David P  Trainer: Wayne Bearden
     KEESEP 1994 Yearling Sale, $82,000, Buyer: STRONACH, F.
1994 Perfectly Nice, f (Silver Deputy). Unraced.
     CBSSEP 1995 Yearling Sale, $12,670, Buyer: STRONACH, FRANK
1995 West An Wewaxation, g (Gone West). 2 wins at 5 Unpl at 3 $9,298 in 13
     starts in NA.   (On turf,  Unpl at 5 $0 in 1 start.)(SSI=0.34)(AWD=6.00)
     2000 In NA 12 2 1 3 $9,123  08-Dec-2000 HOU04 Claiming Fin:11th
     Owner: Schmidt Hilmer C  Trainer: Danny Ogus
     KEESEP 1996 Yearling Sale, $175,000, Buyer: LANESBOROUGH STABLES
     BESMAR 1997 Two-Year Old Sale, $200,000, Buyer: KIMMEL, JOHN C.: AGENT
1996 Sharp Minister, f (Deputy Minister).  Unpl at 3 $760 in 2 starts in NA.
     (On turf,  Unpl at 3 $0 in 1 start.)
     KEENOV 1996 Weanling Sale, $140,000, Buyer: HUGHES, B. WAYNE
1997 Inveterate, c (Deputy Minister).  Unpl at 3 $560 in 9 starts in NA.
     (On turf,  Unpl at 3 $560 in 6 starts.)(SSI=0.02)
     2000 In NA 9 0 0 0 $560  06-Dec-2000 AQU03 Maiden Claiming Fin:10th
     Owner: Kaufman Robert Islein James H & Woo  Trainer: Richard Stoklosa
     KEESEP 1998 Yearling Sale, $0, Buyer:  (RNA)
1999 unnamed b, f, by A.P. Indy.
     KEESEP 2000 Yearling Sale, $100,000, Buyer: MT. BRILLIANT FARM LLC
```

Following is another who doesn't look so bad at first blush.

It is true that with very little help (Lil Tyler is not exactly Northern Dancer) this mare produced Lil Sneeker, a stakes winner of

---

[1] Took me a while to figure this one out—it's Rest and Relaxation as if Elmer Fudd said it.

$463,073, but if you want to talk about a horse who really did it the hard way look at this produce record. You'll see this poor devil made seventy-five starts from the ages of three to nine in cheap stakes and allowance company. Her other foals weren't much better, either.

1st dam
NAMESEEKER, by Run the Gantlet. Unraced. Dam of 8 registered
    foals, 7 of racing age, 4 to race, 3 winners, including—
  LIL SNEEKER (g. by Lil Tyler). 10 wins, 3 to 9, $463,073, Albany H. [L]
    (GG, $31,850), Court Clown H. (GG, $19,635), Seattle H. (EMD,
    $19,250)-ntr, 6 fur. in 1:09 4/5, 2nd Bay Meadows Express H. [L]
    (BM, $20,000), Oakland H. [L] (GG, $20,000) 3 times, Sam J.
    Whiting Memorial H. (PLN, $8,050), 3rd Montclair H.-R (GG,
    $7,500), Montclair S.-R (GG, $7,500), Montclair H. R (GG,
    $6,000), West 12 Ranch H. (BM, $5,250).

As a rule of thumb, you can just assume the more vague a catalogue page is, the more you ought to investigate some alternative form of information.

Also, keep several other things to in mind when you are looking at a mare summary.

Two of the most commonly misunderstood words on the pedigree page are "sire" and "producer." For the record, note that a horse is not a "sire" in a pedigree until one of his offspring has won a race — if people would continue to breed to him, he can sire 2,866 horses that hit the racetrack, and if none of them ever wins a race, he will not be listed as a "sire" in a catalogue. The same thing goes for "producer." A mare is not a producer until one of her offspring wins a race.

On the distaff side of a pedigree, whether you're buying a yearling filly or a broodmare, the first dam that appears on the pedigree page will be the second dam of any offspring you eventually sell, and the second dam will be the third dam, etc. As a consequence, any black type beyond the first dam will be virtually meaningless to buyers insofar as anything you sell out of her.

When you look at a pedigree of a filly or a broodmare, check on her female relatives and the stallions to which they've been bred. If she has several sisters or half-sisters that look like good potential broodmares and they have been bred to good stallions, your mare's pedigree may well improve through no effort of her own.

If you're looking for colts, this doesn't matter quite as much because, to be honest, if your colt can't run he's not going to be worth much as a sire prospect, no matter what his family does.

Race and Produce Records

When you get to a breeding stock sale, the family of the horses you intend to buy becomes less important, while their own performance on the racetrack and their production record become more important. Once again, it simply takes a little research to determine what is behind the scenes in the catalogue.

For example, in a mare's race record, you need to find out the quality of races she won as well as the quality of the races her offspring are winning.

Here's the racing and produce record of a stakes-winning mare that sold in the 2000 Keeneland November sale:

RACE RECORD: At 2, unraced; at 3, one win, once 3rd; at 4, one win, 3 times 3rd; at 5, three wins (Star Ball Invitational H. [LR] (GG, $55,000)), once 2nd (Sacramento H. [L] (GG, $20,000)), 3 times 3rd (Countess Fager H. **[G3]**, Campanile Invitational H. [LR] (GG, $7,500), Chapel of Dreams H. (GG, $4,500)); at 6, three wins (Alameda County H. [L] (PLN, $27,500), Luther Burbank H. [L] (SR, $27,500), Campanile Invitational H.-R (GG, $31,700)), twice 2nd (Mayme Dotson Breeders' Cup H. (STK, $9,000), Mother Lode Breeders' Cup H. (SAC, $9,000)), twice 3rd (Belle Roberts H. [L] (LGA, $22,500), Miss America H. [L] (GG, $15,000)); at 7, one win (Mayme Dotson Breeders' Cup H. (STK, $25,750)), twice 2nd (Mother Lode Breeders' Cup H. (SAC, $9,000), Tulare Breeders' Cup S. (FNO, $9,-000)). Totals: 9 wins, 5 times 2nd, 9 times 3rd. Earned $376,791.
PRODUCE RECORD:
1994 Art Museum, f. by General Meeting. Placed at 2.
1995 College Year, f. by Half a Year. Unraced.
1996 Artistic Art, f. by Woodman. Unraced.
1997 College Class, f. by General Meeting. Unplaced.
1998 not pregnant.
1999 c. by American Day; 2000 not pregnant.
Mated to Event of the Year (Seattle Slew--Classic Event), last service April 23, 2000. (Believed to be pregnant). Vaccinated for virus abortion.

Racing records today are more specific than they used to be, so you can determine right from the pedigree page that this mare won a $55,000 stakes, but the fact that the pedigree writer had to go into all the seconds and thirds she ever had should be a clue to look her up more seriously. If you did, you'd find that she did, indeed, earn $376,791 on the track (which ain't peanuts), but she raced from three to seven to do that, and her family is on the weak side, so they couldn't fill out the page with her half-brothers and sisters.

Further, if you'll look at her breeding record, you'll notice after having four foals of racing age she has not produced a winner, and I would hazard a guess that her owner has given up on her.

Here are a few other red flags to look for in a pedigree:

• If a horse just appears in black type and is merely noted as "stakes winner," or is simply listed as a "winner," with no further specifics, you can pretty much bet that the stakes win was a pretty cheap one or that the "winner" didn't do more than break its maiden.

• You'll see the phrase "no report" in a number of produce records. Ninety times out of a hundred, it means "no foal."

Furthermore, if you look at the following report on the actual catalogue page, your eye may have been sort of trained to look down the left side, and you might have missed the notation "1987 barren; 1992 dead twins; 1996, 1998 no report," which appears on the line that normally just says "PRODUCE RECORD:".

PRODUCE RECORD: 1987 barren; 1992 dead twins; 1996, 1998 no report.
1988 Pavlova, f. by Majestic Light. Winner at 3, $25,240. Producer.
1989 Appointee, c. by Private Account. 3 wins at 3 and 4, $69,140.
1990 **Apprentice**, c. by Forty Niner. 3 wins at 2 and 3, $112,675, 2nd Le-
      Comte H. (FG, $6,665), Risen Star S. (FG, $5,340).
1991 Roaring Camp, c. by Forty Niner. Unraced. Sire.
1993 Danseuse, f. by Mr. Prospector. 2 wins in 2 starts at $38,100.
1994 Green Applause, c. by Mr. Prospector. Winner in 2 starts at 3 in
Japan.
1995 Balletic, f. by Forty Niner. Unraced.
1997 Pivot, c. by Pleasant Colony. Placed at 3, 2000, $9,120.
1999 c. by Our Emblem; 2000 not pregnant
Mated to Our Emblem (Mr. Prospector--Personal Ensign), last service March
      31, 2000. (Believed to be pregnant). Vaccinated for virus abortion.

Here's another example. While the pedigree writer hasn't actually left anything out, the notations "1998 not pregnant" and "2000 aborted single foal" are certainly buried in the produce record. Another case where I'm betting the owners gave up on the mare.

PRODUCE RECORD:
1994 Iron Hombre, g. by Slewpy. 3 wins at 3 and 5, $36,425.
1995 **HOLY NOLA**, f. by Silver Deputy. 5 wins, 2 to 4, $216,812, Great Arizona Futurity Shoot-Out (TUP, $52,825), 2nd Santa Paula S. [L] (SA, $16,230).
1996 aborted single foal; 1998 not pregnant.
1997 Black Iron, c. by Palmister. Winner at 2, $4,780.
1999 f. by Silver Deputy; 2000 aborted single foal.
Mated to Silver Deputy (Deputy Minister—Silver Valley), last service April 13, 2000. (Believed to be pregnant). Vaccinated for virus abortion.

One other thing that ought to raise suspicion. If, after a number of years that are just moderately productive or have been pretty unproductive a mare has been bred to a stallion who is a lot more fashionable than anything to whom she's been bred before, you should take it as a possible warning sign that the owners overbred her a little in anticipation of getting rid of her at the breeding stock sales.

The whole point of this section is that there are bargains to be had throughout the market but be suspicious. Find out why a mare is being sold; you don't want to buy a cull, ever, much less start out with one!

Well, you've spent several weeks doing your homework and, as a result, you've been able to pare your sales prospects down from 2,000 in the catalogue to perhaps 200 that interest you and are likely to fall in your price range. The sale is four days away, so you and your trainer or advisor pack your bags.

Most sales companies require the horses to be on the grounds for two to three days before they are to be sold (this may be cut in half at marathon sales with several thousand horses), and the earlier you get there the better, because a lot of footwork needs to be done before the sale even begins.

Another reason to get to the sales early is that the fewer horses you have to look at in a day the better off you are. When you start looking at 150 or 200 horses a day, they all begin to look alike. As a matter of fact, as the sales have grown to between 3,000 and 5,000 offerings, a lot of bloodstock agents come into town a week or more before the sale to look at prospective horses on the farms, prior to their even being moved to the sales grounds.

The more horses you look at, the better your eye becomes at discerning the fine points. And while people seem to fixate on yearling conformation, remember that conformation is important in breeding stock as well. In the section that follows, I'm only going to discuss some of the basic principles of conformation, because conformation itself can't be learned from a book or videotape. There are books and videotapes that can provide you with an introduction to conformation, though.

Conformation

The study of conformation is an exercise in compromise. There are good-looking horses in this world, and there are great-looking horses in this world, but there are no perfect horses.

If you go into the paddock on Breeders' Cup Day, you'll see more than 100 of the best horses in the world, and you'll also quickly decide that no single "look" defines a good horse. You'll see big horses and little ones; you'll see correct horses and incorrect ones; you'll see a few horses that'll knock your eyes out; and you'll see many more that'll make you scratch your head, trying to figure out how anyone ever paid two dollars for them.

An example of this was pointed out by Roger Mortimer, the British racing writer in the *Sunday Times* following the 1972 English Oaks: "It was the plainest Oaks field I have ever seen, and the paddock critic who expressed a decided preference for the horse of the policewoman on duty was no bad judge."

Only three things differentiate bad horses and good horses, and good horses and great horses. That is courage, desire, and the will to win. At the racetrack, they call it "heart." It's what makes some horses with injuries and bad conformation run faster than those that are physically superior. There's no way to measure "heart" at the sales, and, as mentioned earlier, you won't know until your horse has made several starts whether it's there.

You can get an indication, though. Horses at the sales are in an unusual situation, a strange environment, and the way they react can tell you something about their mental outlook. Are they nervous and fractious? Are they curious about their surroundings or dull and listless (possibly indicating they've been tranquilized)? The way a horse responds to the hustle and bustle of the sale may indicate how it'll respond to the life and competition of the racetrack.

When you look at conformation, what you're doing is hedging your bet — reducing your risk. Every conformational defect is a warning sign that a horse is likely to injure himself in a certain way. From an evolutionary standpoint, the horse is running on the equivalent of an index finger. When you consider that a thousand-pound animal that runs six furlongs in 1:10 is traveling at a speed of 38.56 miles an hour on its finger, you wonder how any of them stay sound. Dr. George Pratt of the Massachusetts Institute of Technology measured the force on a horse's cannon bone as its hoof hits the ground at approximately 9,000 pounds per square inch.

Every horseman has his "pet peeve," a defect that he finds particularly offensive. These are normally the defects with which he's had the worst experience. On the other hand, he'll be inclined to overlook some faults that his good horses have been able to overcome.

A horse must compensate for every conformational fault it has, and often the compensation is as much a cause of lameness as the defect.

As I mentioned earlier, even most of the most successful owners in the world don't judge conformation on their own. When the Coolmore group goes to the sales, when the Maktoums go to the sales, when Bob and Beverly Lewis go to the sales, they bring experts with them. These trainers and veterinarians have spent a lifetime studying conformation, so don't even think you can judge conformation without years of practice.

The most important quality of good conformation is the indefinable "balance." Horsemen normally say "the horse should be pleasing to the eye," which means very little to the layman. He is saying that the horse should be in proportion — the rear end shouldn't be too big for the front end, or vice versa; the head and neck should fit well with the rest of the horse. Most horsemen look at balance first, starting their examination from a little distance away to see whether the animal "looks like a racehorse." If he does not appear to be balanced overall, it will be difficult for him to produce a ground-covering, well-coordinated stride.

Although a horse doesn't run with his head, an intelligent head with a good eye is an indication of good temperament. The size of the head in proportion to the neck and body is important, too, because a horse uses his head for balance when he's running.

The front legs, particularly the way they're set, the slope of the shoulder, and the slope of the pastern are very important. This all sounds simple but it's not.

A long well-sloped shoulder allows a horse to "reach" stride when he's running. The slope of its pasterns determines how well a horse will absorb shock, and therefore is very important. A judge of horses will look for medium length and about a forty-five-degree angle in the pasterns. Any deviation causes strain or a lack of action in the fetlock. Straight pasterns pass the shock directly up the legs, and the horse will likely suffer knee problems. Long, low pasterns do the opposite — they overstrain the tendons by letting the entire leg drop down in each stride.

Being over at the knee is unsightly, but tends to be less of a problem than being back at the knee or calf-kneed. Many trainers will accept horses over at the knee, whereas they will absolutely reject horses that are back at the knee. A tied-in cannon is an indication that the tendons draw closer to the cannon at the knee than they do at the fetlock. This indicates a weakness and a fault at the point where the tendon joins the knee and can be an indication of future unsoundness.

While still looking at the horse from the side, a trainer will look at the strength of his withers, the length of his back, the overall relationship of his top line to his bottom line, the depth of his chest (which houses its heart and lungs), and the strength of his gaskin.

Rear-leg conformation is more important than some people think; after all, this is the pushing power. A long, muscled gaskin with a well-set hock is extremely important, and the hock should appear directly in line with the back of the rump when the leg is vertical. Sickle-hocked horses, in particular, lose some of their motion because they cannot push out far enough in full stride.

From a head-on view, the expert again will look at the horse's general demeanor, and the attractiveness and intelligence of his eyes and head. More significantly, he will look at the musculature of the chest and the way the horse's front legs come out of his chest. A horse's legs should be well separated at the chest and go straight to the ground. A plumb line dropped from the elbow to the ground should pass directly through the center line of the knee. Offset knees are just what they imply. They are offset from the plumb line that extends from the elbow to the ground. Horses also can be knock-kneed or bowlegged, which present serious problems because of the strain on the tendons and joints. Or they can be base narrow, which means that the horse stands closer together at his feet with the legs wider apart at the elbows; or there is the opposite — base wide.

In the foot area, just as in humans, horses can be splayfooted, which means that they point out like a duck; or pigeon-toed, which means that his toes point toward each other. These are very common faults in horses, and generally affect their gait.

A trainer will continue his trip around the horse, observing the off side, looking for blemishes that might be apparent from that side only. Then he will go to the rear of the horse, looking for possible problems with its hocks.

Next, he will ask the handler to walk the horse while he stands directly behind observing the horse's manner of traveling as he walks away and the way the animal handles himself when the handler turns it to walk back. He will look for any indication of incoordination, particularly in the back legs, then will observe the horse walking directly toward him for any toeing in or toeing out. He will try to figure out whether this comes from the knee or from the fetlock. Finally, he will observe whether the horse has a nice long stride, which will be indicated by whether he places his back legs in front of where his front legs had been set down. This is called "overstepping" and is considered very desirable as a gauge of future power.

One point that many observers tend to overlook is the feet. Without the feet there is no horse. Feet must be well made, sound, and free from severe corrective shoeing, which may have been done immediately before the sale. He also will look for wax or epoxy on the hoof, which can be used to mask cracks in the feet. A badly formed foot is a fairly sure sign that there has been some lameness, or some fault in conformation that may have been overlooked.

Once again, conformation is a process of compromise and is very subjective. As you watch your conformation advisor and as you get more experience, you'll learn to like a certain type of horse, just as everyone else does. Just don't like that type to the exclusion of everything else.

Now that you and your advisor have spent two days looking at the horses in the sale, you've eliminated some horses outright for conformation defects, and you've adjusted some of your original estimates, either up or down, to account for their physical appearance.

If you've had a little extra time, you also might have looked at a few horses that you considered to be just slightly above your head. Sales have a rhythm, a cyclical aspect of their own, with soft spots and spots where everything seems to go out of sight. If something you formerly considered over your head happens to come in dur-

Assessing the way a yearling walks.

ing a soft spot, you might be able to get it at an affordable price. This is particularly true in this day when sales of upward of 5,000 horses are not out of the question.

The Repository

The final step before you head for the sales ring is to visit the repository of veterinary information now provided by sales companies.

These repositories were created primarily because the really popular horses were getting examined half to death prior to the sale. Having a veterinarian check out any horse you're really serious about is a good idea, but when multiple groups get serious about one horse, not only is annoying and disruptive to the sales crew, but it can be harmful to the horse itself, for example, repeated scoping of a horse can inflame its air passages.

So, a few years ago, the sales companies, consignors, and veterinarians got together and decided to organize a single repository

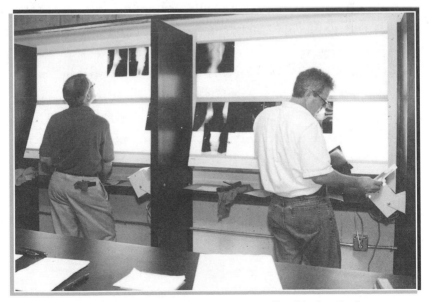

The repository contains pertinent medical information.

where the pertinent veterinary information on horses in a particular sale could be held for all interested parties to view. For instance, at a sale of yearlings or weanlings, the repository will include a set of X-rays of knees, ankles, hocks, statements as to soundness of eye or wind, and information about any major abdominal surgery or invasive joint surgery. At a breeding stock sale it will include reproductive status certificates, etc. — in short, it will contain information about most of the things that are not guaranteed under the conditions of sale. That way the horse does not have to be X-rayed or palpated repeatedly prior to the sale. Once will do very nicely, thank you.

Not surprisingly, I have a couple of comments to make about the repository. First, the veterinarian you send to the repository should be experienced and knowledgeable about whatever aspect concerns you about the horse. In this part of the world, veterinarians are highly specialized, just like real doctors.[2] It doesn't make sense to have a reproductive specialist reading X-rays of ankles, nor does it make sense to have an orthopedist examining pregnancy data. Just as with conformational defects, a veterinarian can probably find something wrong with about every horse in the sale, so you need to have one who knows what is serious, and what he should call to your attention but say, this is something we can live with.

Finally, the repository is not the final word. You should still have your own veterinarian examine any horse you purchase immediately after the sale. Believe it or not, veterinarians have found something wrong with a horse that did not show up in the repository and/or something that is different than what showed up in the repository. With thousands of horses going through the sales, this is bound to happen.

---

[2] This is an intentional dig at some of my very good friends who are veterinarians. They know that I think in many, if not most, ways they actually have to be better than "real" doctors.

If the repository and your own veterinarian's findings differ and the sales company can't mediate an agreement between you and the consignor, a panel of independent veterinarians will adjudicate the issue.

One final thought about veterinary matters and the sales. A buzz is going around about performing drug tests on horses following the sales, just as they do at the racetrack, particularly after sales where soundness counts. It's still up in the air at the time of this writing, but I'll bet we see some form of it within the next few years.

In the Sales Arena

You and your advisor have done all the due diligence, and now it's time to go to the sales ring and find a couple of seats, or take your assigned seats, if it's that kind of sale. As you look around, everything is geared toward creating excitement, toward eliciting one more bid. There are bars frequently spaced around the sales arenas — a drink or two doesn't hurt to loosen up the buyers. Also, if you'll notice when you come into the arena, it's generally fairly chilly; they don't want anyone sleeping in there.

A few people recommend that you tell the bid spotter in your area what horses you'll be bidding on so that he'll be alert to your subtle signals — you don't want other buyers or, especially a consignor, to know you're after a particular horse, so you try to conceal your bids as much as possible. I don't necessarily believe you need to tell the bid spotter what horses you want to bid on, just introduce yourself, tell him you'll be active, and he'll be sure to keep you in the corner of his eye, if he's any good. Personally, my experience is that most bid spotters at the major sales are there for a reason — they're alert and they're sharp — and I feel if you want to bid, you don't need to introduce yourself or anything else, just establish eye contact with him, signal him, and he'll take your bid.

Listen to the rhythm of the sale. Note in your mind the minimum jump in bids. Listen to the auctioneer and the bids he's asking. If he's got a horse at $5,000 and is asking for $6,000, you nod and the horse goes up to $6,000, or you can hold up five fingers and the bid will be $5,500. If he's got a horse for $1 million and you hold up five fingers, that's probably going to be interpreted as $1.5 million.

Also, one further admonition: Don't be shy about correcting the bid spotter and/or the auctioneer. If the auctioneer has a horse, for instance, at $20,000, asking for $25,000, and you hold up one finger meaning $21,000, but he jumps you to $25,000, you can tell the bid spotter you meant only $21,000. You can buy a lot of pride, not to mention hay and oats, for $4,000.

This wonderful picture of two friends of mine at the Spendthrift Farm auction in May 1994 illustrates the necessity to correct a bid spotter occasionally. If you look closely, you can see that the bidder, Jack Graham (seated), is holding up two fingers, indicating a bid of $4,200 per acre, while Steve Dance, the bid spotter, has up three fingers, which would mean a bid of $4,300 per acre. It doesn't seem like much, but at 496 acres, it would have been a mistake of $49,600. Steve was corrected.

The sales move very quickly — from twenty-five to thirty-five horses per hour at most sales — so occasional mix-ups are to be expected. If the auctioneer knocks down a horse to someone else and you thought it was your bid, your bid spotter may be able to get him to reopen the bidding, but it'll be between only you and the other bidder; no new bidders would be allowed to come in at that point. A clue to whether the final bid is yours is that the auctioneer always says the figure as he's about to bang the gavel. You can raise your eyebrows at the bid spotter and point to yourself, to ask if it's your bid.

Another thing that may sound stupid, but it's not — don't bid against yourself! In addition to the bid spotters, the auctioneer and the announcer often spot bids, and sometimes territories of two bid spotters may overlap so, believe it or not, a number of people have become excited and wound up bidding against themselves.[3] The best way to avoid that, I think, is to pick one bid spotter and stick with him. Further, you have to be careful to keep from being "run up" by a consignor or his shill. This is perfectly legal, according to the rules of sale, and some consignors are very good at it.

A final admonition about bidding: Don't ever bid on a horse in the ring if you haven't previously examined it, no matter how cheaply it seems to be going. If you think you're the only smart person in the arena, you're mistaken. There's undoubtedly a reason why the horse isn't going for what you think it's worth. The lighting in the ring is all overhead, which can make Woody Allen look like Mr. America and also can conceal many blemishes on a horse's legs. If you get the impulse to bid on a horse in the ring, go out and have another drink. You'll thank me for it more often than not.

After you've purchased your horse, a member of the sales com-

---

[3] This seems to have happened less in recent years since many auctioneers are paid a salary rather than a commission. Fancy that!

pany staff will bring around an Acknowledgement of Purchase form. You may be shaking like a leaf, but be sure to check the hip number and the price before you sign it. If you have any questions about the purchase, better to ask them at that time than later.

In many states, Thoroughbreds are subject to sales tax, which will be added to the price of your horse, so note that there is a section of the acknowledgement where you can initial to claim an exemption from the sales tax:

• if your horse is purchased for breeding purposes only,

• if the horse is less than two and will be shipped out of state, either immediately or after it's trained, or

• if the horse is a racing prospect and it's being shipped out of the state immediately (and you'll have to give the sales company a bill of lading to prove it). Remember to consult the sales catalogue before the sale for sales tax information.

Also, if you haven't already established credit with the sales company, remember all purchasers are required to settle up within thirty minutes of the end of the session in which they purchase horses. It's just another reason to establish your credit early.

After the Sales

As I mentioned earlier, effective title will not pass until your check has cleared, but the sales company will give you a stable release form that you can use to send your purchase to the farm of your choice.

If you haven't already arranged for insurance, do it now! All kinds of insurance agents are hanging around the sales, in case you don't have your own. If you do have an insurance company with which you normally deal, call and let them know what you've purchased as soon as possible.

See if you can find the consignor at this point, and find out any other special information you need about the horse: vaccinations, stakes not mentioned on the pedigree page, feeding programs, etc. This can save you a lot of time, and possibly money, later on.

Then go to one of the van companies' representatives, who are present at every sale, and arrange for your horse to be shipped to the farm you've chosen to gentle your yearlings or to board your broodmare. If you're from out of state, it might be necessary — or at least cheaper — for you to find an intermediate place to board your purchases locally until the transportation company has a full load ready to go to your area. Most of the reputable van companies will be able to help you make these arrangements if you have no local connections.

Finally, wherever you send your horse, let them know the horse is coming! You wouldn't believe how often a horse van simply shows up at a farm or training center to unload a horse without anyone knowing to whom the horse belongs — or that the horse was even coming. This does not augur well for the future of your horse, or you, in the horse business.

Now, you are through at the sales and you can go back to the hotel, take a shower and have dinner…better yet, go find a church and start to pray.

Some Final Thoughts

The times they are a' changing, and so are the sales.

On balance, because of the level of information available today and because of the interference of lawyers, the auction business is more straightforward and honest than ever before. There are still shysters, certainly, and the philosophy of *caveat emptor* is still prevalent, but the buyer has more of a chance to get a fair shake today than he ever has. I believe this will be the case more and more over the years.

If you have access to the Internet, you can now get live feed of most the world's major sales through the sale's company's web site. It's not like actually going to the sales, but you can now stay home and watch a horse that interests you go through the ring. It wouldn't surprise me if, one day soon, you might be able to bid on line, too.

Apropos of that, you already can bid online for stallion seasons and shares, since the formation of Equine Spectrum, a real-time online exchange. This is a logical successor to the former Matchmaker Breeders' Exchange and to Stallion Access, which were the first companies that offered an open exchange for seasons and shares. Five of the major players in the breeding and sales business are backing the endeavor, including Coolmore/Ashford, Eaton Sales, Lane's End, Taylor Made, and Three Chimneys. If that bunch can't make a go of it, it can't go.

Further, Keeneland has begun an online auction of RNAs following a sale, and, while it has yet to really take off, I expect that it will gain additional acceptance over time.

While online auctions, repositories, and other innovations have made it easier to buy horses, nothing can replace the experience that comes from looking at countless horses at innumerable sales. Make sure to wear a comfortable pair of shoes.

CHAPTER
SEVEN

TAXATION AND YOUR
HORSE BUSINESS

*"...as long as tax rates are less than 100 percent,
there is no 'benefit' in losing money."*

— *Tax Court Decision*

As I have reiterated *ad nauseam* throughout earlier portions of this book, the Tax Reform Act of 1986 did not destroy the horse business, despite almost continuous griping and moaning to the contrary.

On the other hand, it didn't help the business much, either. But, at the risk of raising the specter of realism, it is not the primary function of the U.S. Government or its tax laws to help the horse business.

If you were to look at the situation from a truly dispassionate standpoint, you might just conclude that the Tax Reform Act of 1986 may, in fact, have helped the industry in a certain perverse fashion. If nothing else, the overreaction of those involved in the business went a long way toward stemming the overproduction responsible for the declines we suffered in the mid-1980s and early '90s. And, after we quit moping around and broke out of the doldrums, we entered an era of prosperity that has been unparalleled in the history of the business.

When you consider the current gap between the price of bloodstock and the anticipation of return on the racetrack, taxation is an extremely important consideration from the standpoint of your participation in the horse business.

Before continuing, I want to add one stern admonition for the reader. I am singularly unqualified to give tax advice, and this section of the book is intended only to acquaint you informally with the tax advantages of horse ownership. I cannot emphasize too strongly that all tax decisions pertaining to your horse business, just as with any other business, should be made in consultation with your accountant and/or attorney. In other words, you can take my word for a lot of things in this book, but don't take my word for *anything* in this chapter.

Having said that, I would like to point out that the horse business has a number of important tax advantages. The major one is that you can use the cash method of accounting, allowing you to write off your expenses as you create inventory. This will give you the chance to trade ordinary income (currently taxable to a maximum rate of 39.6 percent) for capital gains for individuals (currently taxable to a maximum rate of twenty percent). Meanwhile, you can write off your expenses of doing business. In other words, you will be using tax dollars to acquire assets

If you remember one thing from this chapter, make it this:

> **"If you treat your horse operation as a business, the IRS will treat your horse operation as a business."**

Bear in mind the flip side, which is if you don't treat your horse operation as a business, neither will the IRS.

Here's something you can take to the bank: The IRS hates the horse business — *despises* it. Although a 1996 economic impact study commissioned by the American Horse Council found that 7.1 million Americans are involved in the horse business and nearly

340,000 of them make their living from it, the IRS regards it as the playground for the extremely wealthy, and every beady-eyed little IRS agent in the country would love to score a big coup by causing someone to lose all the advantages they had gained by participating in the business.

Before going any further, I guess this is as good a place as any to put in a plug for the American Horse Council.

In 1969, some dimwit U.S. congressman whose name I don't remember attempted (with the enthusiastic support of the IRS, I might add) to get the tax code revised so that any losses in a horse business would not be deductible against other income.

A group of horsemen representing all the various segments of the business got together in Washington, D.C., and, in a rare display of unity, formed the American Horse Council for the purposes of representing the horse business — not just the Thoroughbred business, but the entire horse business — before Congress.

In the thirty years since then, the American Horse Council has probably done more good with less money than any other organization I can think of in the horse business. With an annual budget approximately the equivalent of the salaries of the top two or three executives of the National Thoroughbred Racing Association, the American Horse Council has represented the horse business before both the federal government and state governments with an astounding degree of effectiveness, particularly considering the level of resources with which it has had to work.

You should join the American Horse Council as a show of support for when its lobbyists appear before the various government authorities that hold so much control over us, such as Congress, the IRS, and the U.S. Department of Agriculture. Then again, if you can't see past the standpoint of strict self-interest, you should join the American Horse Council because of its tax publications (which are the source of ninety percent of the information in this chapter).

For someone who is only at the point of considering getting into the horse business, I'd suggest *Tax Tips for Horse Owners* by Tad Davis, the tax guru of the business and tax counsel for the American Horse Council for more than twenty-five years. It sells for $10, and is, essentially, a sixteen-page outline of taxation basics of the horse business.

For a complete overview of taxes, you can get *The Horse Owners and Breeders Tax Manual*, which contains something over 800 pages and is *the* tax reference for the horse business. Also written by Tad Davis, it formerly sold for $90, which I thought was a helluva bargain. However, the 2000 Edition is $64.50, which would still be cheap at three or four times the price.

You can get the tax manuals and a lot more information about the American Horse Council from its web site, www.horsecouncil.org.

Finally, also from the standpoint of strict self-interest, as you'll see below, the IRS will consider your American Horse Council membership as another indication that you're operating as a business.

Hobby Loss Provision

To backtrack, the result of the 1969 tax brouhaha was the so-called Hobby Loss Provision, one of the most important parts of tax law insofar as many horse operations are concerned. Briefly, this provision states that if you're engaged in a certain endeavor and your motive is personal enjoyment rather than making a profit, you cannot write off any of the expenses you incur in that endeavor. Conversely, your losses are fully deductible against other income if you can prove it is a business and not a hobby and you were engaged in that activity for a profit .

Oddly enough, you do not necessarily have to *make* a profit to be declared a business, but the facts and circumstances surrounding your activity must indicate that you're in the business to do so. In determining whether the profit motive exists, the IRS will, no doubt, take into consideration the nine factors that they have listed as important indicators of a profit motive.

Before discussing the factors, though, here are a couple of other important admonitions: First, the nine factors may not be the only ones used in determining whether your horse operation is a business or a hobby. Secondly, no single factor carries more weight than another. And, third, a determination will not be made simply on the fact that you qualify under a majority of factors. That is, you just can't expect to say, "I qualified on five counts and didn't qualify on four counts, so it's a business," and be confident the IRS will agree.

Here are the criteria the IRS will use to determine whether you are in the horse business as a business or as a hobby, along with some comments, where necessary:

(1) *Whether the taxpayer carries on the horse operation in a businesslike manner.* This means you should carry on your horse business in a manner similar to other businesses that you are conducting profitably; you should keep accurate books and records; and you should adopt new techniques or abandon unprofitable ones as necessary, etc.

(2) *The expertise of the taxpayer and/or his advisors.* Refer again, please, to Chapter 3. The choice of your advisors will play an important part in the IRS' determination of whether your horse operation is a business.

(3) *The amount of time and effort expended by the taxpayer in carrying on his horse operation.* However,[1] the fact that the taxpayer spends only a limited amount of time on his horse business does not necessarily show the absence of a profit motive, as long as he has competent and qualified people to run the business for him.

---

[1] You're going to see this word a lot in this chapter, because very little is clear-cut with respect to the IRS. So, to see if you're staying awake and paying attention, I'm going to conduct a little contest. The first person to correctly count the "howevers" in this chapter and send the right answer to the publisher will get a nice little prize.

One of the few things that the Tax Reform Act of 1986 did do was add a twist by limiting passive losses and material participation, but I'll discuss those things in further detail.

(4) *Expectation that the assets used in the activity, such as land and horses, will appreciate in value.* However, if, say, you buy a farm primarily because you are anticipating that it will increase in value rather than as an adjunct to your horse business, the tax status of your farming operation may be affected.

(5) *The taxpayer's success in other businesses, whether they're similar or not.*

(6) *The taxpayer's history of profits and losses in his horse activity.* I'll discuss this a little further, too, in the section concerning the "two-out-of-seven presumption."

(7) *The taxpayer's history of profits generated by the activity in relation to the amount of losses, the amount of investment, and the value of the assets used in the activity.* You can't, for example, lose $150,000 a year for five years, then make $10,000 for the next two years and expect the IRS to roll over and say, "Okay, this guy's in the business for a profit."

(8) *Substantial income from sources other than your horse business, especially if the losses from your horse activities create substantial tax benefits.*

(9) *Elements of personal/pleasure recreation.* The fact you happen to like racing and breeding does not necessarily mean you're not in them for a profit. However, the way you treat the "enjoyment" part of your business may have an effect on the IRS' thinking. For instance, if your travel and entertainment expenses are out of line or you deduct an inordinate amount for frills on your farm, you may create a problem for yourself.

Two-Out-Of-Seven Presumption

As mentioned above, a provision in the tax code creates an

important *presumption* that your horse operation is a business, under most circumstances, if you show a profit two years out of any specified seven-year tax period. It seems, however, that anything having to do with the IRS gets pretty complicated, and the "two-out-of-seven presumption" is no exception.

Basically, there are two kinds of presumptions: a "general" presumption, which is automatic, and a "special" presumption. This special presumption applies only to the first seven-year period of a horse operation and requires the taxpayer to make an "election," — in other words, you must choose the special presumption; it will not kick in automatically.

The general presumption comes into play automatically as soon as you have a second profit year in the horse operation in any seven-year period. It protects you for seven years from the first profit year in the period, but does not protect any loss years between the first and second profit years. For example, assume your horse operation has profits (P) and losses (L) in the following seven-year sequence:

1993	1994	1995	1996	1997	1998	1999
(P)	(L)	(L)	(P)	(L)	(L)	(L)

The second profit year is 1996, so, under the general presumption you would be protected in the years 1996 (the second profit year) through 1999 (the seventh year inclusive from the first profit year). You would not be protected in 1994 and 1995 because they came before the second profit year. Therefore, in situations where the general presumption is in effect, it is best to have the profit years come back to back, for instance:

1993	1994	1995	1996	1997	1998	1999
(P)	(P)	(L)	(L)	(L)	(L)	(L)

In the situation shown above you would be safe from 1993 through 1999 because all years after the second year are protected.

Now, suppose you're just starting in the business. At the proper time, you can elect to come under the special presumption, and if your horse operation shows a profit during any two years within the first seven years of its operation, you're safe for the entire seven years. So, at the risk of overexplaining, if you elected to take the special presumption in the first example, you would be safe for the entire period. In the second example you wouldn't need to take a special presumption because your first two years were both profit years.

A word of caution concerning special presumption. Invoking this provision does two things: sends up a red flag at the local IRS office and leaves your business open to audit beyond the normal three-year limit.

There can be overlaps because the seven-year period is a running period and can be any period of seven consecutive years that begins with a profit year and contains at least one other profit year.

One of the most important points to remember with respect to the two-out-of-seven presumption is that it places the burden of proof on the IRS to convince the court that you are not engaged in your horse activities for a profit, rather than vice versa. There's no guarantee your horse operation will be ruled a business if the facts and circumstances dictate otherwise. However, *there is no negative presumption*, so if you don't show a profit in two out of seven years, your horses aren't automatically ruled a hobby rather than a business.

As with other businesses, you are entitled to deduct all ordinary and necessary expenses of breeding, raising, training, and racing your horses. This includes everything from stud fees to labor, veterinary and shoeing costs, and state and local property taxes if you have a farm. Since the cash method of accounting is permitted for a horse operation, expenses are generally deductible in the year they are paid. There are some restrictions on prepaid items, though, mainly if the prepayments are considered to be a deposit toward future expenses or if they materially distort the operation's income picture.

However (aren't you sick of that word?), the amount of losses you are allowed to deduct from your equine activities is limited to the amount you have invested in the business. This is called the "at risk" provision, and it means you can't deduct losses in excess of the amount you have "at risk" in the business.

Not surprisingly, the definition of the amount you have at risk gets pretty complicated, too, but basically includes: (a) the amount of cash you have put into the business, (b) the amount of your *personal* liability on any loans your operation has taken out, and (c) the tax basis of any property contributed to the activity.

A good example of this might be if you were to start out in the business with a five-year installment purchase on a three-year-old filly in training for $100,000. A three-year-old filly falls under property that is depreciable over three years — more about that below — but you've agreed to pay for her in equal installments over five years. You could pay for her and take depreciation on your taxes according to the following schedule:

	Payments on the filly	Depreciation deducted on taxes
Year 1	$ 20,000	$ 25,000[2]
Year 2	$ 20,000	$ 37,500
Year 3	$ 20,000	$ 25,000
Year 4	$ 20,000	$ 12,500
Year 5	$ 20,000	$100,000
	$100,000	

Sounds too good to be true, doesn't it? Well, it is. Under the "at risk" rule, you could only deduct $20,000 a year, plus whatever other losses you have with her in any of the first three years. The

---

[2] Don't even ask right now. I'll explain it below under depreciation.

previous example is very similar to the type of scheme that got the "at risk" rule put into the tax laws in the first place.

One other important form of loss limitation applicable to the horse business did come from the Tax Reform Act of 1986, and it did have a somewhat deleterious effect on the business in that it put a major crimp in the shorts of the people who were doing limited liability partnerships, which will be discussed in the next chapter. The "material participation" provision says you can no longer write off expenses for an endeavor when you don't actively or materially participate in the activities or management of the endeavor. This can also include your participation in a proprietorship, a partnership, or an S corporation.

At any rate, since 1986 you can no longer deduct "passive" losses against salaries; against income from interest, royalties,[3] and dividends; or against profits from your "active" business. In other words, if you do not "materially participate" in your horse business, you can't write off your losses if they are from, say, a limited partnership that owns the horses.

Never one to let us off without complicating matters, the IRS has conveniently provided a list of "facts and circumstances" to define "material participation." Basically, if you spend 500 hours or more on your activity; if you do most of the work yourself; if you do more work than anybody else; if you participate in five out of ten years; or if it's a personal service business, you'll be deemed to "materially participate."

Now here are the final "howevers" for this particular section: (a) you can carry forward "at risk" and "passive" losses to subsequent years and use them when they are allowed, and (b) you can write off "passive" losses against "passive" income.

---

[3] Lord, I'm going to hate this provision when my millions start rolling in from the publication of this book.

Depreciation

A primary benefit of the horse business is that taxpayers are allowed to depreciate (recover the cost) of their horses as an ordinary business expense. Until 1981, horses were required to be depreciated under a fairly complicated "useful life" formula. Under the Economic Recovery Tax Act of 1981, depreciation was simplified, so that horse owners were permitted to depreciate their horses over a three-year period or a five-year period, depending on their use. Another of the minor hits we took from the Tax Reform Act of 1986 was that the latter period was extended, so that now all horses are depreciated over either three or seven years.

The three-year cost recovery period applies to all racehorses more than two years old and breeding horses older than twelve, while the seven-year recovery plan applies to the remainder of the equine population. For several years, there was some consternation and controversy over what was meant by "more than two years old" and "more than twelve," especially in view of the January 1 universal birth date for Thoroughbreds and several other breeds. In February of 1984, the IRS finally got around to defining those two phrases and, of course, they chose the complicated alternative. A horse is "more than two years old," according to the IRS definition, "...after twenty-four months after its actual birth date," and it is "more than twelve" if the horse was foaled more than 144 months and one day prior to being placed into service. So, using the actual foaling date, a horse must be two years and one day old or twelve years and one day old in order to qualify for the three-year depreciation.

Also, because of a thing called the "mid-year convention," the three-year recovery actually extends for four years and the seven-year period takes eight.

The cost recovery schedule for horses is as follows:

	Horses in the 3-year category	Horses in the 7-year category[4]
Year 1	25.0%	10.715%
Year 2	37.5%	19.134%
Year 3	25.0%	15.033%
Year 4	12.5%	12.248%
Year 5		12.248%
Year 6		12.248%
Year 7		12.248%
Year 8		6.128%

Of course, there are a couple of "howevers." Horses you have raised cannot be depreciated if you've already deducted the expenses of raising them, and horses held primarily for sale do not qualify for depreciation. There are also several other alternative forms of depreciation, such as the "half-year" and "mid-quarter" conventions, and alternatives for short tax years and property used outside the United States, but I can already feel you nodding off, so I'll just recommend you discuss this with your accountant.

The first-year depreciation applies to individual horse owners, regardless of the date on which the horse is placed into service. So an individual taxpayer who, for example, bought a horse for $100,000 on December 31, 2000, could take a $25,000 depreciation deduction on it, despite the fact that he's owned the horse for only one day. *However*, and this is *very* important, if the taxpayer is a partnership that was formed in the middle of the year, it must calculate the taxes according to a "short year" and prorate the amount of cost recovery according to the date on which the partnership began business.

You can also depreciate barns, fences, waterers, tractors, cars,

---

[4] Look at the percentages below and then try to tell me it wasn't some government lawyer who worked all this nonsense out to three decimal places.

light-duty trucks, etc. For your interest, I've included a chart of the recovery periods for items normally used in a horse operation.

DEPRECIATION/RECOVERY PERIODS

Type of Property (When Placed in Service)	Recovery Period in Years[5]
• Broodmares or stallions (or stallion shares) if the animal is more than twelve years old	3
• Broodmares or stallions (or stallion shares) if the animal is twelve years old or less	7
• Racehorses more than two years old	3
• Racehorses two years old or less	7
• Show horses, hunters, jumpers, equitation horses, and any other depreciable horse not otherwise specified in the schedule	7
• Cattle, sheep, and other livestock other than horses and hogs	5
• Automobiles and general purpose light-duty trucks (actual unloaded weight of less than 13,000 pounds)	5
• Tractors and other farm machinery and equipment	7
• Horse trailers and vans	5
• Heavy trucks	5
• Fences	7
• Feed and grain bins	7
• Single purpose agricultural structures	10[6]
• Barns, stables, and other nonresidential farm buildings	20
• Office furniture and equipment	7
• Land improvements, such as sidewalks, roads, waterways, drainage facilities, sewers, and landscaping shrubbery	15
• Residential housing	27.5

---

[5] Because of the half-year convention, a three-year item is actually depreciated over four years, a seven-year item over eight years, etc.

[6] One would think that horse barns would qualify as a single purpose agricultural structure, but, as you can see, they don't.

Here are several other points on the subject of depreciation that you should bear in mind:

If a racehorse that is in the process of being depreciated on a three-year schedule is retired for breeding, the remainder of the cost recovery must be converted to a five-year schedule and pro-rated under a fairly complicated formula that is fully explained in *The Horse Owners and Breeders Tax Manual*.

Salvage value is completely eliminated under the current schedules, so all horses and other depreciable assets can be written down to zero.

The cost-recovery schedules outlined above apply to used property, as well as new property.

Capital Gains

As I mentioned at the beginning of the chapter, one of the major benefits of being in the horse business is that in certain instances you can trade straight income for capital gains, which are taxed at a lower overall rate. Under the tax code, if you own a horse for breeding or sporting purposes for more than twenty-four months and then sell it, it will qualify for capital gains treatment, which is taxed at a maximum of twenty percent. Insofar as the Thoroughbred business is concerned, "sporting purposes" is defined as having raced at a public racetrack or having been trained to race at a public racetrack, which qualifies almost everything.

However, if a horse has never been placed into training, it doesn't qualify under the definition of "sporting purposes."

Say, for example, you purchased a weanling filly for $5,000 in October of 1998 but you never put her in training and didn't breed her. Then, her full sister won the Breeders' Cup Filly & Mare Turf on November 4, 2000, and the next day a guy is on your doorstep offering you $500,000 for your filly. You'd have trouble taking capital gains on your profit because she'd never been trained or bred.

If you have partially or totally depreciated a horse and then sell it, before you take capital gains you must "recapture" (pay back) the amount that was depreciated by declaring it as ordinary income. For instance, if you bought a broodmare for $100,000 and held on to her for two years then sold her for $150,000, you'd have a gain of $79,849 ($50,000 actual gain, in addition to which you'd have to recapture the $29,849 of depreciation that you had taken on the mare). The $29,849 that you had depreciated must be treated as ordinary income, however, so you could take capital gains only on the $50,000 in appreciation of the mare.

I don't suppose you'll be surprised to hear that there's another "however" to this portion of the code. Horses that are used "predominantly outside the United States" cannot be depreciated under the normal schedule, but must be depreciated under an alternative depreciation system, which, to put it briefly, is not as beneficial for horses that remain in the good ol' U.S. of A. "Predominantly" is defined as having been outside the United States for more than fifty percent of the time in more than fifty percent of the years in service. To put it another way, if you have a nice filly that you send to race in Europe, say, in mid-June when she's a three-year-old and you keep her there until August of her four-year-old year, you're screwed.

Another twist to this has emerged over the past several years, and it's particularly useful if you're improving your bloodstock holdings. Under certain conditions, you can make a "like kind" exchange without paying taxes on profit in the horse that you have exchanged, or, for that matter, without recapturing the depreciation that you have taken on it. While this is occasionally referred to as a "tax-free" exchange, it is actually a tax-deferred exchange, because somewhere down the road — for example when you sell the horse or horses that you received in the exchange — you're going to have to pay taxes on your profit.

At this time, there's not a lot of case law or regulatory history to fall back on with these like-kind exchanges, but several rules are very clear:

(1) You must have owned the horse for at least twenty-four months prior to the date you dispose of it in order for your horse to be considered as having been used in a trade or business. If not, the IRS will probably try to rule it was held as inventory.

(2) Like kind has also been interpreted as same sex. So, for instance, you can't trade a broodmare or a filly for a stallion or a stallion share. However, you may be able to trade, say, a filly in training for a broodmare, or vice versa, but there is still some uncertainty about that. Also, even though your trade is same sex, you may not be able to trade, say, a Thoroughbred mare for a Quarter Horse mare, etc.

(3) You really don't have to make an actual trade, and the prices don't have to be exactly the same. However, if you do receive money or any non-like-kind property over and above the cost of the property for which you are trading (this is called "boot"), and the boot will be taxed up to the amount of profit that would have been obtained if the horse that you traded had been sold.

(4) You can actually get money for your horse and then spend it later for a "like kind" horse, but there are a number of rules with respect to that, too, notably:

    (A) You must have a written purchase agreement.

    (B) Under the "Starker" rule you can delay your reinvestment for as long as 180 days without losing your tax-deferred status. However, you must identify your prospective replacements within forty-five days from the day you transfer the horse you are trading.

    (C) You should probably only identify three or fewer replacements, and their total value shouldn't exceed twice the value of the horse you sold.

(**D**) You can look at the money you get, but you can't touch it. You must leave the proceeds from your sale in the hands of a "qualified intermediary." (This intermediary must be a "non-agent" and a neutral party, so you can't put the money in your own account, nor can you leave it with your own lawyer or accountant.)[7] The intermediary will help you with all the paperwork necessary for you to document the exchange.

(**E**) You can't exchange horses in the United States for horses that are to remain abroad, even if they are like kind.

Finally, yearlings do not qualify for capital gains, of course, since it is impossible for them to meet the twenty-four-month required holding period, and horses that are held primarily for sale do not qualify no matter how long they are held. This factor comes into play when your horses are considered inventory. For example, if you normally market young horses as two-year-olds in training, they are your inventory and are not eligible for capital gains regardless of time held. On the other hand, if you normally sell yearlings or race homebreds, an occasional two-year-old sale may well qualify as capital gains.

Once again, at the risk of being redundant, probably the best piece of advice that I can give you in this part of the book is to study this chapter very carefully; try to understand it to the best of your abilities, but *do not* try to do your taxes pertaining to the horse business without the help of an accountant — preferably one who has some knowledge and experience with the horse business.

---

[7] This has resulted in a sort of new business of its own. For instance there is a company called Starker Services in California, which specializes in acting as a qualified intermediary on like-kind exchanges. They have very good information on the subject and will be happy to send it to you if you call them at (800) 332-1031.

CHAPTER
EIGHT

WHAT DOES IT COST TO PARTICIPATE?

"Of the two most expensive things in the world, one is a cheap horse..." [1]

— *Arnold's Aphorism #3*

O ne of the most important things to remember in the horse business is the difference between "cheap" and "inexpensive."

According to *Webster's New World Dictionary*, one primary definition of cheap is: "of little value or poor quality; virtually worthless...deserving of scorn; contemptible." Inexpensive is defined: "not expensive; costing relatively little; low-priced."

In horse business vernacular, cheap would define a horse that does not perform or produce well; a useless animal. Over the years, I have seen a lot of people go broke dealing in cheap horses, and I have also seen quite a few make a lot of money dealing in inexpensive ones.

In brief, how much you spend in the horse business is a personal matter.

For example, in 1998, Sarah Jones, who waits on me most morn-

---

[1] This is a whitewashed, sanitized, and censored version of the actual aphorism. If you want a copy of the actual aphorism, which is very pertinent and germane to this chapter and which appears nicely framed on the walls of many horse farms in Central Kentucky, you may drop the author a note at P.O. Box 580, Lexington, KY 40588-0580.

ings at Cracker Barrel, scraped up $1,000 for a small portion in a partnership to pinhook a weanling and resell it as a yearling. The day after the 1999 Keeneland July sales, she sashayed over to my table even more full of piss and vinegar than usual to tell me that the pinhooked weanling had sold for more than $100,000, earning Sarah and her husband a profit of $9,000.

Of course, the pin wasn't the only thing hooked. Today, Sarah and her husband are totally sold on the benefits of being in the horse business.

Another wonderful story is that of "The Lads," a group of ten Irishmen that pooled $5,000 each in 1994, doubled their money in two good years, and broke even in their leanest year. By 1999, the original Lads had expanded to nearly thirty members. At the 1999 Keeneland September sale, they enjoyed several home runs, the largest of which was a Kris S. colt that sold for $900,000 and originally had cost the group $100,000. The group includes a bartender, carpenter, van driver, home builder, insurance agent, pub owner, and other working stiffs in the horse business.

Then, of course, there are the four Maktoum brothers, sheikhs from Dubai who I would estimate have spent well more than a billion (that's billion with a **B**) dollars in the horse business since they first exploded on the U.S. scene in 1981.

Bob and Beverly Lewis have spent tens of millions on yearlings alone, but have had great success by any standard on the racetrack. Some of their top yearling purchases have included champions Serena's Song, the all-time money-earning female, and Timber Country, whom they owned in partnership with W. T. Young and Graham Beck.

With a smaller investment, Mike Pegram has had similar fortune, winning the Kentucky Derby and Preakness Stakes with the bargain-priced Real Quiet and enjoying two championship seasons with the filly Silverbulletday.

227

The point is you don't have to be a multimillionaire to be a success or to have fun in the horse business. But it certainly doesn't hurt.

Unlike investing in stocks, bonds, or commodities, the cost of a Thoroughbred doesn't end with the purchase price. Usually it's only the beginning. Care and maintenance can prove far more costly than what you paid for your horse, particularly with a low-priced one. For instance, keeping a horse in training in New York or California with a top trainer can easily run as high as $40,000 to $50,000 a year. On the other hand, in some areas of the United States where racing is conducted on a more modest scale, costs can run as low as $10,000 or $12,000 per year. Obviously, your horse won't get the same care and attention for $10,000 as he would for $50,000, nor will the trainer have the same ability. In keeping with the disparity in costs, earning opportunities for your horse will be substantially less at the smaller tracks. Training fees also vary widely even at the same track depending on the reputation and success of the particular trainer you choose and the quality of care he gives your horse. In either case, you normally get what you pay for, which reminds me of an old story:

A novice in the Thoroughbred business bought two broodmares and decided he wanted to breed them to a couple of nice stallions in Kentucky. He came to Lexington to find a place to board his mares until they were bred and in foal. His first stop was at one of the more prominent farms, an outfit with an excellent reputation. After setting up an appointment with the manager and discussing a breeding arrangement with him, he inquired about the price of boarding a broodmare. "The price of boarding here is $25 per day per mare," the manager informed him, "and you get the manure."

Now, our novice thought the price was a little high and wondered what in the world he would do with the manure, so he decided to check out another farm in the area to compare prices. He went to a farm that had a reputation for being very competent, although not as awesome as the first place. He found the manager, who showed him around and then told him, "Our rate for seasonal boarders is $23 a day, and you get the manure." Well, this upset our novice because the price was still about fifty percent more than what it cost to board a mare in his home state, and he still didn't have any use for the manure.

After thinking about the situation for a couple of hours, the novice decided that the manure must have some sort of special value since the board prices were so exorbitant. However, being from a state so far from Kentucky, he really had no use for manure and decided to check out one more farm.

While drinking a cup of coffee in a local restaurant, our novice met a stranger who told him about a place on the edge of the horse farm country where he would find the board rates much more to his liking than the rates at "those fancy places."

This was significantly more appealing to our novice. He headed off to find the farm, which turned out to be a little more difficult than he anticipated, but after locating a rusty, dented mailbox, he turned up a gravel road full of potholes and eventually made his way to a trailer. He asked the guy sitting on the deck drinking cof-

Boarding costs can vary, but it's best not to scrimp.

fee about the board rates. "Thirteen dollars a day," the man said without taking his cowboy boots off the railing as he went back to reading his *Racing Form*.

Naturally, the board rate was much more appealing than those he had been quoted previously. However, the manure that had been mentioned at the other farms stuck in his mind, so our neophyte thought he should ask about it.

In response, the man on the deck carefully folded his *Racing Form* and set it aside. He leaned down and looked at the stranger. "Mister," he responded, "at $13 dollars a day, there ain't any."

In Chapter 2, I suggested spending a few days with your potential trainer, not only to determine your compatibility, but to satisfy yourself that his operation will provide your horses with the best opportunity to fulfill their potential as athletes. The same thing applies to the farm where you want to board your mares and foals.

An article that appeared some years ago in the *Wall Street Journal* suggested that if you're interested in buying a store, the only legitimate way to determine its sales is not by looking over the records and ledgers, which could be altered, but rather by spending time standing at the checkout counter watching the operation firsthand — a minimum of seven days, but preferably much longer.

If you are going to invest money in the horse business — where, in many cases, your investment will exceed the purchase price of a small retail establishment — I can't urge you strongly enough to spend the same time and effort to insure that your business investment is in good hands!

Comparative Costs

To help me compare costs, the Thoroughbred Owners and Breeders Association contacted its state and local affiliate trainers' and breeders' organizations in New York, Kentucky, Florida, and California for the information. Keep in mind that the basic board and training costs of care and maintenance do not include any allowances for blacksmith, veterinary, or vanning expenses, and do not include insurance, all of which you can expect to incur. Blacksmith charges vary from area to area and farm to farm. Normal veterinary costs vary even more depending on the herd health program at a particular farm, including vaccination, deworming, and frequency of pregnancy checks (including use of ultrasound).

Average Per Diem Costs For Care and Maintenance
(Vary widely from area to area, farm
to farm, track to track, etc.)

Category	NY	CA	KY	FL
Turned-out year-round boarders	$20	$16	$21	$16
Breeding season boarders	$24	$18	$21	$18
Additional for foal	$4	$2	$2	$2
Foaling fees *(for non-permanent boarders)*	$250	$200	$225	$245
Stallions *(plus breeding rights)*	$50	$28	$50	$35
Sales preparation *(plus 5% commission)*	$25	$22	$30	$20
Breaking yearlings/ two-year-olds *(per day)*	$30	$35	$33	$45
Training costs *(plus 10% of purses)*				
Large tracks	$85	$80	$65	$50
Small tracks	$40	$60	$40	$35
Lay-up costs *(for stall care, blister, fire, swim, etc.)*	$25	$30	$29	$28
Private paddock turn-out *(for racehorse lay-ups)*	$15	$20	$34	$28
Mortality Insurance *(breeding stock)*	3.5–4.5%[1]	3.5-4.5%	3.5-4.5%	3.5-4.5%
Mortality Insurance *(racing stock)*	4-6%[2]	4-6%	4-6%	4-6%
Vet, medication, and shoeing *(Breeding Stock annually)*	$2,000	$1,500	$1,700	$700
Vet, medication, and shoeing *(Racing Stock annually)*	$4,000	$7,500	$5,700	$5,000

---

[1] Varies with age, etc.

[2] Varies with age, quality of horse, etc.

In reviewing the table of costs for care and maintenance, a number of observations and explanations may be helpful.

If you start out in the breeding business, your basic costs will be determined by the board rate for turned-out year-round boarders at the farm where you keep your mare. This is the basic charge for care and maintenance of your mare, and the rate will normally reflect the quality of care and feed your horse gets.

Commercial breeding farms prefer year-round boarders because they provide steady cash flow, which allows the size of the farm's work force to remain constant and because year-round boarders give a farm more control over exposure to disease. In addition, a farm crew more familiar with an individual mare can help her conception rate and her overall care. Believe it or not, horses are like people — they form a society within their group or herd. There will be a "boss" and a "pecking order," friends and enemies, likes and dislikes. The horses will establish which one gets to eat first, which one gets brought to the barn first, which one gets to drink first — all within their own little group, and the group's stability tends to be reflected in each mare's happiness and outlook on life. There is less work with the mares during the summer and fall when the breeding season is over, and with the grass lush, feeding requirements and care are reduced. For these reasons, year-round boarders get a lower rate.

For breeding-season boarders the rate will be higher for the same reasons that the rate on year-round boarders is lower. If you select a stallion that stands in another area, you will have to find a breeding farm that accepts seasonal boarders. Your rate may include a nominal charge for her foal. It's not that the foal eats much, but the additional handling and health care at a well-run farm require much more time and attention to detail than is required for a mare without a foal at her side. If you send your mare to the boarding farm before she foals, you also will probably incur a foaling fee.

Don't scrimp on that! The most critical time of year for your mare and her foal is just before, during, and after foaling. So many things can go wrong at foaling that any fee you pay an experienced foaling crew could be among the best money you ever spent in the horse business. If you keep your mare "at home" and do not have a night watchman, by all means send her to foal somewhere that does. When a mare gets in trouble foaling, things happen very fast, so checking on her every hour or two won't save your mare if she gets in trouble five minutes after you get back in bed.

Be careful of farms that are overloaded with horses. A number of commercial boarding farms have a tendency to load up on breeding-season boarders, which results in overcrowding during the peak season. This can lead to less care and, more importantly, additional exposure to disease. One primary cause of disease in horses is overcrowding. Exposure to horses that are on different health programs, have different immunities, and come from different areas of the country can introduce new and potentially dangerous diseases. This is why some of the better commercial farms will not accept seasonal boarders, or if they do, they might maintain an entirely separate farm for them.

As mentioned in Chapter 5, most mares sent to Kentucky to be bred are not quartered at the same farm as the stallion but at one of the many commercial boarding farms in the area. Make sure that you're satisfied with that farm prior to sending your mare there. Keep in mind that a good reputation takes time to build, and a farm with a good reputation may well be worth the higher rate it charges to take care of your prize mare.

Standing a Stallion

Standing a stallion is a separate and distinct business from boarding mares. It requires specialized facilities, plus a qualified, experienced crew. Whether a farm stands one stallion or ten, a competent stallion man and breeding shed crew are vital. The physical breeding of Thoroughbreds is an intricate operation that can be dangerous both to the horse and the handler if done incorrectly.

Standing a stallion includes not only the physical breeding operation but requires extensive personal contacts, advertising, and public relations on the part of the stallion manager and the farm owner. More organization and a larger staff on the farm are vital to handle the necessary paperwork and public relations required to "make" a stallion.

In addition to the daily board rate, which barely covers the basic cost of caring for the stallion, farms that specialize in standing stallions receive free annual breeding rights. Taking the stallion to the breeding shed every day, showing the stallion, and the attendant promotional duties are all extra work. The reward is the breeding rights. These breeding rights are the farm's commission, much the same as the ten percent trainers receive for winning races and the five percent bloodstock agents get for buying and selling blood-

Standing a stallion requires more than basic care.

stock. Without these breeding rights, the incentive to stand a stallion would be minimal. On the other hand, if a stallion is a success, these breeding rights can be very valuable!

A word of caution: I included a brief discussion of making a stallion in Chapter 5, but as the television programs say when some idiot is trying to jump the Grand Canyon on a tricycle: Do not try this at home. To make a stallion takes at least four years, from retirement to "proof of the pudding." By that time you may have all your eggs in one basket, and the basket may turn out to have a hole in it. As a rule of thumb, one out of ten stallions will be successful, two will be average, and the other seven probably will fail commercially. What happens if the stallion's first foals can't outrun a fat man? By then you'll have a crop of two-year-olds, a crop of yearlings, a crop of weanlings, and a bunch of pregnant mares coming behind the first unsuccessful crop.

Once you start trying to make a stallion, the tendency is to think of the seasons you are using to him as being free — particularly if he is a horse you raced yourself — but, most assuredly, they aren't free. You may pay dearly for them, especially if your mare does not match the stallion either physically or by pedigree, but you breed her to him anyway. After you've been in the horse business for a few years and if you're lucky enough to have a racehorse good enough to retire to stud, keep an interest in him if you like, but send him to a farm that specializes in standing stallions. Sell the major portion of him and hope for the best. You never go broke taking a profit. If the stallion is successful because of the mares the other shareholders sent to him, you will have benefited from the stallion's substantial appreciation and earned the goodwill of happy customers who may well be interested in your next offering.

Sales Costs
Sales preparation is another specialized area of the business.

Prices for these services vary widely, as do techniques. Doing justice to sales preparation at home "after work" is impossible. Proper sales preparation not only includes having the horse in good flesh with a sleek coat, but includes teaching the individual to walk smartly and set up properly for showing. Like stallion managers, sales agents have spent many years developing a good reputation with buyers, as well as sellers, and those buyers often rely on the agents to pare down their large consignments to horses that fit the buyers' tastes. Many a yearling or weanling that would have been overlooked otherwise has been sold because an alert sales agent directed a buyer in its direction. As discussed in Chapter 6, a horse that has been properly prepared for sale will bring considerably more. There are as many different techniques used in sales preparation as there are sales agents. Once again, though, I urge that you investigate your sales agent, his reputation, and his operation before you commit.

The time involved in sales preparation varies from a couple of weeks to thirty days for broodmares and ninety days or longer for yearlings. During that time they are kept in individual stalls, groomed daily, and taught their manners. Young horses are exercised to more fully develop the physique. Properly done, these techniques can add many dollars to the auction price of your horse.

Your agent at the sale will normally get up to a five percent commission on the final bid, which is the real profit for him. (In addition, sales companies charge up to five percent commission to the consignor.) Like the per diem for a horse at the track or on the farm, these charges will barely cover the costs of bringing that horse up to the sale, if that.

Cost of Breaking and Training

Whether you race homebreds or buy yearlings at auction, the location of your yearling's initial education is one of the most critical decisions you'll make. The young horse being gentled is like a child going to school — it requires patience, knowledge, and experience, not necessarily in that order. An equal amount of all three is preferable, with perhaps the emphasis on patience. More than one potentially good horse has been ruined by lack of patience and judgment early in the education process. Bad habits once learned by a horse are almost impossible to break. Like children, young horses can become unruly and rebellious at the first opportunity to do so. Training young horses is properly done at a farm or training center and not at the racetrack. The racetrack is designed and built for racing fully trained athletes — or at least ones that are almost ready to run. Don't let anybody sell you on breaking at the racetrack. The only reason to break yearlings at the racetrack is that the trainer needs the per diem, in which case you don't need him.

Once your two-year-old is ready for racing, you enter into the most thrilling (and expensive) part of being in the horse business. Your horse has been educated to the point where he is ready for final training to reach his ultimate goal of winning races. At this point he requires more attention and more work, and, as a result, he costs more money, but you now have the potential to get a return on your investment.

Training costs vary widely depending upon region, size of track, etc. I would like to reiterate, though, that a daily training rate that is significantly lower than that which is charged by other trainers at the same track almost always means your horse will get a lower quality of feed and care than he would at the prevailing rate, whether that is $40 a day at a small rural track or $80 a day at a major metropolitan track. A trainer who has one groom rubbing three horses and is paying top wages obviously must charge more per horse per day than a trainer who is using a glorified stall cleaner to give superficial attention to six or eight horses. The major portion of a trainer's daily fee goes into direct costs such as labor, grain, hay, bedding, tack, and equipment. The profit for a trainer comes from his ten percent share of purse money rather than from the per diem.

Trainers can be roughly compared to coaches in the human athletic field. As you well know, coaches and managers come and go depending upon the success or failure of their charges. The same is true with trainers. Good horses make good trainers, just

A good trainer helps a horse realize its potential.

like good athletes make good coaches and managers. My definition of a "great" trainer is one who consistently moves up horses in class. There are very few of them. A "good" trainer is one who takes good care of his horses and gives them the opportunity to perform to their potential. If you find a trainer who does that, you will do well to hire him and stick with him through thick and through thin.

If you remain in the horse business any length of time, you will experience lay-ups. Horses are athletes, and they injure themselves in competition, particularly the good ones. The ones that don't are too slow to get hurt or they are the ones that don't try. When you consider the size of horses' legs and the speed at which

Labor is included in the trainer's daily fee.

they run, you have to be amazed that they do not cripple themselves more frequently. Laying up a horse obviously costs less than actual training, but not a great deal less. During lay-up a horse will often require extra veterinary care and stall rest, plus swimming for rehabilitation. A lot of time, effort, and skill are required in such care. After the initial stall care and attention, the horse may be turned out in a private paddock for some weeks or months at a lower rate before commencing his comeback. Normally, farms that do a good job of breaking horses will do a good job on lay-ups.

Cost of Insurance

Insurance in the horse business has changed a lot in the past four or five years. Up until the late '70s, Lloyd's of London was just about the only underwriter of mortality insurance on horses. Because of the large sums that are involved with Thoroughbreds, Lloyd's, with its syndicated underwriting abilities, was most able to cope with the large risk exposure. The rates were inflexible and, as happens in many industries where a monopoly or semi-monopoly exists, enterprising companies saw a profit opportunity in the horse mortality insurance business and jumped in. The result is that now a number of major underwriters offer varying, competitive rates on all types of insurance for horses. These rates vary depending on the age, use, location, and quality of your horse. For instance, a championship-quality horse might get insurance at a lower rate than another horse because the insurance company wants to be able to promote that it insures him. In addition to those rates, you might be able to obtain quantity discounts, experience discounts, and experience refunds available to the larger owners.

Live-foal insurance is also available at costs that vary widely depending on the status of the mare and the length of time she has been in foal. For instance, if you purchase a no-guarantee season you can obtain insurance that your mare will both conceive and produce a live foal. But it is very expensive: twenty-seven to thirty-three percent of the stud fee for a mare of average age and produce record, higher for older mares or mares with marginal produce records. If your mare is of average age and is pronounced in foal forty-two days after breeding, you can obtain live-foal insurance for about twelve percent, or if you buy a mare in foal at the November breeding stock sale, live-foal insurance can run as little as eight percent to ten percent. Basically, it depends on her age, status, breeding record, etc.

The only caution I would offer in buying insurance is to investigate the company's financial soundness and its track record in paying claims. As in other forms of insurance, the promise on the policy is easy to make, but the payoff in time of disaster is not necessarily so easy to collect.

Veterinary Charges

With year-round racing and the increasing advances in veterinary science, medication and veterinary charges have assumed an ever-larger portion of the costs involved in the horse business. Some trainers rely on veterinarians more than others, both for advice and routine treatments. Vitamin injections, routine fluid therapy, bleeder medication, Bute, X-rays, and "scoping" (optical examination of a horse's airways and lungs) have become high-priced, routine practices at the racetracks.

Most major breeding farms will have your mare palpated and checked through ultrasound periodically to get an accurate idea whether she's pregnant and, very importantly, whether she is holding her pregnancy. This makes it difficult to average out veterinary and blacksmith charges and, like many of the other costs in the table on page 242, the numbers I've used are subject to a great deal of variation depending on the location and quality of the operation.

Costs of Owning a Broodmare

If you decide to invest in Thoroughbreds via breeding, you probably will start out by buying a pregnant broodmare at one of the major breeding stock sales held during the fall or winter. With your advisor, you will pore over the catalogue pages representing pedigrees of thousands of broodmares, looking for your diamond in the rough. The average price of broodmares in 2000 was $56,674, which is ninety-seven percent higher than it was in 1984, so I'll just use that price in my example for the cost of purchasing a mare. Since more mares are sold and reside in Kentucky than anywhere else in the world, I've just used figures from there, but you can project your local daily costs. Other variables will be transportation costs (how far from the sale is your boarding facility) and insurance rates (company and type of coverage). Also, some states charge sales tax on horses purchased at public auction.

So, let's just run through a hypothetical purchase of an "average" mare:

Investment Costs

$56,674	Purchase price
2,833	5% agent's fee
$59,507	Total

Operating Expenses For Mare
(first year, assuming purchase at November sales)

$2,267	Mortality insurance @ 4%
75	Transportation to farm
945	Board (forty-five days)
210	Vet/blacksmith (forty-five days)
$3,497	Total operating expenses
$63,004	Total first-year cash outlay

The operating expenses, plus the capital investment, will be your total cash outlay the first year. The taxable deduction for that year will be your operating expenses (including the agent's fee), plus your deduction for depreciation. Depreciation (discussed in Chapter 7) will vary depending on the age of the mare at the time of purchase. Even at the lowest possible deduction (10.715 percent the first year for young mares), the size of the deduction is significant. For a $56,674 mare under the age of twelve, the depreciation comes to $6,072.62 so you'll have a total deduction of $12,402.62.

Your first year of ownership does not include a stud fee since the normal stallion contract, even with a live-foal guarantee, calls for payment of stud fee and cancellation of live-foal guarantee when a mare is sold. When you buy your in-foal mare at auction, the stud fee is already paid, and you get the stallion service certificate, but there is no live-foal guarantee. (As mentioned above, you can get live-foal insurance in the range of eight percent to ten percent for a mare that is in foal in November. Of course, the premium for that insurance will be deductible as well, but for the sake of this example I am going to assume that you opt not to buy it at this time.) The sales company delivers the stallion service certificate to you as the new owner, along with the mare's registration certificate.

Operating Expenses for Mare (second year)

$7,665	Board (365 days)
1,700	Blacksmith and vet charges
2,267	Insurance
16,500	Stud fee (see below)
1,500	Miscellaneous (see below)
$29,632	Total operating expenses

The second-year cash expense of keeping your mare will be likely to include a stud fee. This is because stud fees on many stallions are due in September or October of the year bred, even if there is a live-foal guarantee. For the purpose of this example, I have used thirty percent of the mare's purchase price as the amount of the stud fee. As a rule of thumb, if you get outside a range of one-quarter to one-third of the value of your broodmare for your stud fee, you are probably over- or under-breeding her, and you may be disappointed in the auction price you receive for the resulting foal.

In the likely event that you send your mare away from her regular farm to be bred, you may have to add transportation, a foaling fee, and some additional costs for the differential in seasonal boarder rates, so I have put in a cushion under miscellaneous expenses.

Your depreciation on the mare will be 19.134 percent ($10,844) in the second year, which somewhat makes up for your only being able to take ten percent in the first year, and the IRS has ruled that stud fees are deductible as an ordinary and necessary business expense, so your total tax deduction for the mare in the second year will be $40,476.

Costs of Getting Your Yearling to the Sales

In the fall, your first foal will be weaned from his dam, and at that time will go on the payroll in earnest. Prior to weaning, the periodic work — vaccinations, trimming, etc. — were the only items on the foal's bill since the costs of keeping the mare include the board costs of her foal at most farms. From weaning to sale time, however, the youngster becomes a separate entity with separate boarding and care costs, which should look something like this:

Mare Expenses to Weaning Time

$7,665	Board (approx. one year)
1,700	Blacksmith and vet charges
2,200	Insurance
1,500	Misc. (transportation, etc.)
$13,065	Total

Operating Expenses for Weanling

$1,890	Board (ninety days)
250	Blacksmith and vet charges
$2,140	Total

Operating Expenses for Yearling

$3,780	Board (180 days)
750	Blacksmith and vet charges
1,800	Sales prep (sixty days)
75	Transportation to sale
1,000	Sales entry fee
2,750	5% sales company commission
2,750	5% agent fee
$12,905	Total

To summarize, the total operating expenses of getting your first yearling to the sale should approximate the following summary:

CHAPTER EIGHT

$13,065	Broodmare expenses to weaning
2,140	Weanling expenses
12,905	Yearling expenses
$28,110	Subtotal of actual expenditures
5,893	First-year depreciation on mare
$34,003	Capital outlay of getting yearling to sale

NOTE: Based on experience, I have made several assumptions in the calculations above that you can easily alter to more closely approximate your situation. For instance, in the weanling and yearling expenses, I have assumed veterinary and farrier charges slightly in excess of a strict proration of the average to account for corrective shoeing, etc. I have assumed no insurance is carried on the weanling or yearling since the investment was made in the mare, and she is, so to speak, the factory that produces the foals. Weanlings and yearlings, like children, will find a way to get hurt, but only in rare cases is the injury fatal. Since insurance is for mortality, not for fitness of purpose, justifying the expense of insurance is difficult unless some mitigating circumstance, such as success of a close relative, has suddenly escalated the potential value of your sales candidate. Many breeders will insure their weanlings and yearlings for the amount of the stud fee to protect themselves at least for that direct cash outlay should something dire happen.

In calculating sales costs, I have assumed that an average mare will probably have an average yearling, which would sell for about $55,000 these days.

Although depreciation of your mare is a legitimate tax deduction, the normal course of events in the horse business would certainly suggest that your young mare is not going to depreciate in price nearly as rapidly as the tax code allows. With luck and good mare selection, you actually can anticipate appreciation of value rather than depreciation! This cost therefore is primarily a tax deduction and not necessarily a true cost of production.

Adding one year of broodmare expense to the cost of producing a yearling is not totally accurate because, as discussed in Chapter 5, every so often your mare will probably fall off the calendar and her costs for that year will have to be prorated among her productive years or "eaten" the year she fails to produce a foal. A home-bred yearling has no depreciation deduction since all costs pertaining to raising him are deducted as operating expenses. Keep in mind, too, that there is no stud fee the first year, but this will be an added expense in future years. On the other hand, what you are anticipating is that your mare will be eminently successful and that future foals will be more and more valuable, based on success of her first foals.

In the mid-'80s, John Finney, who was then the president of Fasig-Tipton Company, made the following observations, which, to my way of thinking, are as true today as they were when he made them:

"The breeding business has changed in the last couple of years. Racing has always been the riskier part of Thoroughbred investment. In a successful stable of six racehorses, three will lose money, two will break even, and, hopefully, one will hit a home run and make the stable a paying proposition.

"In the '70s and early '80s, the bloodstock market was so strong that almost every broodmare purchased resulted in a profit for its owners through selling her foals at yearling sales. Not so today, however, with a leveling off of demand and an oversupply of year-lings drawing much more selectiveness by purchasers. Today a breeder needs some home runs, too, to make up for the inevitable crooked yearling that ends up losing money for the breeder."

The only quarrel I have with John Finney's assessment of the market was that he said "inevitable crooked yearling" in the singular and not the plural. Also, John was discussing the market prior to the days when sales contained 3,000 to 4,000 lots, with as many as forty by the same sire. Nowadays, a yearling by a popular sire needs to be more "perfect" than ever before in the history of the business.

As we enter another shakeout period in the Thoroughbred market, a good advisor is all the more important.

When you review the costs of getting a yearling to market, keep in mind that most of them are fixed. Whether the mare and her foal are worth $10,000 or $1 million, the only varying factors are depreciation, insurance, and stud fee! It's much better to own a piece of a good horse than all of a bad one.

Costs of Raising a Homebred

Raising a homebred can be the most rewarding and fun course of all for an investor who is financially and emotionally suited to that endeavor. Unquestionably, the most suitable environment for a youngster is where he can romp and play with his contemporaries in the field during the formative months of his life.

While the practice has been curtailed somewhat, hot-housing — putting a sales yearling in a stall, force-feeding him, and curtailing his exercise for three months — during this important growth stage, in my opinion, is the equine equivalent of trying to develop your son into a star athlete by making him eat nothing but Twinkies, drink nothing but Coke, and do nothing but sit in front of a TV set for six months before he tries out for the team. Neither method is particularly logical and, in fact, is singularly counterproductive in the ultimate scheme of things. End of diatribe!

Because you're not doing sales prep, the costs of raising a homebred yearling are significantly different than raising a sales yearling:

$6,300	Board (300 days)
2,145	Gentling (sixty-five days)
2,125	Blacksmith and vet charges
$10,570	Total

Again, as before, it has been necessary to make a few assumptions. I will assume yearlings that are not going to the sales are not broken until November — and sometimes, depending on their maturity, even later. I'm not an advocate of early two-year-old racing (veterinary studies have shown it's not cost effective in the long run). Therefore, I will assume that you'll allow your yearling adequate time to grow. As a matter of fact, like many homebreds, we'll assume that his early education is done while he is still turned out in his paddock most of the time.

The operating costs of keeping the mare and weanling must be added to the costs of raising the homebred yearling to determine the total investment in him at the start of his two-year-old year.

$13,065	Broodmare expenses to weaning
2,140	Weanling expenses
<u>10,570</u>	Yearling expenses
$25,775	Subtotal (operating expense)
<u>5,893</u>	First year depreciation on mare
$31,668	Total

To this figure you must add the expenses of continuing the breaking process and the final training. Those expenses can vary considerably depending on how much of his two-year-old year is spent at a training center and how much of it is spent at the track. Assuming six months on the farm or at a training center and six months at a major track, the following figures would apply:

$5,940	180 days @ farm/training center
12,025	185 days @ track
500	Transportation charges
<u>3,000</u>	Veterinary/blacksmith charges
$21,465	Total of additional expenses

These costs do not include insurance, which you may want to

add, particularly if your two-year-old is showing great promise. Insurance rates on racehorses are higher than on breeding stock because the mortality risk is higher. Remember, you can insure yourself into the poor house. The rule here applies as elsewhere — insure against any loss (or portion of loss) you can't comfortably absorb and continue your operation.

Other costs not included are nomination and sustaining fees for futurities and stakes, pony fees, jockey's fees, and the trainer's and jockey's ten percent share of winnings. You hope there will be a lot of the latter charges because it means your horse is running and winning, but there is no way to project them.

Buying a Yearling and Racing Him

One final cost projection involves buying a yearling to race. As with a broodmare purchase, you and your advisor will pore over the pedigrees of thousands of yearlings offered at public auction, looking for the proverbial needle in the haystack.

As I mentioned in Chapter 1, the needles are there; finding them is the challenge that makes this such an exciting game. As before, I'm going to assume that you purchase an average yearling, which in 2000 was $54,506, rounded to $55,000.

Costs of Buying a Yearling to Race

$55,000	Cost of the yearling
2,750	5% commission to agent
$57,750	Total

Operating Expenses

$1,260	Sixty days turned out
1,650	Fifty days education
2,750	Insurance (5%)
150	Transportation
750	Veterinary/blacksmith charges
$6,560	Total

Total Cash Outlay in Buying a Yearling to Race

$57,750	Capital investment
6,560	Expenses as a yearling
<u>21,465</u>	Two-year-old expenses (same as a homebred)
$85,775	Subtotal of actual expenditures

Tax Deductions

Yearling Year

$9,310	Operating expenses and commission
<u>5,893.25</u>	Depreciation (seven-year basis)
$15,203.25	Total

Two-Year-Old Year

$21,465	Operating expenses
<u>13,750</u>	Depreciation (three-year basis)
$35,215	Total

Total

$9,310	Operating expenses (yearling)
21,465	Operating expenses (two-year-old)
<u>19,643.25</u>	Depreciation (three-year basis)
$50,418.25	Total

You can see that of the $85,775 investment, almost sixty percent is deductible on your taxes during the first two years of operation, and I haven't included insurance during the second year because by the time your insurance renewal comes around in September, your investment may well be worth a million dollars, or may not be worth insuring at all.

At the risk of boring you further, I just want to reiterate the main points of this chapter, i.e.: Whatever type of investment you choose — a broodmare, yearling, or raising homebreds — be absolutely sure it fits your temperament and your pocketbook.

Quality is your best investment, in advisors, in bloodstock, and in facilities; AND it is far better to own a small part of a good horse than all of a bad one.

CHAPTER
NINE

STRETCHING YOUR INVESTMENT

"It is better to own part of a good horse than it is to own all of a bad one."

— *A.K., Successful Thoroughbred Investment*

I n the past twenty years, Thoroughbred racing and breeding have become substantially more expensive, especially at the top of the market where the percentage for making a profit is also higher.

Those committed to the industry realize if they can't go in at the high end by themselves, they need partners for additional capital. This has opened up investment opportunities for newcomers at the top of the market (which is where you should strive to be; within your means, of course).

Following the horse industry's disastrous foray into the realm of public investment during the '80s, both the investment community and the Thoroughbred business have decided, wisely, I believe, to leave each other alone for a while.

The fact is that neither business understood the other. It's no wonder because the horse business is essentially a game for dreamers, while the investment community has traditionally comprised bottom-line guys — at least it did until the dot-com craze took over the stock market a few years ago.

The innate incompatibility between the hard-nosed number

crunchers, who need to see a profit on a quarterly basis, much less an annual one, and the Thoroughbred business, where the goal is to hang on for a year or two until you hit a home run, was exacerbated by the many public and semi-public offerings that hit an unsuspecting public just about the time the horse business began to turn south.

The results were awful. Many people who had been in the horse business their entire lives went to the cleaners, as did the investors who were only in it for the money and glamour. I strongly believe the presence of those investors exacerbated the "crash" of the mid-'80s. Because they had no real interest in horses and because they had no real interest in the game, they were the first to bail out, and bail they did…in droves. And sue they did in droves. And foreclose they did in droves.

It was a very rough time, but those who were committed to the horse business stuck it out and emerged stronger in the end. And I, for one, don't miss those who are gone for a minute .

Multiple ownership is really nothing new to the horse business. While most people who are involved with Thoroughbreds will tell you that the concept of syndication was developed in our business in the early '50s, *The Thoroughbred Record* reported the first $100,000 syndication in history in its issue of October 19, 1898, when the three-year-old Standardbred Axtell was purchased by a syndicate for $105,000. And, if the whole truth were known, the ancient Romans probably formed syndicates to purchase their favorite teams for the chariot races held at the Coliseum.

What has changed and brought more attention to syndication in the past three or four decades is the level of sophistication and the size of the numbers contained in the deals. Still, to aggravate you with one more repetition, the basic reason for multiple ownership is pretty much the same as it was in the Roman days, i.e., it is better to own part of a good horse than it is to own all of a bad one.

There are variations and elaborations on that theme, which will be discussed in this chapter, but that's it in a nutshell.

Before proceeding, once again I would like to admonish you to consult with your lawyer and/or accountant before going into any sort of multiple ownership deal. Today's trend toward consumer protectionism in many businesses — e.g., cars, real estate, securities, etc. — has turned almost everything you do into a pain in the butt insofar as paperwork and disclosure are concerned...but it's not all a bad thing. The trend hasn't really hit the horse business yet, and, at the risk of angering a lot of my friends, the horse business still has an element of larceny left over that could warrant some oversight.

Anyway, once again, before you do anything in the business, check it out with a lawyer and/or accountant.

Pros and Cons of Multiple Ownership

As with everything else in this world, multiple ownership has certain advantages and disadvantages, but since the concept has stood the test of time, one is forced to conclude that the advantages outweigh the disadvantages. Probably the best way to discuss them is to put them into historical perspective, beginning with the stallion syndications that became a factor in the business in the '50s.

The syndication of a stallion, which gives each shareholder (a syndicate is usually made up of forty shares) one breeding right to a stallion every year for the length of his stud career, is the most popular, and obvious, example of multiple ownership in the horse business.

When Leslie Combs II put together the first million-dollar syndicate in history to buy Nashua for $1,251,200 in 1955, stallion syndication was already accepted in the horse business, and all participants benefited — the horse's owner (in this case the owner was the estate of William Woodward Jr., but the same advantages applied), the syndicator, the people who bought shares (undivided interests) in the horse, and the horse itself.

Even in those days, the owner benefited by sharing the risks and expenses of keeping the horse. Keeping a million-dollar horse was a large risk back in 1955. Since the syndicate manager planned to advertise the horse heavily, the expenses of standing him at stud were greater than they would be if he stood privately, so prorating the expenses among all the share owners really made sense. Further, the syndication of the horse raised the maximum amount of capital. Because he was being sold as a stallion prospect, he brought top dollar at the time.

If the seller had not been an estate, syndicating would have allowed the stable that raced the horse to retain a percentage of ownership rather than having to sell the horse outright. The horse,

Leslie Combs and Nashua, whom he syndicated for $1,251,200.

undoubtedly, would have continued to race in the colors of his original owner, which is the way most of them do today. That way, the original owner could have participated in the appreciation of the horse as a breeding animal following his racing career.

For the syndicator (usually a farm), it offered an opportunity to obtain breeding rights to a stallion the farm might not otherwise have been able to afford. In addition to a nominal fee for board, the farm where the stallion stands usually gets a number of annual breeding rights. The farm can sell those rights or use them to breed its own mares. Whichever it decides to do, those breeding rights are a great incentive for the farm or syndicate manager to do his best to ensure the stallion does as well as possible at stud. Standing a stallion helps promote the farm because every ad for the stallion carries the farm's name. Furthermore, the ad is paid for by the syndicate members.

For the breeder who had some mares but not a really big operation, the syndication was a boon because he was ensured access to a top horse no matter how difficult getting seasons became or how expensive those seasons ran if the stallion became successful. Also, the mare owner didn't have to put all his eggs in one basket; that is, he didn't have to breed all his mares to one stallion, as he might have done if he owned his own stallion. Finally, it gave the breeder the opportunity to participate in the appreciation of a stallion if the horse were a success at stud.

All of this wound up working to the advantage of the horse. First, since his original owners (or anybody, for that matter) didn't have enough top-quality mares to fill his book — and as mentioned in Chapter 5, I feel very strongly that the success of a stallion is probably seventy-five percent to eighty percent dependent on the mares to which he's bred — syndication worked to the benefit of the stallion by improving his book of mares and thereby improving his chances for success at stud. Also, rather than having one owner going around saying what a good horse he was, the stallion would have thirty or more owners promoting him, because each was promoting his or her own interest in the horse.

By 1973, the total yearling crop sold at auction averaged over $10,000 for the first time in history, and the Keeneland July sale average topped $50,000 for the first time (remember, it's more than twelve times that today), despite the fact that the average earnings per runner in North America that year was only $4,263, hardly a sure way of recouping your investment. That year, Jim Scully, a Lexington, Kentucky, bloodstock agent, paid a world-record price of $600,000 for a bay colt by Bold Ruler—Iskra, by Le Haar. After he had signed the sale slip, Scully revealed that he'd purchased the yearling on behalf of a syndicate consisting of himself and six others and that the syndicate also bought two other yearlings, all to go into a racing stable. It was the first really big yearling purchase by a syndicate and, indeed, a precursor of things to come. Interestingly enough, the correspondent for *The Thoroughbred Record* (yours truly) noted in the sales coverage,

Wajima and members of the East-West syndicate.

"With prices the way they were, it was only natural that this was the year of the syndicated yearling. In addition to the syndicate that bought the highest-priced yearling, there were several others active and successful in the bidding, and as yearling prices continue to rise, there will undoubtedly be more and more syndicates active around the sales ring."

That sale was significant in that it introduced two other reasons for forming syndicates — leverage, the use of other people's money for the purchase of horses, and diversification, the purchase of several horses in the hopes that one of them will be successful. As it turned out, that happened. The world-record colt, subsequently named Wajima, went on to be the champion three-year-old colt of 1975 and was syndicated (or resyndicated, actually) for another world-record price, $7.2-million, when he entered stud.

Cot Campbell, a partnership pioneer.

This was followed very closely by the emergence on the scene of a charming and innovative fellow, Cot Campbell, from Atlanta. Under the *nom de course* Dogwood Stable, Cot began bringing new people into the business through small partnerships that would buy a horse (in some cases several horses), race it for two or three years, and if the horse turned out as they hoped, sell it for a profit. Since Campbell was originally in the advertising business, he knows how to treat his clients right, and they are kept well informed through calls from his office, "breezing parties" at his farm in Aiken, South Carolina, and a regular newsletter. He has been very successful both with forming partnerships and buying horses, for instance, Summer Squall, the Preakness Stakes winner in 1990 and the sire of 1999 Kentucky Derby and Preakness winner Charismatic. He now operates quite a number of partnerships and is bringing people into the business in the proper fashion. You can read more about him in his book, *Lightning in a Jar*, which is published by Eclipse Press.

Today, the market is out of sight. The Keeneland July sales average was above $600,000 (of course, if they keep reducing the number of yearlings to keep the averages up, the sale one day might consist of two yearlings that average $6 million); overall averages for broodmares and yearlings are both above $50,000 (with medians of $12,000 for both), and shares in untried stallions — shares, not stallions — selling for sums in excess of $1 million.

It's no wonder, then, that you see syndicates getting together to purchase everything from racehorses to shares in other syndicates.

Before discussing some of the pros and cons of multiple ownership, this might be as good a place as any to discuss some of the types and elements of multiple ownership.

Types of Multiple Ownership

While there are almost as many types of multiple ownership as there are deals floating around today, for the present purposes they can be divided into the six most common categories: partnerships, syndicates, joint ventures, Subchapter S corporations, regular corporations, and limited liability companies.

None is contingent upon the amount of money you have to

spend — two people could, for example, form a general partnership to purchase a mare for $10,000, while other partnerships are formed to buy multimillion-dollar yearlings to race, or broodmares to breed, or farms, etc. What is important are the goals that the participants want to achieve.

Partnerships. According to the *Horse Owners and Breeders Tax Handbook*, a partnership is when two or more people get together to "carry on a business endeavor with each person contributing money, property, labor or skill, and all are expected to share in the profits and losses of the business." Today in the Thoroughbred business, there are racing partnerships, breeding partnerships, pinhooking partnerships...in short, if you look hard enough you can find a partnership to indulge in just about any area of the business you want.

The Internal Revenue Code defines a partnership as "a syndicate, group, pool, joint venture, or other unincorporated organization, through or by means of which any business, financial operation, or venture is carried on and which is not...a corporation or a trust or estate." It can be formed by a written or an oral agreement, although I don't recommend the latter (see below).

Whether your partnership is a general partnership, a syndicate, or a joint venture generally depends on the amount of control you want to have and the reasons it is established. In all forms, though, the income tax credits that accrue to the partnership "pass through" to the partners on a pro rata basis for their portion of the partnership. In other words, the partners pay taxes or take tax deductions on their individual returns in proportion to their participation in the partnership, which can either be in proportion to their contributions to the partnership or according to the partnership agreement. While the partnership files an income tax return, it is an informational return only, and the partnership itself doesn't have any tax responsibility.

In a general partnership, the partners have a relatively equal say in its operations, and, as a result, they are equally liable for its obligations. This liability can extend past the partnership to the personal assets of each of the general partners. General partnerships can be formed for a specific purpose, such as racing or breeding, or for a combination of purposes, such as breeding, racing a few fillies, owning stallion shares, etc.

A limited partnership is similar to a general partnership, except normally there is only one general partner who is responsible for all the business decisions of the partnership and also is personally liable for the obligations of the partnership. The personal liability of the limited partners is held to a specific amount, typically the limited partner's capital contribution. These were among the most popular forms of doing business in the early '80s, but, as I pointed out in Chapter 7, they became substantially less popular with the passage of the Tax Reform Act of 1986, which has a "passive loss provision" that only permits a limited partner to write off "passive"

Partnerships can have many advantages, both emotional and monetary.

losses, such as would accrue from a limited partnership, against "passive" income.

While I realize a lot of people will probably disagree vehemently with me on this, I think the effective demise of the limited partnership wasn't all a bad thing. As alluded to above, it helped weed out a lot of the people who weren't committed to the horse business in the first place and helped eliminate some of the shysters who were populating the business.

As an egregious example of what was going on in those days, let me cite the following actual quote from a limited partnership agreement, which, believe it or not, actually raised $2 million in the early '80s:

> *Inexperienced Management.* No member of management of...the General Partner of the Partnership, has any experience in commercial thoroughbred breeding or farm management. Moreover, [the company]...has limited financial resources and a substantial portion of [the company's] operating budget for the foreseeable future is likely to be a direct result of this offering. Such inexperience and limited financial resources could have a materially adverse effect on the operations of the Partnership.

Well, I guess you could take the position that anyone stupid enough to invest in a partnership that had a statement like that in the prospectus deserved anything he got, but I, for one, am not in the least bit sorry to see most of them gone.

Syndicates. A syndicate can be either a co-ownership or partnership depending on its purpose; and the purposes of a syndicate are usually more limited than those of a partnership, i.e., owning a stallion for racing or breeding but usually not crossing over. If a syndicate doesn't engage in any business activities of its own and delegates control to somebody else, for example, a stallion syndicate, it is usually regarded as a co-ownership, while if it does engage in a business activity, for example, selling excess seasons and distributing the proceeds, it is regarded as a partnership.

Joint ventures. A joint venture is a business structure legally similar to a partnership (and taxed as such), but typically narrower in purpose and scope, and often used simply for a single, specific business purpose. The benefit of a joint venture is that it can often be accomplished without a complicated written document.

Subchapter S Corporations. A corporation that has seventy-five or fewer stockholders (husbands and wives count as only one) can elect to be treated as a Subchapter S corporation for income tax purposes. Basically, a Subchapter S corporation is just like any other corporation, with limited liability to shareholders and easy transferability of stock (although transfer restrictions may be placed on shares of any privately held corporation), except it has one great advantage: profits and losses are passed through to shareholders, as in a partnership, so you avoid the double taxation that plagues most corporations. The drawback is that a Subchapter S corporation is more complicated than a partnership, and sometimes income and loss may pass through to a shareholder less favorably than in a partnership. For instance, there is very little flexibility in the income and losses (which are calculated at the corporate level) between shareholders. In some rare circumstances, a Subchapter S corporation may be subject to taxes at the corporate level. A Subchapter S corporation, however, might offer an attractive middle ground between not having any say as a limited partner in a limited partnership and worrying about the liability in a general partnership. However, corporations and foreign individuals are not allowed to be shareholders in a Subchapter S corporation.

Regular Corporations. In the early '80s, several major (and a couple of minor) Thoroughbred operations decided to become public corporations. While they offered the investor participation in the Thoroughbred business at a very nominal level, I noted at the time that "it seems…that the only real benefit, generating capital, accrues to the company. In the meantime, the stockholders get all of the disadvantages of corporate investment (double taxation, etc.) and none of the advantages of the horse business (i.e., tax advantages, thrill of participation, etc.)."

The result was disaster. Not to end this discussion precipitously, but because the cash flow in the horse business is sporadic, which doesn't suit Wall Street analysts, and because of the necessity to act quickly without consulting an army of lawyers and accountants, the Thoroughbred business is not suited to this form of business. I don't think you'll find any major Thoroughbred operation even thinking about going public today. And, if you did, I don't think you'd find any firm willing to underwrite the offer. End of story.

Limited Liability Company. The new kid on the block is the limited liability company or partnership, which is very popular because it contains the liability immunities of a corporation and the flexible tax treatment of a partnership. As pointed out in *Tax Tips for Horse Owners*, "[It can incorporate] the best of both worlds. In other words, think of an LLC as a corporation for purposes of lawsuits and legal liability, and as a partnership for federal tax purposes."

An LLC has other important characteristics:

(1) The owners are considered "members" rather than shareholders.

(2) You can select whether to be taxed as a partnership or a proprietorship by making an election with the IRS.

(3) The LLC is formed by registering your articles of organization with the secretary of the state where you will be headquartered. (A caveat here is that very few states aren't registering LLCs yet.)

(4) An LLC is managed by its members or by managers who are designated by its members.

(5) It is controlled by an operating agreement that results from agreement by all the members.

(6) Profits and assets can be allocated disproportionately among the members by agreement.

While I'm beginning to see LLC plastered over almost everything in the horse business, there are a couple of drawbacks, i.e., difficulties in transferring your interest in this type of company, and since this is a relatively new development, the case law and regulations may be a little sketchy at this time.

At any rate, you can participate in multiple ownership of Thoroughbreds in a number of ways, but before you make the decision where to put your money, do your homework.

Before You Invest

The late Samuel Goldwyn once said, "An oral contract isn't worth the paper it's written on." He was absolutely right! While some case law today has upheld oral contracts, it is far better to write everything down.

Whether you and a friend are going together to claim a filly for $5,000 or you're putting together a $10-million limited partnership, make sure you write down some sort of agreement. It can be scribbled on the back of a napkin in the former case, or it can be a 200-page legal document in the latter case, but the fact remains you should basically write down: (a) who's going to pay for what; (b) who's going to have what management responsibilities; (c) what's going to happen to the profits, if any, and; (d) what happens if you have a disagreement and decide to dissolve the partnership.

In many cases, this will all be set out for you in a long, complex document. Read it! Read it carefully, and ask questions about anything you don't understand.

Look out for certain things that will almost guarantee that you won't make money if you invest. Be especially attentive to the qualifications of the people you'll be dealing with and leaning on to make the vital decisions that will mean profit or loss for your enterprise. If you see anything like the paragraph I reproduced earlier, don't think, just run like hell.

If you're going to make any substantial investment, you should at least have some sort of business plan or pro forma from your partner.

Here are some of the other warning signs you should look for in your choice of a partnership or in looking at a business plan or pro forma:

Profit motive. It makes no sense to enter into a deal based on tax benefits alone. Remember the quote from that tax court judge in Chapter 7: "As long as tax rates are less than 100 percent, there is no 'benefit' in losing money." If the primary goal isn't to show a profit, you will never make money. Besides, if you cannot prove a profit motive, the IRS will probably disallow any write-offs associated with the enterprise. In the past few years, it has been vigorous in attacking "tax shelter" deals, those that do not project a profit.

The business plan should contain specifics of where the money is to come from and where it is to go. Income projections are difficult at best in the horse business, and some business plans may not even include them, but if they are included, you should be aware they are simply projections and are subject to wide variations.

If an agreement has been written properly by the organizing partner, there is seldom any real legal way to hold his feet to the fire, but a specific business plan and a pro forma will at least give you something to point to in times of trouble.

Large front-end load. Making money in the horse business is difficult enough without giving thirty-five percent to fifty percent up front in commissions, management fees, etc.

The organizing partner should not get rich until the other participants have at least been paid back. I believe management should be compensated only nominally until all the other participants have recouped their original investment. Then, as a reward for doing a good job, the manager can receive a percentage of the net proceeds, but not before then.

Self-dealing. Some partnerships include purchasing horses from the general partner, allowing the general partner to breed to his own stallions or buy the seasons that come with the shares he owns. Worse, they often permit a general partner to sell seasons and horses back and forth from one partnership to another and take a commission on the sale. All of these things become very tempting if the general partner needs money, which he probably does or he wouldn't be forming the partnership in the first place.

Insofar as the purchase of horses from the general partner, it doesn't have to be bad, but I'd advise getting an independent appraisal of the animals included in the deal because, whether honestly or not, often horse owners have an inflated value of the animals they own.

Conflicts of interest. Undoubtedly, unless you participate in a partnership in which no one has any previous connection to the industry, you'll be faced with certain conflicts of interest. This isn't necessarily all bad. Many general or managing partners will own other horses on their own or in another partnership, which by definition creates conflicts of interest since they will be competing for buyers and/or seasons or shares.

However, while you don't want someone to use the partnership to unload his own seasons and fill up his own stallions, you don't want a total stranger to the industry. Most conflicts of interest are offset by useful contacts within the industry, but you should bear them in mind while studying the offering memorandum.

On the subject of conflicts of interest, it might be appropriate here to discuss the proposition of a "blind pool" vs. purchasing named horses that are already owned by the general partner. As mentioned above, if the horses are put into the partnership by the general partner, they could be inflated. On the other hand, you can have them appraised by an independent source. Most partnerships, though, are put together to raise capital for the general partner to take to the sales in order to purchase horses, and you don't know what you're going to get. In the latter case, though, the prices will probably be dictated by the market, so it will be public knowledge what the horse is worth (at least if he hasn't purchased the horse or an interest prior to the sale and run it up in the ring, which does happen).

What it all boils down to is whether your partnership manager is a person of integrity. If he isn't, you're not going to get an even break either way.

Other Forms of Stretching Your Investment

Even before the business began to look outward for additional capital, other ways of expanding investments were available.

First, syndicators and others in the business began to offer deferred payment plans. Then banks, leasing companies, and other financial institutions began looking toward the business as a place for expansion, especially when the market was going up at a solid thirty percent a year and interest rates were fifteen percent or better. Now, despite the tender ministrations of Mr. Greenspan and the Federal Reserve, interest rates remain relatively low. Even in this heated economy, growth in the horse business is at a rate that is a little unbalanced but not totally insane. Nevertheless, financial institutions have not forgotten their previous foray into the business and are not so eager as they once were.

To put it more succinctly, I asked a friend of mine what he

thought the difference was between the 2000 Keeneland July sale and those of the mid-'80s. "They're spending their own money" was the reply.

To backtrack a little, the first major trend toward offering terms or deferred payments came in the early to mid-'70s, as stallion syndication was becoming attractive to outside investors. Some of the innovators in the business reasoned, correctly, that a mul-tiyear payout might prove beneficial to the people for whom they were syndicating the horses (capital gains were on a sliding scale in those days, with a maximum rate considerably higher than the current twenty percent). By offering terms, the syndicator could get a higher price per share than he otherwise would and, at the same time, make ownership of syndicate shares more attractive to outside investors.

They began offering variations on a basic theme: an initial pay-ment followed by three or four subsequent annual payments, depending on the syndicate manager.

At first, the rationale for a five-year payment on a stallion share was that the purchaser would be able to make the share payments from the sale of seasons and amortize the share before the horse was proven to be a failure at stud, if that were going to happen. In year one, the horse was just off the track and the syndicate manag-er could still promote him using the glitter of his race record; in year two the hype would surround the arrival of his first foals; year three would see his first yearlings coming to market; and year four would feature his first two-year-olds getting to the races. If they couldn't run, the stallion's seasons would begin to decline in value, but the shareholder would have paid for his share through the sale or use of seasons while they held their price, and the subsequent sale of seasons, even at a reduced rate, would be gravy.

This formula became even more attractive in 1981 when the ACRS (depreciation) guidelines were reduced to five years and the depreciation of a share closely approximated the payment schedule for the share. However, as discussed in Chapter 7, as part of the Tax Reform Act of 1986, an "at risk" provision was added to the tax code, and the ACRS was changed to the MACRS (Modified Accelerated Cost Recovery System), which extended the depreciation guidelines to seven years and made them pretty much incompatible with the five-year payout of a share that was prevalent at the time.

For example, if one were to buy a share for $100,000 under the ACRS, the payment schedule and depreciation allowances would look something like this:

Year	Share Payment	Depreciation
1	$20,000	$15,000
2	$20,000	$22,000
3	$20,000	$21,000
4	$20,000	$21,000
5	$20,000	$21,000
	$100,000	$100,000

Today, under the MACRS the payment schedule and depreciation schedule for a $100,000 share looks like this:

Year	Share Payment	Depreciation
1	$20,000	$10,715
2	$20,000	$19,134
3	$20,000	$15,033
4	$20,000	$12,248
5	$20,000	$12,248
6		$12,248
7		$12,248
8		$6,126
	100,000	$100,000

Obviously, the second example is not as attractive as the first, so stallion shares have become less of an item of speculation than they were in the early '80s, but, once again, I'm not totally certain that's a bad thing. I may be a little old fashioned about this, but I think that speculators not only drive up the business in the good times, but they intensify declines when the business goes through rough times.

Still, when breeders, owners, and other people began seeing how effective payments over time were becoming, and as prices continued to escalate, the trend caught on with other forms of bloodstock. Now you can get terms on almost any bloodstock purchase you make privately. As a heavy participant in the business is fond of saying, "the terms make the deal," and I have to agree. The terms can also create a great temptation to overextend yourself, though, and that, I'll remind you several times in this section, is very, very dangerous.

Bank Loans

Prior to 1975, very few financial institutions were willing to take a flyer on horses, but during the late '70s and early '80s, many banks nationwide actively sought investors who wanted to borrow money on horses. If there ever was a red flag waved in front of a bull, it was banks offering to lend money to people wanting to buy horses.

A lot of banks were not overly discriminate in selecting their loan recipients, either. For instance, the former First Security Bank in Lexington is conservatively reported to have written off in excess of $30 million in equine loans in the early '90s; First City National Bank in Houston took a bath to the tune of $65 million on Calumet Farm alone in a case that involves fraud, bribery, calumny, and deceit (all those things we hold near and dear), and which is still being played out in the federal courts. One of the primary causes cited in the widely publicized failure of the Penn Square Bank in Oklahoma was a number of questionable horse loans, although in all fairness, they were mostly Quarter Horse loans.

Apparently, greed is a stronger motivator than fear or memory, because, even after the beating they took in the '80s, banks are beginning to get involved in the horse business again, and I'm not too sure I like it.

Your banker may be your best friend in the good times — he'll be more than happy to stand beside you in the winner's circle after the Kentucky Derby or to drink champagne with you after you've sold a yearling for $1 million — but when the going gets tough, as the saying goes, with friends like this, you don't need any enemies. To be truly objective about the matter, banks are in the business of money, and that's all they really care about. When things go bad, as they inevitably will from time to time, the bank won't be your partner and pal anymore. They want their money; they want it now; and they want it…period.

Fortunately, I escaped that trap because I divested myself of most of my horse interests in 1984 and 1985 in anticipation of the downturn that was to come, but I firmly believe that excessive leverage was another factor that exacerbated the decline in the horse business during the late '80s. When the business began to turn down, the bankers panicked and began to force people to sell, when under different circumstances, those people might otherwise have been able to hold on until the business turned up again.

While a number of banks today make loans of fifty percent on breeding stock and up to sixty percent on stallion shares, today's equine lenders are rightly much more discriminating about the people to whom they lend money than they were in the '80s (which is probably another reason I'm not borrowing money for horses today). If the bankers did learn anything, it is that while the prices of horses may accelerate rapidly, they can fall just as rapidly.

Today the bank will want to have people they can rely on to make up the difference if, for some reason, your equine asset declines drastically in value.

So, to borrow a euphemism from the banking profession, today's bankers are making asset-based loans rather than collateral-based loans, i.e., they will rely on your overall financial statement and not on your equine portfolio's value. Translation: They'll be happy to lend you the money, provided you don't really need it.

Nevertheless, several factors should be kept in mind as you go to the bank seeking an equine loan. As mentioned, you, yourself, will make the most important difference in the bank's decision. An important factor will be your preparedness — you should have a definite business plan and/or projections of income and expenses, including when and how you plan to repay the loan. Be prepared with copies of income tax returns for the previous two or three years and a current, easily verifiable financial statement — emphasizing liquidity, as much as possible. Lastly, but very importantly, if you're not established and experienced in the business, you should bring some information about your advisors. It helps if you go to a bank where you're well known, and if your regular bank absolutely does not give loans on horses, you'll be better off in the long run if you begin to establish a relationship with one that does.

Finally, I have several other bits of advice for you when going to the bank.

First, and foremost, choose a banker who knows something about horses and the horse business. If you have someone who knows about the ups and downs of the business, he may be more sympathetic when you have to ask for an extension or some help with your loan. He probably won't be able to give you a lot of help, because most of today's banks have merged into some megalithic corporation, and he probably has to answer to some hardass who works in a city 300 miles away and couldn't care less whether you live or die, much less go bankrupt. But if he knows about the horse business, at least he might take a stab at it.

Secondly, don't overvalue your horses. I realize that you are probably convinced your horses are worth more than most other people think they are — that's just human nature — but try your hardest to make an objective valuation. Much of the trouble encountered by the banks when the business turned south in the '80s came about because the banks' ability to recoup their money was compromised not only by the decline in value of the horses themselves, but because the horses were overvalued in the first place. Like much of the horse business, the appraisal sector is relatively unregulated, so they are not subject to the same stringent educational and licensing requirements as, say, real estate appraisers. In fact, the bank may have an independent appraisal done on your horses. A lot of them just rely on the expertise of their lending officers (who, remember, are basically loan salesmen) to value the horses, but if they do have an independent appraisal and there is a large discrepancy, it'll send up a red flag.

Third, banks are very reluctant to lend money for horses at the track. As mentioned in Chapter 4 and in the Glossary, the effective title to a horse is carried by The Jockey Club Registration Certificate. Since the certificate must be on file at the racing secretary's office in order for the horse to race, this, in effect, causes the bank to make an unsecured loan since it does not have title to the horse. That doesn't give the banker much of a feeling of confidence.

The problem with bank financing today, as I see it, is the same as that of a partnership with a large front-end load, i.e., making it in the horse business is tough enough without adding on a ten percent to eleven percent additional burden to your operation in the form of interest. However, if you decide leveraging is good for your business, you should include the interest at a reasonable rate in your business plan.

Leases

The last form of alternative financing that merits discussion here is leasing. Leasing has been prevalent on the racetrack for many years as a way for people who are interested in racing but not breeding to have some fun with a well-bred horse that has potential, while the breeder who is interested in breeding but not racing can benefit from the appreciation of the horse during its racing career.

During the mid-'90s leasing became an increasingly popular aspect of the breeding industry, too, as more and more owners of stallion shares couldn't sell a season or they found an appropriate broodmare too expensive to purchase. Occasionally, a mare owner will find himself in a cash bind and want to generate some fairly immediate income without losing his best broodmare. There are, of course, certain advantages and disadvantages for both sides in a lease deal, but, in general, the lessor (the person who owns the horse) comes out on the better end of the deal.

For the lessee, the advantages are that all expenses of the deal are deductible in the year they are paid, and the lease probably permits him to get a foal out of a mare that he might not be able to touch otherwise. However, while he can get a guarantee that the mare is in foal at the time the lease is signed, he cannot get a live-foal guarantee because tax rulings have stated that a live-foal guarantee removes all risk of loss, and therefore the lease money is being paid for the purchase of the foal and must be capitalized as such. Also, since the tax rules essentially rule out multiyear leases (renewals are permissible, though), the lessee is not necessarily tied for life to a mare that doesn't fit into his breeding program.

For the lessor, a lease permits some cash flow without making the lessor permanently divest himself of a major and valued asset. Also, since he retains actual ownership of the horse, the lessor continues to take depreciation on it, even though it may be in the possession of the lessee.

Until relatively recently, leasing basically was an activity between individuals. During the '80s and '90s, leasing companies sprang up for the wholesale purchase of horses for people who would then lease them from the company. The brochure for one of those companies that was prominent in the '80s cites the benefits of leasing as permitting the lessee to:

> Conserve investments and other assets by making the lease payments out of earnings or other income. Be able to purchase more horses, or horses of better quality, than funds available permit. Permit investment of available funds in other needed items.

TRANSLATION: "We'll help you get in over your head and do it fast."

In summary, there are major advantages and disadvantages to participation in all forms of alternative ownership and/or financing. The important thing to remember, though, whether you're buying shares of common stock at $4.50, limited partnership units at $100,000, or taking out a million-dollar loan, is to plan ahead, allow for contingencies, and, above all, stay within your means.

Although it's close to a dead heat, greed has probably caused more failures in the horse business than ineptitude.

GLOSSARY*

Acepromazine — A common tranquilizer for horses; often used in small quantities during vanning or other instances when a horse may become agitated, such as hair clipping or dental work. Also known as Ace.

Added money — Money added by the racing association to the amount paid by owners in nomination, eligibility, and starting fees. All added-money races in North America are stakes races.

Allowance race — An event other than claiming for which the racing secretary drafts certain conditions.

Allowances — Weights and other conditions of a race.

Also-eligible — Horse officially entered but not permitted to start unless field is reduced by scratches below specified number.

Apprentice allowance — Weight concession to an apprentice rider. This varies among states from five to ten pounds. Slang term is "bug." Indicated by an asterisk next to the jockey's name in the program.

Backstretch — Straight part of the track on far side between turns; slang term to describe the stable area.

Bandage — Strips of cloth wound around the lower part of horses' legs for support or protection against injury.

Bar shoe — A horseshoe on which the heels are connected by a bar rather than being open like a normal shoe. The purpose is to keep the hoof from spreading on impact. Normally used when a horse has a foot problem, such as a quarter crack, but it adds weight to the horse's foot and impedes his traction, which results in some loss of efficiency during running.

Barren — Denotes the status of a mare that has not conceived after being bred.

Bit — Metal bar in a horse's mouth that guides and controls him. There are many types with varying degrees of severity.

Black type — Boldface type used in sales catalogues to distinguish horses that have won or placed in a stakes race. If a horse's name appears in capitalized boldface type, he has won at least one stakes. If capital and lower-case letters both appear in boldface type, he has placed in at least one stakes.

Bleeder — Horse that bleeds from lungs after or during a workout or race.

Blinkers — Device to limit a horse's vision to prevent him from swerving from objects, other horses, etc., on either side of him.

Blister — A counter-irritant causing acute inflammation; used to increase blood supply and promote healing in the leg.

Blood typing — A procedure implemented by The Jockey Club to verify parentage.

Bloodlines — The genealogy of a horse.

Bloodstock — Thoroughbred horses and interests therein.

Bloodstock agent — A broker who represents the purchaser or seller (or both) of Thoroughbreds at public or private sale, generally for a commission.

Blow out — A short, timed exercise, normally a day or two before a race.

Bog spavin — Puffy swelling on the inside and slightly to the front of the hock. Caused by overwork or strain, usually indicative of an OCD (osteochondritis desicans) lesion. Should be X-rayed.

Bone spavin — Bony growth inside and just below the hock. Even with good hocks a bone spavin may occur as a result of undue concussion or strain, causing lameness.

Book — The group of mares being bred to a stallion in one given year. Today, a "normal book" is about sixty mares, but many stallions are bred to books in excess of 150 mares.

Bots — Ova stage of a common parasite that are visible on a horse's legs. Ingested, they become larval parasites. The ultimate form is the bot fly.

Bottom line — Thoroughbred's breeding in female, or distaff, side.

Bowed tendon — Damage to the deep flexor tendon, superficial flexor tendon, or both, located below the knee (or hock on back leg) and running behind the cannon bone, usually in a front leg. Often caused by a bad step, poor conformation, or strain. A bowed tendon requires a long layoff and can mean the end of a horse's racing career.

Break (a horse) — To accustom a young horse to racing equipment and carrying a rider, usually done as a yearling in the fall. Also referred to as "gentling."

Breakage — At pari-mutuel betting tracks, the rounding off to a nickel or dime, as required by state laws, in paying off winning tickets. If breakage is to the nickel, the bettor on a horse that should pay, say, $6.91, receives $6.90. If breakage is to the dime, the payoff on a $6.91 horse would be $6.80. Generally, the breakage is split between the track and the state in varying proportions.

Breakdown — When a horse suffers a severe injury resulting in lameness.

Bred — A horse is "bred" at the place of his birth. Also, the mating of a horse.

Breeder — The owner of the foal at the time the foal is born.

Breeding farm — A farm for Thoroughbreds used for breeding and/or potential racing stock.

Breeding right — The right to breed one mare to one stallion for one or more breeding seasons, generally not including an ownership interest in the stallion.

Breeze — Work a horse at a brisk pace.

Broodmare — Female Thoroughbred used for breeding.

Broodmare prospect — A filly or mare that has not been bred.

Bucked shins — Inflammation of the periosteum on the front of the cannon bone. It is confined chiefly to young horses, although it is possible for older horses to buck shins. It is not a serious ailment, but requires about three weeks of rest. Known as bucked because of humped or bucked appearance on front of cannon bone.

Bug — See Apprentice allowance.

Butazolidin (Bute) — A racetrack term for Phenylbutazone (see Phenylbutazone).

Buy-back — A horse put through public auction that did not reach his reserve and so was retained by the consignor. Also called charge-back or RNA.

Cannon bone — The bone between the knee or hock and the fetlock (ankle). A common site of fracture in racehorses.

Champion — In the United States, a horse voted best of its division in a given year by members of *Daily Racing Form*, the Thoroughbred Racing Associations, and National Turf Writers Association, and thus earner of an Eclipse Award. In other countries, either voted upon in a similar fashion or top-weighted on a published year-end handicap list.

Chute — Extension of backstretch or homestretch to permit straightaway run from the start.

Claiming race — An event in which each horse entered is eligible to be purchased at a set price.

Clerk of scales — Official whose chief duty is to weigh the riders before and after a race to insure proper weight is being carried.

Clocker — A person on duty during morning training hours to identify the horses during their workouts, time them, and report to the public their training activities. Some clockers work for the racetrack, others are employed by Equibase.

Clubhouse turn — The first turn past the finish line, where the clubhouse is usually located.

Coggins test — A test named after its developer, Dr. Leroy Coggins, to determine whether a horse is a carrier of swamp fever.

This test, almost universally required today, has essentially wiped out this disease in Thoroughbreds.

Colors — The individual owner's racing silks, jacket, and cap, worn by riders to denote ownership of horse. All colors are different and many are registered with The Jockey Club.

Colt — A male Thoroughbred horse (other than a gelding or ridgeling) that has not reached his fifth birth date or has not been bred.

Condition book — Publication produced by a racetrack that lists the races to be run, usually covering a period of two weeks. Horsemen use the book to decide in which race to enter a horse, based upon its eligibility. If the minimum number of horses is not entered, meaning the race did not fill, it will not be contested and a substitute race is written and used in its place.

Conformation — The physical makeup or qualities of a horse; its physical appearance and structural makeup.

Consignor — The seller of a horse at public auction. The consignor can be the horse's owner or the owner's agent.

Contract rider — Jockey under contract to specific stable or trainer.

Controlled medication — A term widely used today to mean that some drugs, primarily Phenylbutazone and furosemide, are permissible under controlled circumstances that allow veterinary administration of predetermined dosages at predetermined intervals prior to race time.

Cooling out — Restoring the horse to normal body temperature and heart rate, usually by walking, after he becomes overheated in a workout or race.

Coupled — Two or more horses running as a single betting unit. Also known as an entry.

Cover — A single breeding of a mare to a stallion. If a mare were bred to a stallion three times before becoming pregnant, then she was covered three times. Cover date in a sales catalogue refers to the last time a mare was bred that season.

Cribber — Some horses develop a habit of swallowing air. A cribber or crib-biter swallows air by taking hold of the feed manger or other objects with his teeth. It is discouraged by using an unpalatable substance such as cayenne pepper, covering objects with metal, or using a cribbing strap around his neck.

Cuppy track — A surface that will break under a horse's hooves; usually such a surface will be sandy in nature.

Curb — A painful swelling and thickening of one or all of the ligaments or tendons at the lower part of the hock. The swelling is seen on the rear legs from the point of the hock to the cannon bone.

Cushion — Top layer of the racetrack, normally three to four inches deep, maintained to absorb the concussion of horse's legs uniformly during running.

Dam — Mother of a horse. In a pedigree, the first dam is the horse's mother; the second dam is the first dam's mother; and the third dam is the second dam's mother.

Dead heat — Two or more horses finishing on even terms.

Declared — Horse withdrawn from a stakes race in advance of scratch time on the day of the race.

Derby — A stakes race for three-year-olds.

Detention barn — The barn where horses are required to go until blood tests or urine samples have been taken for testing (see Spit box).

DNA testing — May supplant blood typing for the verification of parentage of Thoroughbreds one day.

Dogs — Barriers placed on a track away from the inside rail to indicate that the inside strip of the track is not to be used during morning workouts to preserve the surface. Workouts around these barriers are noted, and the times are correspondingly slower due to the longer distance it adds on the turns.

Dual hemisphere breeding — Quite a few popular stallions today stand a breeding season in the Northern Hemisphere then are sent to the Southern Hemisphere for an abbreviated service season. A way of increasing a stallion's production and income.

Easily — Horse running or winning without being pressed by rider or opposition.

Eighth — An eighth-mile; a furlong; 220 yards; 660 feet.

Eligible — Qualified to start in a race according to conditions.

Entrance fee — Money paid to start a horse. Usually required only in stakes or special events.

Exercise rider — Person who exercises horses during morning workouts.

Fetlock — A horse's ankle, located above the pastern and below the cannon bone.

Field — One or more starters running coupled as single betting unit. Usually horses calculated to have small chance to win are grouped in the "field." Also used as a term for all the horses in a race.

Filly — A female Thoroughbred that has not reached her fifth birth date or has not been bred.

First turn — Bend of track beyond starting point. Usually same as clubhouse turn.

Flat race — Contest on level ground as opposed to a hurdle race, a steeplechase, or harness race.

Flatten out — When a horse drops his head almost on a straight line with his body while running. Indicates exhaustion.

Foal — A baby horse. Also, the process of giving birth. A pregnant mare is termed in foal.

Foal heat — The first time a mare comes into season after giving birth, about nine days afterward (also called nine-day heat).

Foal sharing — An arrangement between the owner of a stallion share or season and the owner of a broodmare to breed them and (generally) to share the foals by either owning one-half interest in each foal or owning every other foal the broodmare produces.

Founder — See Laminitis.

Fractional time — Intermediate times in a race, as at quarter-mile, half-mile, three-quarters, etc.

Free handicap — Race in which no liability is incurred for entrance money, stakes, or forfeit until acceptance of weight. Also, a term used to describe an end-of-the-year assessment of individual horses expressed in weight or pounds.

Full brother (sister) — Horses that have the same sire and dam.

Furlong — One-eighth of a mile; 220 yards; 660 feet.

Furosemide — A diuretic medication often used to treat bleeders at racetracks. Legal under certain conditions in most states. Commonly called by its brand name, Lasix.

Gallop — A type of gait; a fast canter. To ride horse at that gait.

Gelding — Male horse that has been castrated.

Get — Progeny of a sire.

Girth — Band around the horse's body to keep the saddle from slipping.

Good bottom — Track that is firm under a surface that may be sloppy or muddy.

Good track — Condition of track surface between fast and slow as surface dries out.

Granddam — Grandmother of a horse.

Grandsire — Grandfather of a horse.

Groom — An employee who works for a trainer and is in charge of taking care of the horses. A groom may take care of three to six horses, depending on the circumstances.

Half-brother (-sister) — Horses that have the same dams. Does not apply to horses that share only the same sire.

Halter — Like a bridle, but lacking bit. Used in handling horses around stable and when they are not being ridden.

Halterman — One who claims horses on a routine basis.

Hand — Four inches. Unit used in measuring the height of all horses, from withers to ground.

Hand ride — Urging a horse with the hands and not using a whip.

Handicap — Event in which the racing secretary determines the weight to be carried by each horse according to his assessment of the horse's ability. The better the horse the more weight he would carry to give each horse a theoretically equal chance of winning.

Handicapper — One who handicaps races, officially or privately; expert who makes selections for publication. Also, name given to racing secretary who assigns weights for handicaps at his track. Also, a horse that usually runs in handicap races.

Handicapping — Study of all factors in past performances to determine the relative qualities of horses in a race. These factors include distance, weight, track conditions, trainers, owners, riders, previous race record, breeding, idiosyncrasies of the horses, etc.

Handily — Working or racing with moderate effort; not under the whip.

Handle (mutuel) — Amount of money bet on a race, a daily card, or during meeting, season, or year.

Head — One unit of measurement of distance between horses in a race; approximately an eighth of a length.

Health certificate — A standard form certificate concerning a horse's health. Universally required for interstate travel.

Horse — In broad terms, any Thoroughbred regardless of sex. Specifically, an entire male, five years old or older; or any male that has been bred.

Hotwalker — A person or a mechanical device to lead a horse after exercise to cool it down.

Hung — Horse tiring but holding position. Usually used in negative context; a horse not being able to pass another horse.

Identifier — The person assigned the job of identifying all horses coming to the paddock before a race. The identifier uses the registration form, which has the color, sex, markings, and age of the horse, as well as its tattoo number.

In-foal contract — An agreement by the owner of a stallion share or season that all or a portion of the stud fee will be refunded or will not become due if the mare does not produce a live foal.

In hand — When a horse is running under moderate control at less than his best pace; with speed in reserve at call of rider.

Inquiry — An investigation into the running of a race or claim of foul brought by a racing official. Called an objection when lodged by a rider.

Jockey Club Registration Certificate — One of the most important pieces of paper you'll have in the business. Like the registration for your car, one is assigned to each horse and should go wherever he goes. It includes a race record and a record of transfers. While it does not technically carry title to a horse, you can't race, sell, or register a foal without it.

Laminitis — A debilitating foot disease that is the subject of much research. An inflammation of the sensitive laminae that can be triggered by changes in blood flow to the foot, overeating, high temperature, toxemia, and concussion. Also known as founder.

Lasix — A brand name for furosemide, a diuretic commonly administered to racehorses.

Lay-up — A racehorse sent from the racetrack to recuperate from injury or illness or to be rested.

Lead — The leading leg of a horse. A horse usually leads with his inside leg around turns and with his opposite leg on straightaways.

Lead pony — Horse or pony that heads parade of field from paddock to starting gate. Also, horse or pony that accompanies a starter to the post to quiet him.

Length — Length of a horse from nose to tail, about eight feet. Distance between horses in a race; calculated as one-fifth of a second in terms of time.

Maiden — A racehorse of either sex that has never won a race; a female horse that has never been bred. Also a classification of race open only to horses that have never won a race. Straight (non-claiming) maiden races are considered of a higher class than maiden claiming races.

Mare — Female Thoroughbred five years old or older, or younger if she has been bred.

Morning line — Odds quoted in the official program at the track and are the odds at which betting opens.

Mudder — Horse that runs best on muddy or soft track.

Muzzle — Nose and lips of a horse. Also a guard placed over horse's mouth to prevent biting.

Near side — Left side of a horse, the side on which he is led or mounted.

Neck — One unit of measurement of distances between horses in races. Approximately equal to a quarter-length.

Nom de course — Assumed name of an owner or racing partnership.

Nominator — Person who paid nomination fee when entering a horse for a race in the future.

Nose — One unit of measurement of distances between horses in races. The smallest such unit.

Not sold — In sales results, a horse that went through the auction ring but did not change owners, usually because the consignor did not receive a price high enough (see Reserve).

Oaks — Stakes event for three-year-old fillies.

Objection — Claim of foul lodged by a rider against another. Called an inquiry when lodged by a racing official.

Odds-on — A payoff that would be less than even money.

Off side — Right side of horse.

Official — Sign displayed when result is confirmed. Or, racing official.

On the bit — When a horse is eager to run.

Osselet — Calcification deposit in the area of the fetlock joint that impedes movement of that joint. Depending upon severity, it can be very debilitating.

Overweight — Surplus weight carried by a horse when a rider cannot make the required poundage. Limited to five pounds or less.

Ownership registry — The Jockey Club's registration arm; registers the owners of all stallions and broodmares and requires ownership to be transferred when these horses change hands.

Paddock — Structure or area where horses are saddled and paraded before a race.

Paddock judge — Official in charge of paddock and saddling routine.

Palpation — The physical examination of a mare to feel or "palpate" her ovaries and uterus to determine breeding soundness, follicular activity (readiness to breed), uterine condition, or pregnancy.

Pari-mutuel — Form of wagering existing at all U.S. tracks today in which odds are determined by the amount of money bet on each horse. In essence, the bettors are competing against each other not against the track, which acts as an agent, taking a commission on each bet to cover purses, taxes, and operating expenses.

Patrol judges — Officials who observe progress of race from various vantage points around running strip.

Pedigree — A written record of a Thoroughbred's immediate ancestors. Usually one that gives four generations, called a four-cross pedigree.

Phenylbutazone — A nonsteroidal anti-inflammatory medication legal in certain amounts for horses in many states. Normally administered twenty-four to forty-eight hours before race time. Also called Butazolidin or Bute.

Photo finish — Result of a race so close that the placing judges cannot decide it with the naked eye and must consult a photograph.

Placed — Finishing second or third in a race. A stakes-placed horse is one that has finished second or third in a stakes but has not won a stakes. Not to be confused with betting terms place (second) and show (third).

Placing judge — An official who, in conjunction with other officials, determines the order of finish of a race.

Plater — Horse that runs in claiming races.

Plates — Shoes horses wear in races. Racing plates.

Pole — Markers placed at measured distances around the track and identified by distance from the finish line.

Pool — Total money bet on entire field to win, place, and show.

Post parade — Horses going from paddock to starting gate (post), parading past the stands.

Post position — Position in the starting gate from which horse breaks. Numbered from the rail outward.

Post time — Designated time for race to start.

Preferred list — Horses with prior rights to starting in a given race.

Prep (or prep race) — Training; an event that precedes another, more important, engagement.

Produce — The offspring of a mare.

Producer — A term applied to a mare only after one of her offspring wins a race.

Public trainer — One whose services are not exclusively engaged by one owner and who accepts horses to train for a daily fee.

Purse — A race for money or other prize to which the owners do not contribute.

Quarter crack — A crack in a horse's hoof wall near the heel on either side. This area of the hoof wall is known as the quarter and a crack in it is debilitating depending upon its severity and the extent to which it involves the coronet band. It can be the result of a concussion or poor shoeing, or it may be hereditary and result from weak hoof walls.

Quarter pole — Marker one-quarter of a mile from finish.

Race-day medication — Medication given on race day. Most medications, with the exception of Lasix, are prohibited in almost all racing jurisdictions.

Racing secretary — Official who drafts conditions for races, writes condition book, and usually serves as handicapper.

Receiving barn — Structure at some tracks where ship-ins, and, in some cases, all horses entered are isolated for a certain period before post time. Used to minimize chances of tampering.

Repository — Area or building at the sales set aside for pertinent medical information.

Reserve — The minimum amount for which a consignor will allow his horse to change hands at public auction.

RNA — Reserve Not Attained. Used by some sales companies rather than Not Sold or Charge Back.

Restricted race — A race restricted to certain starters either because of their place of birth or their previous winnings.

Ridgeling — Male horse with one or both testicles not descended into the scrotum .

Run down — When the pasterns of a horse hit the track in a race or workout, causing abrasion. Also a bandage to prevent injury from running down.

Saddle cloth — Cloth under saddle on which number denoting post position is displayed during races.

Scale of weights — Fixed imposts to be carried by horses in a race, determined according to age, sex, season, and distance.

Schooling — Getting a horse accustomed to starting from gate and racing practices.

Select sale — A public auction in which the entrants have been chosen on specified criteria, usually high-quality pedigrees and good conformation.

Sesamoids — Two small bones at the back of the fetlock held in place by ligaments. With stress and fatigue in a race, they can fracture. Although a horse can return to the races after such a fracture, it usually means the end of the racing career.

Shadow roll — A device normally made of sheepskin that goes over a horse's nose to keep him from seeing shadows on the ground. Some horses tend to jump shadows or become nervous at what they see, and the shadow roll is a method of limiting the horse's vision downward in the same manner that blinkers limit his vision to the sides.

Shedrow — An aisle outside the stalls in a barn.

Short — A horse needing more work or racing to attain best form.

Silks — Jacket and cap worn by riders.

Sire — Father of a horse; a stallion that has produced a foal that has won a race.

Sire production index — A statistic that compares a stallion's offspring from the mares to which he has been bred with the offspring of those mares with other stallions. Useful in determining whether a stallion is moving up his mares.

Sixteenth — One-sixteenth of a mile; a half-furlong; 110 yards, 330 feet.

Slipped — A pregnancy aborted or resorbed spontaneously. When a mare that had been bred and conceived aborted forty-two or more days following her last service. Usually referred to as aborted.

Sound — A term used to denote a Thoroughbred's health and freedom from disease or lameness. Physically able to perform an intended task, i.e., racing or breeding.

Spit box — Place where urine and/or blood are taken from a horse for testing after a race (see Detention barn). An anachronism from the days when saliva tests were prevalent following a race.

Splint — A hard swelling below the knee or hock indicating a fracture or damage to the splint bones, two bones on either side of the cannon bone, or their connecting ligaments.

Stakes — The highest class of race. A race in which an entry fee is paid by the owners of the horses starting and those entry fees are added to the purse. Often all of such entry fees go to the winner. (Entry fees are not required for any other type of race.) Also, invitational races (no entry fee required) with a large purse (usually $50,000 or more) are regarded as stakes races. Stakes races qualify horses for black type in sales catalogues.

Stakes producer — A mare with at least one foal that has won or placed in a stakes race.

Stallion — Entire male horse used for the purpose of breeding.

Stallion prospect — An entire male horse that has not been bred.

Stallion season — The right to breed one mare to a particular stallion for one particular season.

Stallion share — An undivided fractional interest in a stallion, which customarily entitles the owner to breed one broodmare to the stallion each year, plus an occasional extra season, depending upon the syndicate agreement (syndicate agreements usually provide for forty shares).

Standard starts index (SSI) — A statistic to compare a horse's racing class based on earnings per start per year. It is calculated and divided into male and female categories. Any horse earning the average for his or her sex has an SSI of 1.00. A horse with an SSI of 2.00 would have earned twice the average per start of his crop, one with 0.50 would have earned half the average, etc.

Starter — Racing official in charge of the starting gate. A horse that runs in a race.

Starter allowance — A particular kind of race written to allow claiming horses that have improved from their earlier form to run in a non-claiming event. Conditions of starter allowance races allow horses that have previously started for a certain lower-level claiming price to run under allowance conditions. These races are normally found at longer distances.

Starter handicap — The same type of race as a starter allowance except that the horses are assigned weights by the handicapper rather than determining them from allowance conditions.

Starting gate — Mechanical device with stalls from which horses exit when the starter releases doors to start race.

Stayer — Stout-hearted horse; one who can race long distances.

Stewards — The three individuals who uphold the rules of racing at a racetrack. They answer to the state racing commission, and their decisions can be appealed to that body.

Stifle — The joint of a horse's rear leg comprising the femur, tibia, and kneecap.

Stimulant — An illegal substance given to a horse to increase his normal physical activity temporarily for the purpose of improving his racing performance.

Strangles — A contagious bacterial disease caused by *Streptococcus equi* infection.

Stretch — Straightaway portion of racetrack in front of the grandstand. More particularly, the homestretch.

Stride — Manner of going. Distance progressed after each foot has touched ground once. More broadly, a step.

Stud — Male horse used for breeding. Also a breeding farm.

Stud book — The registry and genealogical record of the breeding of Thoroughbreds, maintained by The Jockey Club. Only Thoroughbreds of accepted lineage are eligible for inclusion.

Stud fee (or service fee) — A fee for the right to breed a mare to a stallion during the breeding period.

Subscription — Fee paid by owner to nominate horse for stakes or maintain eligibility for it.

Suckling — A young horse still nursing his dam.

Suitable for mating — A mare having two normal ovaries, a normal uterus, and a genital tract. Within normal reproductive limits. In stallions it indicates fertility.

Tack — Riders' racing equipment; applied also to stable gear.

Take (mutuel) — Commission deducted from mutuel pools that is shared by track, horsemen, and state.

Teasing — Using a male horse to approach a mare to determine whether she is in heat. Often farms have a horse or pony specifically for this purpose called a teaser, and he is usually not the stallion to whom the mare will be bred.

Thoroughbred — A distinctive breed of horse used for flat and steeplechase racing. Generally, a Thoroughbred must be registered with The Jockey Club of the United States or a similar registry in other countries to participate in sanctioned events.

Tongue strap — Strap or tape bandage used to tie down a horse's tongue to prevent it from choking him in a race or workout. Also known as a tongue tie.

Top line (sire line) — A Thoroughbred's breeding on sire's side. Also the visual line created by the horse's back.

Totalizator — Intricate machine that sells betting tickets, records total of straight place and show pools, and keeps track of amount bet on each horse in the three categories; shows odds to win on each horse in field and complete payoff after finish.

Track record — Fastest time at various distances made at a particular course.

Triple Crown — In the United States: the Kentucky Derby, Preakness Stakes, and Belmont Stakes. In England: the Two Thousand Guineas, Epsom Derby, and St. Leger.

Turf — Grass as opposed to dirt racing surfaces. When capitalized denotes the entire racing industry.

Twitch — A device generally consisting of a stick with loop of rope at one end that is placed around horse's upper lip and twisted to curb fractiousness. Used to assist in controlling a horse for veterinary treatment, etc.

Under wraps — Horse under stout restraint in race or workout.

Untried — Not raced or tested for speed.

Urinalysis — A series of laboratory tests of the urine to determine whether horse has been drugged. Also, occasionally used to determine whether a horse is normal or shows evidence of a disease or pathology.

Valet — Person who attends jockeys and keeps their wardrobe and equipment in order.

Veterinarian — God in beige coveralls.

Walk hots — To cool out a horse after a workout or race.

Walkover — Race that scratches down to one starter who merely gallops the required distance. A formal gesture required by rules of racing.

Warming up — Galloping a horse on way to post.

Washy — Horse that breaks out in a nervous sweat before a race.

Weanling — A Thoroughbred after being weaned from his dam until he becomes a yearling on the New Year's Day following his foaling.

Weight-for-age — Fixed scale of weights to be carried by horses according to age, sex, distance of race, and month.

Wind puffs — A soft fluid filling found to the rear and above the ankle in the area of the suspensories. Usually the result of strain.

Withers — Point where the neck of the horse meets the shoulders and turns into the back; the point at which the horse is measured for height.

Work — To exercise a horse. A workout.

Yearling — Thoroughbred between the first New Year's Day after being foaled and the following January 1.

* For a more detailed and comprehensive glossary, refer to the National Thoroughbred Racing Association glossary of racing terminology (www.ntra.com/glossindex.html).

SUGGESTED READING

Almost any educational process worth its salt will require some homework, and your education in the horse business is no different. As you go through the various learning segments, reading some sort of pertinent information at the same time is a big help.

As I've mentioned in this book, the Thoroughbred industry is an information-intensive business, and the more you read and keep up to date, the better off you'll be. Naturally, some of these publications will be more important to you than others, and those are preceded by an asterisk. The others, though, will be useful in providing you with insight into the business.

* *The Blood-Horse.* P.O. Box 4038, Lexington, KY 40544.

Weekly magazine, with excellent annual supplements, including *Stallion Register, Stakes Annual, Auctions of 2000*, and *Dams of 2000*. Numerous articles on current racing, breeding, sales, personalities, and horses, complemented by extensive statistics, statistical analyses, and other articles of interest to the industry. In addition, they are the publishers of numerous equine books (Eclipse Press) and the excellent newsletter *MarketWatch* (see below).

**MarketWatch.* Published by The Blood-Horse.

A bi-monthly newsletter containing extensive statistical information and analyses about breeding that is not available in the regular publications.

**The Thoroughbred Times*. 496 Southland Drive, Lexington, KY 40503.

Formerly *The Thoroughbred Record*. Weekly slick tabloid with very good annual supplements, including the *Stallion Directory*. Numerous articles on current racing, breeding, sales, personalities, and horses, complemented by extensive statistics, statistical analyses, and other articles of interest to the industry.

*Racing Update. P.O. Box 11052, Lexington, KY 40512.

An excellent bi-monthly newsletter containing extensive statistical information about breeding that is not available in the regular publications. Spiced with a liberal dash of opinion. Also publishes very comprehensive sales updates that give you a lot of good information on each lot, including stud fees, previous sales of mare's offspring, etc.

* Davis, Thomas A., Esq. ***Horse Owners and Breeders Tax Manual.*** American Horse Council, 1700 K Street NW, Suite 300, Washington, D.C. 20036.

Invaluable reference on taxation in the horse business. Nearly 1,000 pages containing everything you wanted to know about taxation of the horse business and a lot you didn't. This reference is a must for your lawyer and accountant. As for you, there's a seventeen-page pamphlet entitled *Tax Tips for Horse Owners*, which is available free with a membership in the American Horse Council.

* Rossdale, Peter D., M.A., F.R.C.V.S. (2000) ***The Horse From Conception to Maturity***. London: J.A. Allen & Co.

One of England's leading veterinarians describes, in lay language, the life cycle of the Thoroughbred horse, with most of what you can expect to encounter along the way.

* Smiley, Jane. (2000) ***Horse Heaven***. New York: Alfred Knopf.

Has supplanted *Laughing in the Hills* as the best book ever written about horse racing. Fiction, liberally spiced with fact. Great insight into the emotions and motivations of horse people.

* Barich, Bill. ***Laughing in the Hills.*** (1993) St. Paul, MN: Hungry Mind Press.

Beautifully written memoir that contains an excellent explanation of life at the racetrack without glamorizing it, including a lot of things people may not think to explain to you as you enter the business. Originally published by Viking in 1980, it has been recently reprinted in paperback. Good reading, really, whether you're interested in racing or not.

Robinson, Patrick with Robinson, Nick. (1993) *Horsetrader, Robert Sangster and the Rise and Fall of the Sport of Kings.* London: HarperCollins.

Wonderfully written account of the influence of the Sangster Group, the Maktoums, etc., on the Thoroughbred industry. Excellent reading, with education along the way, I must say, even if I did have a little bit to do with it.

Way, Robert F. , V.M.D., M.S., and Lee, Donald G., V.M.D. (1983) *Anatomy of the Horse.* Sharon Hill, PA: Breakthrough Publications.

Excellent, understandable treatment of equine anatomy.

Burch, Preston M. (1992) *Training Thoroughbred Horses.* Neena, WI: Russell Meerdinck Co.

Hints on purchase, development, and training Thoroughbreds from a Hall of Fame trainer.

Pons, Josh. (revised edition, 1999) *Country Life Diary: Three Years in the Life of a Horse Farm.* Lexington, KY: The Blood-Horse, Inc.

Also of Note:

Auerbach, Ann Hagedorn. (1996) *Wild Ride: The Rise and Tragic Fall of Calumet Farm, Inc., America's Premier Racing Dynasty.* New York: Henry Holt and Company.

Toby, Milt and Perch, Karen. (1999) *Understanding Equine Law.* Lexington, KY: Eclipse Press.

Toby, Milt and Perch, Karen. (2001) *Understanding Equine Business Basics*, Lexington, KY: Eclipse Press.

Campbell, W. Cothran. (2000) *Lightning in a Jar: Catching Racing*

Fever. Lexington, KY: Eclipse Press.

Mearns, Dan. (2000) **Seattle Slew**. Lexington, KY: Eclipse Press.

Bowen, Edward L. (2000) *Dynasties: Great Thoroughbred Stallions*. Lexington, KY: Eclipse Press.

Internet Resources

American Association of Equine Practitioners (www.aaep.org).
Comprehensive site for horse health care. Contains an owner's education section as well as information on locating a veterinarian in your area.

American Horse Council (www.horsecouncil.org).
Learn about the horse industry's voice in Washington, D.C. New or prospective owners can obtain the *Tax Tips for Horse Owners* booklet and other helpful publications via this site.

Bloodstock Research Information Systems (www.brisnet.com).
Provides racing, pedigree, sales, and handicapping information as well as the online newsletters, *Bloodstock Journal* and *Handicapper's Edge*. The original provider of computerized data for the Thoroughbred industry.

Daily Racing Form (www.drf.com)
The online version of the venerable daily. Features include racetrack entries, results, and Stable Mail, which allows a person to follow specific horses on the track.

Del Mar Turf Club (www.dmtc.com)
Like everything else about Del Mar, this site is top class and user friendly. Includes information about the track and its race meetings, a directory of trainers, information for new owners, and a 450,000-horse pedigree database that you can access free. The database includes pictures of many of the horses.

Equibase (www.equibase.com).
The official supplier of racing information and statistics to the NTRA, TVG, and ESPN.com. A key source for entries and results as well as links to a number of racetrack web sites.

Equine Online (www.equineonline.com).
  Provides links to the web sites for The Jockey Club, The Jockey Club Information Systems, EquineLine2000, Equibase Company, among others. Also has a glossary of equine terms and an international calendar of racing and sales events. Has just developed a revolutionary online portfolio management system for your equine holdings that will continuously update your horses' records, etc. *This program will be an enormous boon to owners.*

Keeneland Association (www.keeneland.com).
  A good site to learn more about Thoroughbred auctions as well as racing. Provides information for the first-time buyer at the sales, plus the Conditions of Sale.

National Thoroughbred Racing Association (www.ntra.com).
  Primarily aimed at horse-racing fans, but a good place for those new to racing to learn more about the sport.

Thoroughbred Times (www.thoroughbredtimes.com).
  Another good resource for racing news and results and other racing industry information.

The Blood Horse (www.bloodhorse.com).
  Comprehensive site for racing news, results, and breeding information, plus a wide array of links to other racing and equine sites.

The Jockey Club Home Page (home.jockeyclub.com).
  A key site for new or prospective owners. Contains information on registration, including rules and regulations and fee schedules, plus an online names book and recently released names for use, Thoroughbred industry statistics, and general information.

Thoroughbred Owners and Breeders Association (www.toba.org).
  Another important site for new or prospective owners. Provides information on buying your first horse, owner seminars, state organizations, and more.

INDEX

PHOTO CREDITS

Chapter 1 — Anne M. Eberhardt, p. 18, 29; The Blood-Horse, 22; Barbara D. Livingston, 23; Skip Dickstein, 25.

Chapter 2 — The Blood-Horse, 32; Anne M. Eberhardt, 36.

Chapter 3 — Anne M. Eberhardt, 49, 58, 65, 67.

Chapter 4 — D&S Photo, 72; Barbara D. Livingston, 73, 88; Anne M. Eberhardt, 77, 85, 90, 106; Pat Lang, 115; Tom Hall, 119.

Chapter 5 — Anne M. Eberhardt, 128, 132, 133, 137, 146, 150, 154; Christine M. Schweizer, 131.

Chapter 6 — Anne M. Eberhardt, 165, 168, 169, 200, 201; Charles Bertram/Lexington Herald-Leader, 204.

Chapter 8 — Anne M. Eberhardt, 229, 234, 238, 239.

Chapter 9 — The Blood-Horse, 254, 256; Anne M. Eberhardt, 257; Rick Samuels, 260.

ACKNOWLEDGMENTS

I would like to dedicate this book to my family, who inspired me, each in their own way, to keep on writing. Also, it is dedicated to the memories of Rich Rolapp and Jack Lohman, who did so much for this business, received too little recognition, and left us too soon.

A number of my friends pitched in and helped with this thing...either providing information or reading sections to insure that my errors or omissions were not overly egregious. They include (in alphabetical order): Howard Battle, racing secretary of Keeneland and equine artist; Rogers Beasley, director of sales for Keeneland; Tom Biederman, auctioneer, realtor, and president of Equine Spectrum; Happy Broadbent of Bloodstock Research; Sam Brown, partner in Radwan-Brown CPAs; Gary Carpenter of The Jockey Club; Chris Clay and Jim Cox of *MarketWatch*; Sherry Craig, Central Kentucky representative, and Rochelle Stone, CEO, of Starker Services; Jack Jones, partner in the law firm of Wyatt, Tarrant & Combs; Jay Hickey, president of the American Horse Council; Ron Kirk, president of Kirk Horse Insurance; John Kropp, president and premier pettifogger of Graydon, Head & Ritchie (The Firm); Reiley McDonald, wine connoisseur and partner in Eaton Sales; R. Bates Newton, president of Vinery; Walt Robertson, auctioneer extraordinaire and president of Fasig-Tipton Company; Dan Rosenberg, general manager of Three Chimneys Farm and extensive commentator on the Thoroughbred business; Mark Simon, editor of *The Thoroughbred Times* and of *Successful Thoroughbred Investment in a Changing Market*, who again provided invaluable assistance, even though this time his prime competitor is the publisher; and Jim Smith, DVM and Walter Zent, DVM, of Hagyard-Davidson-McGee, who, if you'll pardon the pun, vetted most of the book.

My most heartfelt thanks and apologies to Kelly Beattie, Ed Houlihan, and Cindy Rullman, who put up with all my complaining, griping, moaning, and short temper during the production of this book.

Finally, Jackie Duke and Rena Baer, my editors at Eclipse Press, along with Judy Marchman. Thanks for all your hard work and good suggestions. Now that we're finished, I hope you-all learn that slavery is against the law.

ABOUT THE AUTHOR

For four decades, Arnold Kirkpatrick has been extensively involved in the Thoroughbred business. He has served as editor and publisher of *The Thoroughbred Record*; director of racing and research for the American Horse Council; executive vice president of Spendthrift Farm (in the days when the stallion roster included Nashua, Raise a Native, Exclusive Native, Caro, Seattle Slew, and Affirmed); president of the Kentucky Jockey Club (operator of Latonia Race Course during the formative days of the Jim Beam Stakes); and now as president of Kirkpatrick & Company, a real estate and Thoroughbred brokerage, appraisal, and consulting firm.

Kirkpatrick also helped organize the Breeders' Cup and was founding president of American Horse Publications.

He has received major industry awards as both a writer and a breeder, having won an Eclipse Award for magazine writing in 1983 and a Keeneland Consignor Award as co-breeder of Taisez Vous, stakes winner of $372,185 and the best Keeneland-sold three-year-old of her year.

He has been an officer and/or director of the Thoroughbred Racing Associations of North America, National Turf Writers Association, Australian Breeders Co-Operative Society, Central Kentucky Riding For The Handicapped, The HOPE Center, and Thoroughbred Club of America and has been featured in the *International Who's Who of Authors & Writers*, *International Men of Achievement*, and *Who's Who in the South and Southwest*.

Kirkpatrick lives in Lexington, Kentucky.

OTHER TITLES

from **Eclipse Press**

Baffert: Dirt Road to the Derby

Cigar: America's Horse (revised edition)

Country Life Diary (revised edition)

Crown Jewels of Thoroughbred Racing

Dynasties: Great Thoroughbred Stallions

Etched in Stone

Four Seasons of Racing

Great Horse Racing Mysteries

Lightning in a Jar — Catching Racing Fever

Matriarchs: Great Mares of the 20th Century

Olympic Equestrian

Thoroughbred Champions:
Top 100 Racehorses of the 20th Century

Thoroughbred Legends series:

Citation: Thoroughbred Legends

Dr. Fager: Thoroughbred Legends

Forego: Thoroughbred Legends

Go for Wand: Thoroughbred Legends

Man o' War: Thoroughbred Legends

Nashua: Thoroughbred Legends

Native Dancer: Thoroughbred Legends

Seattle Slew: Thoroughbred Legends